History of Housing in the U.S.
in the U.S.
1930-1980

Gulf Publishing Company
Book Division
Houston, London,
Paris, Tokyo

History of Housing in the U.S. 1930-1980

Joseph B. Mason

History of Housing in the U.S., 1930-1980

CONTENTS

PREFACE

This is a true story, a first hand and perhaps, therefore, limited historical account told by an editor who still marvels at the deeds, drama, and events that unfolded in his many years as journalist and housing observer.

My career as a building editor began in 1928 on the staff of *Building Age* magazine and has continued to this date (1981). Thus my personal experience, editorial work, and observation closely parallel the 50-year history of this volume.

I first learned about construction from the most notable and enterprising builder in my hometown, Niagara, Wisconsin, population 2,347. Here, I must admit, the saga of Paul Bunyon was more in the vernacular of the residents than that of Frank Lloyd Wright ever could be. This builder, Art Wilson, felt that putting up a half-dozen houses a year was ample fulfillment of his dreams, and he paid me 50 cents an hour to lay good, solid hardwood floors, and 60 cents for clinging to the roof to lay shingles, my mouth stuffed with nails, to work my way through school.

At the University of Wisconsin at Madison I acquired some knowledge of civil engineering and journalism—an unlikely combination, but one that stood me in good stead as I worked my way through later assignments. By 1928 I had, through good fortune, arrived at the very job I had dreamed of, Editor of *Building Age*, an old and respected journal with some 80,000 builder subscribers. Thus I was in New York on the night of October 29, 1929, when the newsboys hawked the headlines: "Stocks Collapse—16 Million Shares Sold!" So I witnessed the stock market crash and lived through the subsequent collapse of housing and the nation's mortgage-finance structure, and the worst economic debacle in U.S. history.

Through the years, as Editor of *American Builder*, Building Editor of *Good Housekeeping*, Executive Editor of *Architectural Record*, and Senior Editor of *Professional Builder*, I have participated in many of the events described in this history. For example, in 1933 and 1934 I wrote *American Builder* editorials helping bring about the Federal Housing Administration, the Home Loan Bank Board, and the Home Owners' Loan Corporation which rescued more than a million foreclosed homes.

And in 1940-1943 I participated actively in the movement to found the National Association of Home Builders, writing editorials and attending many of the early meetings.

The most important result of these many years of editing, writing, covering conventions, meetings, seminars, and press affairs is the host of friends I have made among architects, builders, planners, editors, and industry leaders. In 1976-1977 I carried on extensive research at the behest of the National Association of Home Builders to list and describe some 350 persons who had made "outstanding contributions to the advancement of housing in the U.S." Establishment of the Housing Hall of Fame occurred in 1976. This history is an indirect outgrowth of that research.

Progress in the housing industry proceeds on a thousand fronts, the result of the efforts of many thousands of small firms. Home building is one of the last bastions of small, private enterprise—an industry in which a small entrepreneur, a carpenter, a bricklayer, or a gifted college student can start from nowhere and become great.

One of my hopes is to help the American people understand this industry and to realize how it works and how much they are the beneficiaries of the sacrifice, the struggle, the heartaches of such men. In every crisis, leaders have risen who have forged new ways to progress. They have the true genius of American enterprise and ingenuity which gets houses built despite obstacles.

In writing this history I have had the support, help, and encouragement—but not necessarily the endorsement—of the National Housing Center Board of Governors and many officers and members of the National Association of Home Builders. To Martin L. Bartling, Jr., and George C. Martin, past presidents of NAHB, and to Mildred M. Druckery, able assistant and confidante of NAHB presidents, go my special thanks. I must here add an emphatic statement that the NAHB assumes no responsibility for the completeness or accuracy of the work or for any other aspect of its contents.

I have been helped by many others, whose numbers are too great to mention. Specifically, I wish to thank the publishers and editors of *American Builder, Professional Builder, Architectural Forum, Architectural Record, House and Home, Housing,* and *NAHB Builder* for background information, illustrations, and advice; Edward C. Birkner who so skillfully directs Marketing Information Network; and a special word of thanks to Denver builder Samuel Primack.

My apologies must go to many men and institutions of the industry whose contributions to progress have been great, but whose work I do not have space to report. It should also be apparent—and I hope understood—that the scope and objectives of the work are limited. I have covered those events that interested me most, and, unavoidably, that entailed passing over large sectors. I trust, however, that the major objectives remain clear: To show how the American Dream of better housing for all was advanced in these 50 years by the effort and individual genius of builders large and small, working largely under an unfettered private enterprise system.

Joseph B. Mason
December 1981

History of Housing in the U.S.
in the U.S.
1930-1980

CHAPTER ONE

1930-1940

DEPRESSION AND REVITALIZATION

The Legacy of the Big Crash

The stock market crash of 1929 was the major event that changed the course of U.S. housing and affected it for many years. It seems appropriate, therefore, to open this history of the decade of the thirties on October 29, 1929, when panic selling of stocks hit the greatest and most devastating proportions.

Newsboys on that chill and ominous evening were hawking the headlines: "STOCKS COLLAPSE—16 MILLION SHARES SOLD!" Few of the persons who crowded the newstands, the stock tickers, and the Wall Street brokers' offices fully comprehended what was happening and what the terrible consequences would be. Certainly very few of the millions who depended on the housing industry for shelter or jobs grasped the full import.*

It was only later that the public realized that on that disastrous, historic day they had been witnessing the start of the greatest deflation and the worst economic debacle in this country's history. The whole structure of U.S. housing, building, and mortgage finance was about to crumble and collapse about their ears.

The effect of the crash was cruelly far reaching: investors lost some $75 billion, U.S. Steel and General Motors stocks dropped to 8% of their 1929 highs, and the total value of all stocks dropped ultimately to less than 12% of their former prices. The deflation and depression that followed have been well documented, but many who read about it today may not appreciate the sad consequences for so many.

There were the pitiful men who sold apples on street corners near Greenwich Village. Neighbors could only weep at the haggard men and women who stood in block-long lines in the nearby Bowery, waiting for a crust of bread and a bowl of watery soup. Some of the depression-day signs on restaurants and barber shops in the Bowery recall the picture:

---

*Editor's note: J.B. Mason was living in New York at this time and was Editor of *Building Age* magazine.

Meat Balls & Beans—10¢
Ham & Eggs—20¢
Yankee Pot Roast—20¢
Oxtail Stew—Coffee—15¢
Shave—Bay Rum & Hot Towel—10¢

But even these prices were out of sight for the man out of work.

Yes, do not forget the cruel depression years and their effect on Americans everywhere. The major effort in this history, however, is to put the spotlight on the consequences of the market crash on housing. Builders stopped work overnight, mortgage finance dried up, housing starts plunged, millions of building men were thrown out of work, and more than one-and-a-half million homes were foreclosed. It was not until 1936 that housing was able to begin a feeble comeback.

This and much more will be reported as this 50-year housing drama unfolds: there were new financial acts that brought gradual recovery, the growth of new building techniques, the effects of war, tight money, and material shortages, the rise of new communities and planning, and the emergence of a stronger, more sophisticated industry.

Objective reporters will usually agree that the full story of what builders and developers achieved for this country has not been completely told or appreciated by the American public. Builders have had little credit for the risks they took, the losses they suffered, and the problems they faced from war controls, scarce materials, tight money, outmoded codes, zoning, and most recently, environmental and no-growth restrictions.

Yet the record of houses built is astonishing and far surpasses that of any nation in the world. The amazing 57 million homes produced in the 50-year period 1930-1980 has unquestionably changed the face of America and vastly improved the living standards of its citizenry.

The Nature of the Industry and Its Self-Made Men

At this point it seems pertinent to review a few of the facts and figures of the housing industry, its workings and its men. The first fact to note is that residential building is made up of so many hundreds of thousands of mostly small-volume builders, carpenters, sub-contractors, real estate persons, and many other workers, that it is difficult for anyone to control, organize, or even understand its intricacies.

The second is that the actual construction of houses is carried on in thousands of isolated sites or on small lots in and around more than 20,000 towns and communities, as well as in an infinite number of scattered locations in suburbia, exurbia, and rural areas. Each of these has its own local codes, zoning, environmental demands, distribution methods, and servicing requirements.

The result of this vast dispersion of men, materials, and land has been to discourage large-scale production. People often ask, "Why in the world are builders so old-fashioned? Why don't they turn out houses like autos and bring the cost down?"

The only answer is that each piece of land—the local building site—is an individual problem relating to its terrain, water, sewerage, and local codes and customs. The problems of local land use cannot be mass solved by Detroit production methods. Over the years many articles have been written about exciting industrialized and prefab systems. But the record reveals that progress has been made slowly, by evolution. Many of the early prefab techniques have been adapted and adopted by both large and small builders.

Today homes are being produced much more efficiently than they were a few decades ago. But even so, the typical U.S. builder in 1975 produced less than 20 units a year, and large producers of 1,000 or more a year accounted for less than 5% of total production.

A trend toward larger operations was discernible in the late seventies, but a report by a professional builder magazine indicates that in 1978 and 1979, fewer than 500 "giants" whose volume was at least $10 million a year built less than 20% of all new housing. There were an estimated 127,000 active residential builders.

A third observation is that American housing is powerfully controlled and often drastically curtailed by U.S. monetary and fiscal policies. The tragic consequences of "tight money" and high interest rates have pushed thousands of builders into bankruptcy. The nation has gone far in 50 years to improve housing finance methods, but it has not to this day found a way to even out the ups and downs of building volume caused by federal monetary policies.

A fourth observation is that housing can be a powerful engine of prosperity when properly turned on. It touches every spot in the economic system and is a major contributor to business growth, employment, and higher living standards. Perhaps the best way to illustrate this point is to quote from the *Statistical Abstract of the United States*, giving construction industry totals, of which housing is a major segment.

In 1977 there were 478,000 "construction establishments" with 4.2 million employees.

There were 154,000 general building contractors and 289,000 special trade contractors, which included 24,300 carpenter contractors, 24,800 masonry firms and 56,500 plumbing, heating and air-conditioning firms. Also note 27,300 painting and decorating firms, 36,800 electrical contractors, 20,600 roofing and sheet-metal firms, and 16,000 excavating contractors. When architects, real estate persons, lumber and material supply firms, and the vast U.S. manufacturing industries that produce and distribute housing products, equipment, and furnishings are added, it becomes clear why, when housing booms, the economy is strong. When it drops, a recession is usually in the making.

In 1930, hardly anyone could speak for builders or the housing industry. In fact, neither private nor government agencies could tell how many builders there were or where they worked. Things have changed and there are much better statistics today, but the industry is still difficult to grasp and understand, and it still has an enormously vast and complicated sales and distribution system.

One thing that does become crystal clear to a housing analyst or historian is that home building is a profession of *individualists*. Anyone with energy, initiative, and a small amount of expertise can get ahead, or, as often happens, go broke. Many builders get started by building one house—if it sells at a profit, they build another; if not, they sometimes move in. John Long, the enormously successful Phoenix, Arizona, builder, started this way, with his wife helping build his first house. Many such men have made great contributions, as he did, to research, production techniques, the number of good homes, and a higher standard of living.

Perhaps many builders were successful because of the very difficulties with which they were faced during their early years, and because they were able to rise from humble beginnings to wealth and power through their own diligence. There are many such men, but the stories of four will suffice to illustrate the point.

Robert F. Gerholz of Flint, Michigan, was one of 12 children born on a farm in Lincoln County, Wisconsin, in 1896, of poor, German immigrant parents. "Mine was a rich heritage—the *work ethic*," he relates. "I learned to work as soon as I learned to walk."

Indeed, at age nine he started working on truck farms in summer for 25 cents an hour. At 14 he put in ten hours a day in a box factory for 20 cents an hour. At 18 he worked his way through Ferris Institute at Big Rapids, Michigan, raking yards, stoking furnaces, milking cows, and selling books, and he completed the four-year course in two years.

Gerholz taught school, fought in the First World War, worked as a part-time real estate salesman, and finally became a home builder in 1923. All of his drive and initiative were fully tested in home building—he almost went broke during the depression—but persevered and ultimately built more than 5,000 houses, became well-off, and was elected president of the National Association of Home Builders (NAHB) in 1944, the National Association of Real Estate Boards in 1950, and the Chamber of Commerce of the United States in 1965.

In 1977 he received the Horatio Alger Award of the American Schools and Colleges Association—a fitting climax to his rags-to-riches career. "I've been lucky all my life," he says. "But I learned that the harder I worked the luckier I got."

Richard G. Hughes of Pampa, Texas, was born in a Texas dugout following a cyclone that killed his father and crippled his mother.

He worked in a gas station and as a janitor, milked cows, and then sold insurance to get through West Texas State College.

He says, "Since I left college at 19 I have never drawn anybody's pay check but my own. I have never slept more than four or five hours a night."

"He was born working," said one of his staff.

Hughes got into home building in 1940 because he felt something should be done about better living conditions in Pampa. He continued to work 18 hours a day building homes and communities, including many for the poor and minorities. He became president of the NAHB in 1954.

W. P. "Bill" Atkinson was born in Midwest City, Oklahoma. His father was a carpenter, his mother died when he was nine, and he went to work at the age of 11 as a printer's devil on the *Panola Watchman*, a weekly paper in Carthage, Texas. He worked his way through high school and Texas Christian University in newspaper jobs. He struggled upward as journalist, editor, advertising salesman, and later real estate salesman, which brought him into home building in 1936.

The Horatio Alger aspects of Bill Atkinson's career are hard to compress in a few paragraphs. Suffice it to say he became enormously successful as a builder. He developed the great Midwest City planned residential complex and many others, has been a candidate for governor, and became publisher of the *Oklahoma Journal*. He was president of the NAHB in 1951. He continues to develop and build homes, shopping centers, and well-planned residential complexes.

Carl T. Mitnick of Cape May, N. J., the son of Russian immigrants, quit school and went to work at the age of 13 as a delivery boy, then as clerk in a clothing store. "In 1918 I either had to quit school or quit eating," he relates. He went to work for a builder relative, and when he was 21, branched out on his own. He later built 10,000 houses, many of them retirement homes, became head of real estate and mortgage companies, and was elected president of the NAHB in 1959.

Such men as these, in the often stated opinion of industry leaders, testify to the strength and greatness of the private-enterprise system which allows housing to function. The building record detailed in this volume may help the American people understand more fully how much they are the beneficiaries of this system and of the builders who struggle, take risks, suffer losses and heartaches, encounter appalling and unpredictable problems—but do get houses built.

Builders generally tend to extol Adam Smith's philosophy of production for progress and the benefits of hard work, also endorsed by Benjamin Franklin. In housing, the greatest advances have always been the result of inventiveness, research, enterprise, and a favorable financial climate. Public housing has usually failed, while private building, aided, it is true, by federal financial agencies such as the Federal Housing Administration (FHA), Veterans Administration (VA), Federal Home Loan Bank (FHLB), and Federal National Mortgage Association (FNMA), has produced needed homes. George C. Martin, the brilliant Louisville, Kentucky, builder and past president of the NAHB expresses it this way:

"The builder has to be a gambler, risk-taker, and an optimist. He's also a problem solver—he has to be, in this complicated field, or he would not last a month," Martin adds, "Housing is the most essential ingredient of the American way of life, and yet it lacks clout in state and national capitals and recognition by the public at large."

Over the years, observers have recorded the remarkable growth of the NAHB and its industry leadership. They have also seen the rise and fall of giant shelter conglomerates and large corporate builder entities. But through all this, one theme emerges, which is that there is a driving, personal, and aggressive spirit in most builders—small or large—that propels them forward, and which is the basic cause of progress.

The housing industry is one of the last bastions of small, private enterprise—a place where a small entrepreneur, a carpenter, a bricklayer, or a gifted college student can start from nowhere and become great. Janis Risbergs, a rugged Latvian immigrant who came here with only $5 in his pocket, rose to become head of a multi-million-dollar building corporation, trained three sons to succeed him, and, among many other distinguished accomplishments, brought new excellence to the planning and design of high-rise condominium apartments and communities in Florida and elsewhere.

Progress in the housing industry proceeds on a thousand fronts, regardless of government actions, no-growth activists, or the problems created by overzealous environmentalists. In every crisis, leaders have risen to forge ahead with new ways of satisfying human needs. They have come from many sources and many lowly backgrounds. They are blessed with a spirit of enterprise and ingenuity that will lead to further housing advances in the years ahead.

Depression's Effects on Home Financing

The stock market crash of 1929, as we have stated, changed the course of housing for the decade of the thirties, and for many years thereafter. Its effect on housing was pervasive and far reaching, as the rapid march of events soon showed.

The excesses and errors associated with the stock market had been great, but housing, real estate, and mortgage finance in 1930 were equally troubled. The nation was plagued with poorly planned projects, badly designed homes and apartments, overextended financing, second and third mortgages on homes at high interest, and huge mortgage bond issues on vastly inflated real estate projects. The mortgage-finance structure was weak and almost bankrupt.

The outlook in early 1930 was bleak, and it was hard for most building-industry observers to credit the optimistic predictions of President Herbert Hoover, Andrew Mellon, J. P. Morgan, and even Nicholas Murray Butler, president of Columbia University, when they declared that "economic conditions are basically sound."

Certainly this was not true of housing and the entire construction industry, which had just completed a decade of expansion and overbuilding. Housing starts had peaked at 937,000 units in 1925; they declined every year after that, and in 1930 were at the 330,000 level.

The gloom was bad enough among the ranks of builders, developers, and real estate persons, not one of whom was planning another project. But the real crunch came in the desperate circles of the savings-and-loan and mortgage-finance men. The outlook was tragically bad and was soon bound to get worse. Here is what was happening:

Deposits in home-savings institutions were dropping toward zero. At the same time, cash withdrawals mounted rapidly as depositors, thrown out of work, were forced to call on their savings to survive.

Savings, building and loan, and mortgage-finance institutions were drained heavily for funds to meet stock market and collateral loan requirements. Investors, depositors, and owners were all affected, and the result was a complete drying up of mortgage-finance funds.

All mortgages that came due, or that could be foreclosed, were called. This was particularly unfortunate for home owners saddled with second and third mortgages.

Soon there was not only an acute shortage of money to finance new building, but an explosive increase in home foreclosures. Home owners out of work simply could not pay anything on their mortgages, and often packed up and moved out. By 1933 more than one-and-a-half million homes were in default, foreclosed, or in process of foreclosure.

Evictions were a stark blow to formerly proud home owners who subsequently moved to rented rooms or joined the millions of migrants moving from town to town, living in cars, trailers, trucks, tents, shacks, or hobo jungles.

The sad stories of the displaced home owners, the nomad unemployed, the Hoovervilles, the 15 million out of work, the Bonus Army, Hoover's firm-jawed but ineffectual efforts, have been well documented. But the catastrophic story of the effects of all this on housing can be simply stated: the industry just died.

Housing starts plummeted from 330,000 in 1930 to 254,000 in 1931; 134,000 in 1932;

and to the irreducible minimum of 93,000 in 1933, still an all-time low, and a 90% drop from 1925. No funds were available to builders to finance anything—a house, a chicken coop, an apartment, or even the tiniest remodeling job. Huge mortgage bond defaults on apartment, commercial, and real-estate projects approached scandalous proportions. For many years the gaunt, bare-bone steel frames of unfinished buildings stood to remind investors of these bond defaults: it took a long time for them to forget.

Interestingly enough, a few big projects which were getting under way in 1929 to 1933 were successfully finished during the depression. Rockefeller Center—the $250 million dream (and a depression bargain!)—still delights the eye of both New Yorkers and tourists from all over the world. The huge Metropolitan Life Building complex set a high standard of conservative design. The George Washington Bridge was thrown over the Hudson River in 1931, and the Golden Gate Bridge soared to new heights of design, daring, and delicacy.

The problems of the building industry in the early thirties were immense. More than two million construction workers were unemployed, and thousands of builders went out of business. A million and a half homes foreclosed meant no mortgage-payment income for the financial institutions that made the loans, and many closed their doors.

Three outstanding builders have related how they "hung on" during the depression.

"My builder father went broke," says *Earl "Flat Top" Smith*, of El Cerrito, California, "so I got a job as carpenter's helper. I worked at anything that could produce a buck."

Nels Severin, builder and mortgage banker of San Diego, said, "In the thirties I worked at parking cars, as a bill collector, and as a bank clerk at $125 a month. Later I became an auto salesman."

Joe Haverstick of Dayton, Ohio, relates: "My father's building business collapsed in 1931 and I went to work as a carpenter and cement finisher. Then I worked as surveyor, production-line worker, and later sold Buick cars. By 1936 I was able to get back to work as a carpenter."

All of these men later became highly successful builders, constructed many thousands of homes and apartments, and among other achievements were elected president of the NAHB.

A little known casualty of the depression was Radburn, the "Town for the Motor Age," which had been started with great fanfare and promise in New Jersey in 1928. It could not withstand the depression problems, and work was stopped in 1932 with only a small portion completed. There were many similar cases.

FDR's Extraordinary 100 Days

"The people have asked for action," Franklin Delano Roosevelt declared in his vibrant, high-pitched voice on that snowy inauguration day in March, 1933. "We have nothing to fear but fear itself," he said reassuringly to a bewildered populace which had little idea what its new president was going to do.

He thereupon proceeded, swiftly and confidently, to provide action—action on a nationwide basis such as the country had never experienced from a new president. Early the next morning, March 5, he entered the Oval Office, shouted for his aides, declared a four-day bank holiday, and called Congress into session to pass an emergency banking bill.

It was the start of what historians have described as one of the most remarkable periods of political and social action in American history. FDR hammered Congress with 15 major messages, culminating in 15 major pieces of legislation. Before the exhausted Congressmen adjourned three months later, he had taken the country off the gold standard, announced a new foreign policy, authorized $4 billion for public relief, legalized beer, and instituted reform on Wall Street.

In those exciting first 100 days, followed by another period of equal length and vigorous action, New Deal legislation insured all bank deposits, refinanced foreclosed home mortgages, established the Federal Housing Administration (FHA), the National Recovery Administration (NRA), the Public Works Administration (PWA), the Works Progress Administration (WPA), the Civilian Conservation Corporation (CCC), the Tennessee Valley Authority (TVA), the Farm Credit Administration (FCA), the Glass-Steagall Banking Act, the Rural Electrification Act (REA), and, later, in May 1935, the Social Security Act, believed by many people to be the most significant piece of long-term New Deal legislation.

The astonishing swirl of bills affected every facet of American life and industry. But on none did it have a more profound long-term influence than on housing. We will analyze shortly both the short- and long-term effects, but let us first look back at the conditions that preceded this whirlwind reconstruction period.

By March 4, 1933, when FDR took office, housing and construction were at absolutely irreducible levels. Poverty and fear stalked the land, 15 million formerly employed people were out of work, industrial production was at a record low, and a staggering run had closed most U.S. banks. More than $1 billion had been withdrawn in panic during the preceding two weeks, and many solid citizens began hoarding gold.

The years 1931-1933 continued the complete deterioration of the construction industry and, indeed, of the entire financial and economic structure of the nation. Hoover had attempted to shore up financial institutions with the Reconstruction Finance Corporation, which came into existence in 1932 with capital of $500 million and authority to borrow $1.5 billion to make loans to banks, insurance companies, building and loan associations, farm-mortgage associations, and others. One of its first loans was $8 million to Fred F. French's Knickerbocker Village apartments on New York's lower East Side. The 12-story buildings had 1,662 apartments which rented at $12.50 per room.

In December, 1932, President Hoover, recognizing the desperate plight of housing, called his President's Conference on Home Building and Ownership. More than 400 prestigious specialists took part, including 25 fact-finding committees and six auxiliary groups. One of these urged an improved mortgage-credit system "to make it as easy to buy a house as a car." But this was far too radical an idea for Hoover, and little came out of the conference. The genesis of an idea may have been born here, however, which later blossomed into the FHA amortized-mortgage system of the New Deal in 1934.

One Hoover achievement was the passage of the Federal Home Loan Bank Act in 1932, creating 12 regional banks with capital of $125 million to act as a reserve system for savings and loan associations and thrift and home-finance firms. Under the next U.S. president FHLB was expanded and a subsidiary, the Home Owners' Loan Corporation, was set up and performed a monumental service by refinancing and saving more than a million foreclosed homes.

Hoover worked long and hard and tried desperately to stop the nation's downward thrust, but his approaches did not work.

In startling contrast, FDR and the New Deal brought a bold and confident approach to the nation's problems. "Try it—but get action," was the watchword. He considered his landslide victory a mandate for change and action. His brain trust advisors and administrators included men eagerly open to new ideas—men such as Rexford Tugwell, Henry Wallace, Marriner Eccles, Harry Hopkins, Hugh Johnson, Lewis Douglas, Harold Ickes, Frank C. Walker, and many others who were attracted by FDR's exuberant personality.

One purpose of this volume is to discuss the impact of these men and the New Deal legislation on housing. It took a long time for home building to recover. But the immediate effect of FDR's bold actions and legislation was to start restoring public confidence in the banks, in the economy, and in the future. Homes are only built and bought by people with jobs, an assured financial base, and confidence in the future.

Aids to Housing, 1933-1935

The record of New Deal acts, laws, legislation, and programs that had an important impact on housing is impressive. Together with the restoration of confidence in the economy, these acts produced a remarkable expansion in building. They also strongly affected the course of the housing industry over the next decades.

Heading the list must be the *Emergency Banking Relief Act* and the *Glass-Steagall Banking Act of 1933*, which saved, reorganized, and established a permanent and sound U.S. banking system. The *Federal Deposit Insurance Corporation* (FDIC) was created to guarantee deposits and maintain the confidence of depositors. The beneficial effect of this sound banking system on housing can hardly be overstated.

The *Public Works Administration* (PWA) was created in 1933 to finance a wide range of public construction, including slum clearance, low-cost housing, and subsistence home-steads. In the next six years it spent or invested more than $6 billion and created some five billion man-hours of job labor. Grants to states for bridges, grade crossings, sewerage plants, airports, highways, and hospitals were included.

This was a help to architects, contractors, and construction workers, as well as to the thousands of communities it served. Projects included Key West roads and bridges; a water supply for Denver; a mental hospital in California; the Zoo and Mall in Washington, DC; a band shell in Phoenix, Arizona; Lincoln Tunnel in New York City; flood control for Ohio; a port for Brownsville, Texas; Hoover Dam; and a swimming pool for Wheeling, West Virginia. Harold Ickes headed PWA and made the sparks fly.

The *Federal Emergency Relief Act* (FERA), a controversial bill to aid the poor and hungry, was in sharp contrast to Hoover policies, and it became even more controversial under the direction of socially minded Harry Hopkins. Some $500 million was made available by grants to state and local agencies, and this amount was later increased. The funds did aid the poor and hungry, but also pumped needed cash into the depleted economy.

The *Civil Works Administration* (CWA) was planned to create immediate employment, faster than was possible by the long-term PWA projects. More than four million workers got jobs, many of them from the construction field.

The *Works Progress Administration* (WPA) was another controversial act which, however, employed thousands of architects, artists, designers, composers, actors, and others in the cultural fields. A surprising amount of cultural and artistic advances was generated.

The *Civilian Conservation Corps* (CCC) was one of the most popular of the New Deal ideas. It took some three million young men, aged 18 to 25, from the ranks of the unemployed and put them to work in minor construction, reforestation, fire and flood control, road building, and improving forests, parks, and recreational areas. The pay was $30 a month, most of which went into immediate circulation via the needy folks back home.

The *Farm Credit Administration* (FCA) and *Federal Farm Mortgage Corporation* granted production loans and favorable terms for refinancing farm debts. These aids made many debt-ridden farmers solvent and stimulated spending for equipment, farm improvement, and building.

The *Tennessee Valley Authority* (TVA) was authorized to operate Muscle Shoals and embark on a vast development program of dam and power plant construction and rural electrification. Along the way it built housing and recreational areas, and engaged in flood-erosion control and reforestation. Much of this had a direct impact on construction and jobs for millions in a seven-state area.

The *Home Owners' Loan Corporation* (HOLC), a daring project set up under the aegis of the Federal Home Loan Bank Board, was given $200 million capital and authority to raise ten times that amount by selling bonds. This amazingly successful agency rescued more than a million home owners whose mortgages had been foreclosed or were in trouble. HOLC paid off the old short-term, high-interest mortgages and replaced them with one long-term loan at 3%. It was a financial success and closed its books in 1936 without costing taxpayers a dime.

The *Federal Housing Administration* (FHA) has been aptly described as the most significant housing legislation in U.S. history. It established in June, 1934, a new concept of insuring long-term amortized mortgages. It revolutionized housing finance and set the stage for an enormous expansion of home building in later years.

The *Social Security Act*, which became law in August, 1935 was probably the greatest social achievement of the New Deal. It has also had far-reaching influence on housing, retirement communities, and homes for the elderly. It was indeed a venturesome program, aimed at safeguarding most Americans against the poverty of old age, unemployment, and illness. Its retirement pensions greatly increased the ability of older people to acquire and live in decent housing. Later chapters will describe the growth of such housing and retirement communities.

The New Deal legislation took a disturbingly long time to produce its effect on housing and create a revival of home building. The first beneficial result was to secure jobs for many thousands of architects, construction workers, and related industry employees. As the financial system gained strength, home buyers gained confidence and private builders started—gingerly, to be sure—to take the risks that would have to be taken to resume building.

The three direct major contributors to the revival of this industry were the Home Loan Bank Board, the Home Owners' Loan Corporation, and the extremely successful Federal Housing Administration's FHA program, a new concept in low-cost, long-term amortized home-mortgage finance. A brief excursion at this point will describe the origins of the programs and the tremendous long-term benefits these government programs have had on U.S. housing.

The HOLC Story— Rescuing a Million Homes from Foreclosure

No chapter in the history of the federal government's involvement in housing is brighter or more refreshing than that of the Federal Home Loan Bank Board and its offspring, the Federal Home Owners' Loan Corporation. FHLB was organized in 1932, expanded by the Home Owners' Loan Act of 1933, and strengthened by the National Housing Act of 1934, which set up the Federal Savings and Loan Insurance Corporation.

In June, 1933, President Roosevelt appointed John H. Fahey, a prominent New England investment banker and publisher, to the post of Chairman of FHLB. He held the job for many years and must surely be credited for much of its success.

What Fahey and his associates did was to reorganize and restore the completely demoralized U.S. mortgage-finance structure. The Home Loan Bank, operating through 12 regional banks, acted as a reserve system similar to the Federal Reserve. It brought stability and liquidity to thousands of savings and loans, savings banks, and thrift institutions. It chartered hundreds of new Federal Savings and Loan Associations that brought added funds into the hard-pressed home-finance field. Its Insurance Corporation insured accounts of member institutions up to $5,000. The result was that funds began to flow once more into thrift institutions, and they, in turn, were able to resume making loans for new home construction.

In one of his rare interviews, John Fahey describes the conditions that led to the daring multi-billion-dollar Home Owners' Loan Corporation program to refinance defaulting mortgages:

"In the spring of 1933 the home-financing system was drifting to complete collapse. Foreclosures rose to 26,000 for the month of June alone. The value of underlying real estate was being undermined. I felt we must end the downward spiral and forestall complete disaster."

The HOLC operation was a classic example of the well-managed use of the financial power of central government. HOLC raised the billions it needed for the gigantic refinancing operation by selling low-interest bonds. It then offered to pay off the short-term, high-interest mortgages of distressed home owners and replace them with one long-term, amortized loan at 3% interest.

The program was an immediate success. By September, 1934, HOLC had refinanced 492,700 mortgages, totaling $1.48 billion, and had 500,000 under processing. Fahey reported that more than $200 million had gone directly to closed thrift institutions to release frozen assets. The program not only rescued more than a million home owners, but brought solvency and strength to the savings and loans and thrift institutions of the country. Many had become insolvent because they could not collect on their foreclosures.

By this giant and risky act of finance, HOLC put the home-mortgage industry back on its feet. This, and the new support and strength of the expanded Home Loan Bank system, enabled the financing of home construction to resume, and paved the way for a sharp increase in housing in later years. Best of all, the entire HOLC program did not cost taxpayers any money. When it went out of business in 1936, HOLC was even able to show a modest profit.

We must also point out that the Home Loan Bank system continued to expand and increase its services to the home-finance field. One of its major functions has become extending loans to its member institutions to help them finance their mortgage lending. Especially in periods of tight money, such advances have proved most valuable.

FHA, 1934: Housing's Most Significant Achievement

When President Roosevelt signed the Federal Housing Act putting FHA into business in June, 1934, he thought of it largely as a pump-priming device to get home building going. It was, and it did. But FHA has achieved much, much more. It revolutionized finance with its long-term amortized mortgage, and it changed the whole structure of the housing industry.

It is said that in 1933 FDR had expressed his desire for at least one agency that could stimulate building without government spending, and which would instead rely on private enterprise. He asked Marriner Eccles to work on the idea with Frank Walker, chairman of the National Emergency Council, and a small study group. A key member was Winfield Riefler, an economics and statistics expert of great talent and imagination, who is now credited with many of the basic concepts. Other members included Albert Deane of General Motors, Miles Colean, an economist,

Corrington Gill, Matt Daiger, and Tom Corcoran.

The study group worked hard and came up with a bill early in 1934. At the time, numerous editorials calling for such action were appearing in the building press, including one titled "Federal Loans Needed for Home Building," and another, "Home Loans for the Forgotten Man," In February 1934 the professional magazine *American Builder* conducted a survey of 500 builders who reported in strong terms their dire need for home financing help. Some 400 letters were bound into a volume which was presented to the Congressional committee working on the bill. This may have helped, but at any rate the bill made good progress and was soon signed into law by the president.*

---

*Editor's note: J.B. Mason was an editor of *American Builder* at this time.

The history of FHA is now well-known, but it seems worthwhile to summarize the major advances it pioneered:

1. It permanently established the concept of the long-term, amortized mortgage, and also the acceptance of low down payments.
2. It helped create a strong national market for mortgages by establishing insurance standards, property standards, and economic soundness.
3. FHA's forward commitments to builders and building projects made possible better large-scale planning and wider use of mass-production techniques.
4. FHA's technical, design, and land-planning standards contributed greatly to more sophisticated builder and tract housing work. Architects and land planners have been particularly impressed by the improvement in subdivision layout and design which grew out of the leadership of Seward H. Mott, FHA's first director of land planning.

Twenty-five years after FHA's beginning, the distinguished architect and housing economist, Miles L. Colean, who was one of the original study group, wrote that it was "the most significant innovation in the home-building industry, and has been a prime stimulant to subsequent innovation." He later opposed the trend to use FHA "for social housing reforms."

On the occasion of FHA's thirtieth birthday in May, 1964, *American Builder* magazine summed up its achievements:

The House of Representatives has celebrated FHA's thirtieth birthday by chopping $6,065,000 off the agency's 1965 budget. This seems to us an ungrateful acknowledgment of an agency which:

● pays all its own bills and turns in a profit to Uncle Sam;

● has done more than any agency inside or outside government to encourage private home ownership;

● is undoubtedly the most useful potential force to aid President Johnson's proposed war on poverty.

We strongly deplore the Congressional budget cuts. We also take issue with those who say FHA's useful days are over. The need for a strong, effective FHA is greater than ever. Only the *directions* are different.

In 1933 and 1934 we campaigned vigorously for FHA. Our editorials and supporting research pictured the unbelievably bad state of home building and home financing; many were read into the Congressional Records. We can testify to the desperate state of builders before FHA came into being.

FHA and its companion, the Home Owners' Loan Corporation and the Federal Savings & Loan Insurance Corporation restored confidence in private home ownership and finance. FHA's revolutionary long-term mortgage ideas, although strongly opposed by most banking and loan groups at the time, have become accepted practice.

It is a fact, nonetheless, that FHA and FSLIC—although federal agencies—have contributed significantly to private home ownership and private-enterprise building. We think it fair to state that without them the U.S. housing industry might have gone far along the socialist route of Great Britain and France.

Let us not lose sight also of FHA's contributions to higher technical standards, better land planning, good design, and quality construction; also its aid to low income and elderly housing, urban renewal, and other socially important building. Without it, demands for outright government building would surely increase. FHA exerts a strong stabilizing influence on the entire private home-finance system.

There is a big job ahead for FHA, working with private-enterprise builders, to achieve President Johnson's goal of 'a decent home in a decent neighborhood' for every American. Congress should give it the money and the tools for this job.

To this may be added a few statements from FHA's *30 Years of Progress*, a booklet produced in May 1964 by Robert C. Weaver, Housing and Home Finance Agency Administrator, and Philip N. Brownstein, FHA Commissioner, as part of FHA's thirtieth-anniversary celebration.

> Congressional approval of this concept did not come easily. There were dire predictions that it would (a) doom private lending institutions or (b) bankrupt the government.
>
> As to soundness, FHA repaid its indebtedness to the Treasury in fiscal 1954: $65 million in principal and $20 million in interest.
>
> This, the thirtieth year, is the twenty-fourth in which FHA has met all expenditures for salaries, expenses, and losses from insurance funds. It is entirely self-supporting.
>
> The FHA has been a tower of strength for the home buyer and the home-building in-

dustry. Today about one of every four non-farm dwellings built since 1934 has been insured with FHA.

As it has grown, FHA has expanded its services. Our programs now include housing for the elderly, for low-income families, for those displaced by the urban renewal, for servicemen, nursing homes, condominums, and cooperatives.

The first house to be built with FHA-insured financing was for Mr. and Mrs. Warren H. Newkirk of 30 Hoppe Avenue, Pompton Plains, New Jersey. The Newkirks obtained a $4,800 mortgage on a $10,000 house that could certainly today be valued at more than $50,000.

FHA also stimulated remodeling and home improvement with its low-interest terms and "Better Housing" campaign in 1935, when 700,000 such loans were made. In 1938, new home mortgages were hiked to 90% of appraised value with 25 years to pay. Also, in 1938 a new FHA Section 207 was added to permit insurance on rental-housing mortgages.

Through the years FHA has continued a solid base for home finance in war, postwar, and peace time. Its rental-housing programs produced more than 465,000 sorely needed apartments in the postwar period, and its aid to housing still continues strongly.

Architecture, Heritage, and Progress

James Ford, director of the influential "Better Homes in America" architectural committee in 1931, remarked unhappily that "the majority of small homes built in America are ugly in design and inconveniently planned." The jury regretted that "so few houses of good design are entered."

Better Homes in America was a group founded in 1922 by then Secretary of Commerce Herbert Hoover. It had 8,000 committees working to improve home design through lectures, tours, and architectural contests.

Despite the poor quality deplored by Ford, awards were made in both 1931 and 1932, and they included some charming and influential work that continued to affect U.S. home design in later years. The six winners who impressed the jury were:

1. *William Wilson Wurster*, San Francisco, for his eclectic Monterey Colonial at Santa Cruz, with great appeal to the California style of living.
2. *Royal Barry Wills*, Boston, for his authentic, livable, Cape Cod Colonial, which won a gold medal and was widely copied.
3. *Dwight James Baum*, Fieldston, New York, for his classic two-story Colonial, another trend setter for years to come.
4. *H. Roy Kelley*, Los Angeles, for his well-sited, tile-roofed Mediterranean cottage in Palos Verdes Estates, the famous early planned community.
5. *W. L. Risley*, Los Angeles, for his quaint one-story Colonial cottage, also at Palos Verdes Estates.
6. *Roland E. Coate*, Santa Barbara, for his elegant Monterey-style California design.

These were all outstanding for this era and far above the average which James Ford described. It is important to note, however, that during the depression years architects, builders, and land planners had the time—and took the time—to do much rethinking and restyling of residential work. Progress was slow, but there were brilliant and often inspired men whose work appeared in the mid-thirties and who greatly influenced design in later years.

One of the most outstanding, of course, was *Frank Lloyd Wright*, a busy, provocative, trend setter. His Broadacres City appeared in 1934, and when he died in 1959 at the age of 89 he left a seven-decade legacy that had touched the lives and work of every architect and every builder. He was indeed *the* great architect, designer, and innovator of the century.

Few persons today, including most builders, appreciate the amazing array of ideas and concepts he originated which are now taken for granted, even in speculative homes (i.e. for sale)—advanced ideas like the open-space plan, low-pitched roofs, huge overhangs, and "horizontality" of design. He opened tight interiors to outside light and garden views by the use of glass-window walls, and his glass corner windows have been the delight of home decorators. He pioneered radiant floor heating, carports (he invented the term), and the idea of built-in wardrobes and other furniture.

Not only did Frank Lloyd Wright create great concepts, but he trained and inspired hundreds of young men in his Taliesen schools who have carried on his ideas. History has already firmly recorded that here was a man who left a vivid imprint on the housing of the twentieth century.

Stories about him are legion. On one occasion a luncheon was held for him by the *Architectural Record* at the Century Club in New York City which, however, refused to have photographs taken in its restrained milieu. So the editor and Tommy Weber, a New York photographer, hustled him across the street to the Columbia Club, where they proceeded to pose him in front of the famous Columbia stuffed lion, a rather ratty-looking animal. FLW liked the idea, then grinned and said, "Just be sure you get it straight which one is Frank Lloyd Wright."

On another occasion FLW created a lively stir at a ceremony in Houston when he was finally, after many years, awarded the prized Gold Medal of the American Institute of Architects. He paused, drew himself up to his full five-foot five-inch stature on the podium and remarked, "Should have had this long ago."

Another architect of the era who exercised great influence on later home design was *Bernard R. Maybeck* of San Francisco. He was the favored forerunner of the "Bay Area" school, which many West Coast architects admired and followed. His houses reflected high craftsmanship in use of wood, with natural redwood exteriors, huge rough-sawn beams, and wood members "aged by nature." He particularly sought to have materials, color, and form blend his houses into their natural setting. He designed the Palace of Fine Arts in San Francisco and was awarded the AIA Gold Medal in 1951 at the age of 89.

An interesting sidelight on Maybeck is that the Bay Area concept with its natural wood and rough-sawn timbers became the hottest selling model home design of the project builders of the seventies.

William Wilson Wurster, one of the Better Homes in America award winners in 1931, also greatly influenced U.S. home architecture. In his early years, in the thirties, he designed lovely homes in wood and natural materials, well-fenestrated, well-structured, with low profiles, and well-sited to their area. One of the greatest was a small California design at Santa Cruz for the noted landscape architect, Thomas D. Church. Wurster also designed exceptional San Francisco apartments, and later, as dean of the School of Architecture at the Massachusetts Institute of Technology, continued his influence as an advocate of restrained, well-thought-out contemporary home planning and design.

Credit must certainly be given to another winner, *Royal Barry Wills,* who, many believe, had the greatest influence on small home design of any architect of the thirties,

forties, or fifties. He brought authentic Colonial design to the small home field, and he did it with style and éclat. Within his authentically designed exteriors he managed to produce very livable, modern floor plans. His designs and published works were admired, copied, and popular with millions of home buyers. He had a thriving practice, and designed not only expensive custom homes but many low-cost projects which brought new insights to the speculative builders.

The mid-thirties also brought some rapprochement between high-thinking architects and profit-minded builder/developers. In earlier eras most well-qualified architects would have little to do with speculative builders. But now the builders began to discover that quality of design and planning might be worth a respectable architectural fee. And a few well-trained, well-qualified architects decided they could pry at least *some* income from the tight-fisted builders—who had previously used stock plans—and at the same time make a contribution to the advancement of home design, especially in lower priced houses, which sorely needed their help.

A prominent architect who followed this route with great success was *Randolph W. Evans* of New York. One of his outstanding jobs was the Harbour Green project of Harmon National Corporation on Long Island. It was well planned with well-sited cottage Colonials of an authentic homespun variety. He later did Orchard Hill in Westchester County, New York, and Chatham Hills in New Jersey. All his houses had a friendly, low-profile, early-American look that was a vast improvement over the speculative houses of the twenties. These were "simple, countrified Colonial cottages" on 100 × 100 foot lots, with many trees, no curbs or sidewalks, and open green space kept up by the residents. The prices ranged from $6,000 to $10,000.

Evans caught the public trend toward conventional Colonial design, and his work had wide acceptance. He was retained to do a "Blueprint House of the Month" for *American Builder* magazine which was very popular with builders, and he developed a plan service which provided a higher quality plan and design than most operators had used before.

There are hundreds of architects who perhaps should be mentioned for their influence on improved home design in the thirties. But a strong contributing factor was that all of the burgeoning government agencies—especially FHA and the Home Loan Bank Board—were pressing for higher design standards and better community planning. Also, projects were bigger and builders could afford, often under protest, to spend a little more for architectural services.

An architect of this period who truly understood the requirements of the bigger builders was *Arthur E. Allen* of Jamaica, New York. He developed a specialized mass-production architectural service for mass-production builders. He had training, talent, and a down-to-earth respect for the needs of the speculative builder. For a long time his firm produced plans for some 5,000 homes a year, including work for most of the biggest Long Island firms, such as Gross-Morton. While his exterior designs rarely won any prizes, his floor plans were marvels of efficiency. He helped many builders produce good, livable houses at very low cost.

Looking back to the poor quality of small-home design in the twenties it can only be said fairly to lie at the door of both the architectural profession and the builder/developers. The architects preferred the more lucrative custom homes and larger structures where they could also express their aesthetic and cultural ideals. But builders seldom even considered an architect. They preferred a stock plan

with perhaps a few changes they made themselves or with the help of a draftsman in the local lumber yard.

There was a change in the thirties, and one of the best expressions of this change is a report issued in 1932 by the AIA Committee on Site Planning and Housing at the annual convention of the American Institute of Architects. A distinguished group of architects and planners participated. They reported that:

1. Architects should acquaint themselves with the financial and other procedures of building projects.
2. Architects should more fully cooperate with land owners, site planners, creditors, building developers, and others, in order to devise better-planned projects.
3. Excessive subdivision of land into small lots, many of which remain unoccupied, is costly. Builder/developers should carry through the whole process of subdivision, utilities, project, and dwelling construction.
4. For the foreseeable future, large-scale operations will produce the most efficient planning, the maximum economy, and the most extensive amenities as well as social gains.
5. Encouragement should be given to inventiveness and ingenuity to permit the greatest design and good construction.

A prescription for housing today could hardly improve on this 1932 statement. But many of these thoughts did not produce action. It took several decades to achieve these ideals, which were just beginning to be approached in the seventies. Let us now turn to the great pioneering residential architects and community planners who pointed the way to the progress aimed for in this manifesto.

Pioneer Community Planners

The decade of the thirties, which could be called "threadbare thirties" for economic reasons, was not in fact threadbare at all in regard to the pioneering of advanced concepts of community planning and design. Special honor must be paid to four talented men whose work powerfully affected the community design and development of the nation for many decades. Their ideas and influence are still pervasive among architects, land planners, builders, and home owners.

Frederick Law Olmstead of Baltimore was a landscape architect and community planner who easily takes preeminence as the first and greatest designer of large, environmentally planned communities. He and his firm, Olmstead Brothers, were retained by Edward H. Bouton of the Roland Park Company around 1900, and continued to design successful areas such as Guilford (1912), Homeland (1924), and Northwood (1932).

Olmstead brought entirely new and brilliant concepts: parks, playgrounds, curvilinear streets, landscaping, open space, preservation of trees and natural environment. He also assisted builder developers in setting up covenants and restrictions to preserve open space, architectural quality, and long-term values of their communities.

Olmstead and his firm had a long and distinguished career and planned many of the outstanding environmental projects of the twenties and thirties. In addition to Roland Park these included Forest Hills Gardens, Long Island, New York; St. Francis Woods and Park Hills, San Francisco; Juniper Hill, Belmont, Massachusetts; and Palos Verdes Estates, Los Angeles. His towering influence on better landscaping, site planning, community life, and environment continue to this day.

Henry Wright, architect and town planner, lived a notable career as the foremost town and site planner in the twenties and thirties. Born in Kansas, he studied architecture and city planning at the University of Pennsylvania and quickly went on to his favorite subject, community planning. He helped design the St. Louis World's Fair and many municipal parks and city projects. In 1926 he participated with Clarence Stein as architect and planner of Sunnyside Gardens on Long Island, New York, then Radburn in New Jersey, and later planned Chatham Village for Pittsburgh's Buhl Foundation. These were outstanding planned communities which have had great impact on city planning. Later Henry Wright continued his contributions to better living as associate in town planning at Columbia University's School of Architecture. His contributions to concepts of environmental planning, open space, playgrounds, recreation, and better land use have made a major impact.

In the twenties and thirties *Clarence Stein* captured the imagination of developers and home owners alike with his daring concepts of good neighborhood design. He led the way in such land and site planning ideas as the cul-de-sac, the super block, green-space areas around homes and apartments, rear gardens off living rooms, and safe walkways for children.

Stein worked closely with architect Henry Wright, as we have said, in Sunnyside, Radburn, and other projects. He went on to new achievements as he laid out Greenbelt, Maryland, in 1938, and Baldwin Hills Village in

Los Angeles, both meriting accolades in top-echelon community planning. He has exerted a strong and beneficial influence on the quality of American dwellings.

Seward H. Mott was the first director of FHA's land-planning division and as such carried out the monumental job of setting up improved standards for site and subdivision planning for builder projects. He brought new neighborhood design, siting, and environmental concepts that transformed the old traditional approaches for the better.

FHA was new in the mid-thirties and had inherited many in-built past errors of the industry. It is to Seward Mott's credit that he brought and enforced new ideas that transformed neighborhood planning methods.

Mott later became head of the Urban Land Institute, where he carried on his influence for improved community planning. He then entered a distinguished career as land planning consultant and as such laid out many outstanding U.S. communities, including Midwest City in Oklahoma.

These were the thinkers, dreamers, and planners. Now consider the *builders*, whose money, know-how, and willingness to risk using new ideas led them to put these concepts into home and living communities.

Great Builder/Developers
of Planned Residential Communities

When historians review the progress of residential community planning they inevitably arrive at the fact that each stage of progress and each project grew out of the work of brilliant men in an earlier period.

A good example is *Leicester Square* in London, which was laid out and developed around a park as a controlled community in the early seventeenth century. The Earl of Leicester had built his fine townhouse there and wanted to be assured that the area would live up to his standards. The property owners later set up what would today be called a community homes association, and adapted a legal setup to assure firm control of the area and use of the park. It is one of the first examples of a planned residential project with a community owners' association.

Americans are no doubt more familiar with Louisburg Square on Boston's famous *Beacon Hill*, developed in 1826. Here a 21-acre pasture was turned into an elegant, planned community around a park, or square, by a syndicate of four developers—Mason, Otis, Joy, and Jackson. Many of the 28 homes were constructed by carpenter builders, but the control of planning, design, and setting up a residential home owners' association was firmly in the hands of the developers.

Through the years, this project has continued to increase in value and appeal due to its strong protective covenants and its active home owners' association.

Perhaps the most outstanding U.S. examples of early residential home development were carried on by the *Roland Park Company* of Baltimore. There were four major areas, as we have noted: Roland Park, Guilford, Homeland, and Northwood. All were skillfully planned by the acknowledged dean of American home community planners, Frederick Law Olmstead and his firm, Olmstead Brothers.

The president of the Roland Park projects in the mid-thirties was the dashing, dedicated, and well-trained *Major John McC. Mowbray*. He was a close friend of, and consultant for, J. C. Nichols, Hugh Potter, and other leading developers. These men were all active in founding the Urban Land Institute, which will be described in Chapter 2. In fact, all became officials and McC. Mowbray was the first president.

Jack McC. Mowbray had inherited and done honor to a high tradition of community planning established by the original founder of Roland Park, Edward H. Bouton, who was considered the leader in advanced development ideas and was friend and advisor to many builders. Bouton discovered and employed the Olmstead Brothers' firm which later moved on to many famous assignments in planning. The Roland Park projects became an example of the finest accomplishments in early residential land development in this country and they strongly influenced builders and developers for decades to come.

All these projects included parks, playgrounds, ponds, malls, open space, skillful street plans, covenants, and community home owners' associations to assure long-lasting control of the common areas. The Urban Land Institute says of Roland Park, "It stands today as a monument to creative planning and the pioneering spirit of its developers. They set a pattern for immediate successors—among them J. C. Nichols—and the present generation of developers and planners."

Jesse Clyde Nichols, builder/developer of the famous Country Club District in Kansas City, is honored today as the greatest pioneer in community planning. His concepts of sit-

ing, landscaping, environmental control, open space parks, and use of home owners' associations to maintain community values are still inspiring builders all over the world.

"J.C." as he was often called, started with ten acres in 1905 and built his Country Club District to more than 6,500 acres, 15 communities, 14,000 homes, many shopping centers, and a population of more than 60,000.

In his planning Nichols was strongly influenced by the work of his friends at Roland Park, and he expanded and improved on their experience. One highly important concept was his setting up of community home owners' associations with mandatory requirements for membership. He developed legal covenants that ran with the land which proved a powerful force in maintaining both high community standards and the resulting high values.

In the early thirties during the depression, Nichols was one of the few builders still active. His Indian Hills area of 400 homes continued slowly, but he started the 350-unit Tomahawk Road project in 1935, and the 470-unit Fairway Homes in 1938. The Country Club District continued to develop, community by community, through the depression, war, postwar, and on to the present day. It rightly deserves its reputation as the highest quality, large scale, planned residential development in America.

Through his long career, Nichols was a leader in many community and industry affairs, and was one of the founders of both the Urban Land Institute and the National Association of Home Builders.

Hugh Potter of Houston, Texas, was another one of the relatively small handful of talented builder/developers whose work strongly influenced succeeding generations. His River Oaks project established new standards of en-

Royal Barry Wills' Cape Cod Colonial, built in 1933, was the winner of the Better Homes in America design competition.

Interior detail of the Cape Cod Colonial.

Colonial Williamsburg restoration (1927-1937) had a lasting impact on U.S. home design. (Photo courtesy Colonial Williamsburg.)

Early California ranch-style home, designed by Cliff May. This was built in 1933 at San Diego. (Photo courtesy Maynard Parker.)

Falling Waters, the famous Kaufmann House by Frank Lloyd Wright, built at Bull's Run, Pennsylvania, in 1936. (Photo courtesy Hedrich-Blessing.)

The A.C. Goodyear house in Old Westbury, Connecticut, designed by architect Edward Stone in 1939. It is an example of the contemporary style of the period. (Photo courtesy Ezra Stoller.)

In 1949, Levitt's Strathmore at Manhasset provided homes such as this at exceptionally low prices.

The Sloan house, designed by pioneers George Fred and William Keck, was included in the first solar community at Glenview, Illinois, in 1940. (Photo courtesy Hedrich-Blessing.)

Solar prefab design by Keck and Keck in 1940. This model was built by Greens Ready Built Homes. (Photo courtesy Hedrich-Blessing.)

The home of architect Carl Koch on Snake Hill near Cambridge, Massachusetts, built in 1941. (Photo courtesy Ezra Stoller.)

Snake Hill interior. (Photo courtesy Ezra Stoller.)

New trends in panelization, gypsum decking, and metal framing were displayed in this 1954 U.S. Gypsum Research Village house (above), designed by architect A. Quincy Jones and built by famed modernist Joseph Eichler. At right, a contemporary interior in Eichler style displays open webb joists. (Photos courtesy Hedrich-Blessing.)

Indoor-outdoor living was the trend of the fifties. This model was designed by Hugh Stubbins. (Photo courtesy Hedrich-Blessing.)

Modern interior with large glass areas—a trend-setting style created by Don Scholz in the mid-fifties.

Aerial view of Levittown, Long Island, in early stages before landscaping.

This original Levittown Cape Cod model had 720 square feet of living space and sold for $6,990 in 1947. Similar models with improvements were selling at $40,000 in 1979.

Vacation cottage of the fifties shows plywood in new forms and with new uses.

vironmental planning, land use, and architectural controls. Potter, as has been noted, was a close friend of John McC. Mowbray and J. C. Nichols, and employed many of the same advanced planning ideas. He sited houses skillfully on large, well-landscaped plots along wide, curved streets. The towering trees were preserved and many more were added. Esplanades and small parks were beautified with landscaping, and covenants were established to assure their upkeep.

Potter was one of the founders and an early president of the Urban Land Institute. In 1940 he became chairman of the Home Builders' Emergency Committee, which did a notable job of helping builders untangle the confusing web of priorities, rules and restrictions that almost throttled private war housing construction.

Duncan McDuffie, of San Francisco, has the distinction of having been one of the first community developers in the U.S. to provide landscaped parks, recreational and open-space areas, curvilinear streets, and a mandatory homes association to maintain common areas.

McDuffie's St. Francis Wood (1912) and Park Hills (1939) in San Francisco were both skillfully planned and landscaped by the celebrated Olmstead Brothers. They have today become showcases of the best in community design, planning, and landscaping.

Notable in these projects are the small landscaped parks, the playgrounds, and the elaborate and beautiful gateway entrances, one with a lovely fountain. The parks and common property are maintained by the home owners' associations set up by McDuffie before opening the projects. Membership is mandatory, and over the years the associations have maintained the common properties in excellent fashion, and indeed enhanced the beauty, livability, and value of the properties.

Sunnyside Gardens (1926), in the heavily populated Queens area of New York City, was a pioneer high-density townhouse project intended for low and middle-income buyers. The builder was the City Housing Corporation, headed by Alexander Bing, and the designers and planners were Clarence Stein and Henry Wright.

Sunnyside arranged its 565 units around private, landscaped interior courts which were intended to recall the "close" of Old England. This project also included playgrounds and a 3.5-acre recreational area—all daring concepts for the period.

Important also was the establishment of a home owners' association to maintain the common property. Over the years, Sunnyside has continued to hold its place as a desirable, well-maintained residential community.

Radburn, the "Town for the Motor Age," was another project of the City Housing Corporation, and like Sunnyside, had Clarence Stein and Henry Wright as architects and planners. It started with an ambitious and remarkably far-sighted plan in 1928—a bad year for the building industry. It originally was intended to be a complete satellite community with an industrial area to provide employment. The depression forced a large cutback in the project, but the portion that was completed remains world famous as an example of superb community planning, and a good place to live.

Radburn's pioneering plan created superblocks with interior recreation and park areas, cul-de-sacs, cluster plans, open green space, and safe walkways for children.

A striking feature of the cul-de-sac house arrangement was a motor entrance on one side and a private walkway entrance on the other.

The amenities provided were superb, even by today's standards, and included two swimming pools, 23 acres of parks, tot lots, ballfields, tennis courts, and a maze of interior walkways with underpasses permitting children to get to school without crossing heavily trafficked streets. A mandatory home owners' association maintained the common property and the high standards of the community.

Palos Verdes Estates near Los Angeles is an example of a large, high-quality residential community that has flourished over the years because of its fine location, excellent planning, protective restrictions, and a strong home owners' association.

The project was developed by the Vanderlip Syndicate, headed by Frank Vanderlip and

planned by Olmstead Brothers. Although started in the mid-twenties, it got caught in the financial problems of the thirties, was delayed, and not completed for many years. By then the original tract of 16,000 acres on a striking headland overlooking the Pacific Ocean was reduced to 3,200 acres.

Olmstead's plan made the most of the beautiful rolling terrain and provided for three separate communities with schools, playgrounds, shopping centers, parks, and open space. The project developed as a high-priced area with large plots, well-designed homes, and restrictive covenants plus home owners' associations that have maintained its high principles.

Chicago World's Fair, 1933— Showcase for Architectural Innovation

The glittering, colorful World's Fair in Chicago opened during the depth of the depression—a dramatic contrast to the drab state of the construction industry elsewhere at that period. Building editors* had plenty of time to visit and photograph the strange and wonderful structures they saw rising from Chicago's lakefront; there was not much other construction to write about.

The Fair's theme was "Science is the determining factor in progress," and it well lived up to its promise. The imagination of millions of visitors was caught up in a fantastic world of color and architectural forms. They gasped in awe at the cable suspension systems, glass walls, steel in strong, delicate forms, over-

whelming light and color, the skyride, rocket cars, "enchanted island," fountains, pools, gardens, and the amazing and exotic exhibits.

There can be little question that the Fair had an indisputable effect on architecture, design, construction methods, and, especially, new materials. It was a great showcase and testing ground for building-product manufacturers, and they made the most of it.

The houses were exciting and full of new ideas, inside and out. The "House of Tomorrow," designed by architect George Fred Keck, was a 12-sided structure of glass and steel sections bolted together and supported on a cantilevered frame. It had an airplane hanger in the basement and, most astounding of all, was fully air-conditioned.

There were houses of many different types and styles, ranging from Cape Cod to classic to modern. Inside they had the most elabo-

---

*Editor's note: J.B. Mason, then with *American Builder*, attended and wrote extensively on it.

rate, elegant, and innovative kitchens, baths, and equipment ever seen. Here, too, U.S. manufacturers went all out to display their newest ideas in equipment and also designs for the areas where they would be installed.

Two of the houses were prototypes of the latest in prefabrication. American Houses of New York displayed a compact model designed by Holden, McLaughlin and Associates which foretold a trend to the prefab panel systems of later years. It had a lightweight steel frame and open-truss steel joists for floors and roofs. Wall panels four feet wide fitted into the steel frame and were built of asbestos cement sheets with insulation in-between. Heavy insulating composition panels were used in floors and roofs. American Houses later became one of the largest prefab home manufacturing companies using this basic system, with many later variations.

Another leading prefab-home firm, General Houses, Incorporated, of Chicago, displayed its compact prototype, and it attracted wide attention. Designed by architect Howard T. Fisher, it used factory-made, sheet-steel panels with cork insulation. The frame was of light steel designed for fast and easy erection. It was available as a complete prefab package of standardized parts, with heating and cooling. The firm claimed, "Expected life span of house, if properly maintained: *forever.*"

Williamsburg Restoration, 1927-1937

Our remarks on architecture, design, and planning may fittingly be concluded with a brief account of the saga of Williamsburg, which got under way about 1927 and was largely completed by 1937. Thus it benefitted by the low costs of the depression years, but more importantly, it enjoyed the financial backing of John D. Rockefeller, Jr., without whose support it would probably not have survived.

It is the belief of many authorities that the Williamsburg, Virginia, restoration has had a greater influence on U.S. home design than any other program, project, or person. Not only did it have impact on home building of that time, but it continued through the forties, fifties, and on to this day. In fact, one of the project fads of the late seventies was a return to "authentic Colonial," in which architects and builders drew heavily on the popular Williamsburg Colonial themes.

Williamsburg was, of course, extremely publicized, and its home designs, colors, interiors, fireplaces, chimney details, and even picket fences were glorified in many books and articles. One magazine editor* took a special trip to Williamsburg in 1948 just to photograph the picket, rail, board, serpentine brick, and other "authentic" fences, which were published along with details showing how they were built.

The story of how the restoration got its start is an historical tale worth telling. It began as a daring dream and desire on the part of Dr. W. A. R. Goodwin, rector of the local Bruton Parish Church, who for many years had been striving to preserve and restore the lovely local architecture and historical landmarks. In

---

*Editor's note: In fact, it was J.B. Mason, then with *Good Housekeeping*, who made this trip.

1925 he gave a lecture on his favorite topic before the Phi Beta Kappa Society in New York, which was heard by John D. Rockefeller, Jr.

Within a few months Dr. Goodwin had persuaded Mr. Rockefeller to come down to Williamsburg, and he presented him with hi plan for a complete restoration of the area to its original Colonial appearance. Shortly after, the Rector was authorized by Rockefeller to buy the needed properties and launch the project—certainly one of the happiest instances of a dream that came true.

At the time of the American Revolution, Williamsburg had been a town of beauty and great architectural significance. Its College of William and Mary had been designed by Christopher Wren in late Renaissance style, and the building was carried out by Thomas Hadley, master builder. Its Governor's Palace, Capitol, Old Court House, Raleigh tavern, Ludwell-Paradise House, and many homes, taverns, and public buildings were examples of the best architectural heritage of the time and of Colonial Virginia.

"The stamp of Wren's interpretation of the later Renaissance is clear throughout," said William Perry, one of the principal architects of the restoration. "As in England, the mannerisms of the Netherlands . . . are to be seen in plan, composition, scale detail of brickwork, and furnishings.

"We see that process of change and adaptation of the later Renaissance which has produced what is known to us as Virginia 'character'."

When the original town was surveyed and laid out by Theodorick Bland in 1666, it projected a "noble great Street"—the Duke of Gloucester Street—100 feet wide, with numerous broad, tree-lined avenues and cross streets. It called for public greens and squares and effective use of open spaces.

The plan also included restrictions governing the types of buildings which could be constructed on the large, one-half-acre lots. It thus appears to have been one of the first "planned communities" in America.

The process of research, restoration, and rebuilding was a monumental one. The Williamsburg Restoration, Incorporated, directed the work, aided by the City of Williamsburg, the Association for the Preservation of Virginia Antiquities, and numerous public and private donors, including Mr. Rockefeller. A team of architects headed by the firm of Perry, Shaw and Hepburn carried on extensive historical and even archeological studies and meticulously supervised each reconstruction detail. Arthur A. Shurcliff directed the landscaping and city planning, and contractors Todd & Brown, Incorporated, carried out the construction.

Some concept of the size and magnitude of the operation is shown by the fact that 440 buildings were torn down, 18 were moved outside the area, 66 Colonial buildings were repaired or restored, 84 were reproduced on Colonial foundations, and streets, open spaces, and gardens were restored to their Colonial appearance, with lampposts, fences, brick walks, and proper plantings. In addition, the vast influx of visitors has required building numerous inns, lodges, restaurants, and, in fact, an expansion of the whole area that has continued to the present.

Dr. Goodwin's dream has indeed grown to wondrous proportions, and the entire nation is indebted to him for it.

Research Paves the Way for Progress

Housing advances in the thirties were hidden by the dismal disasters of the depression. Yet progress was there—as has been noted—in architectural design and far-sighted community planning. Now turn to another aspect of that hidden advance: housing research, techniques, new products, and prefabrication.

During the late twenties and early thirties a dedicated number of little-known scientists, researchers, architects, engineers, and technicians were at work on many forms of building technology. We cannot describe all of them, for like most activities in this huge and dispersed industry, research and development are carried on by hundreds of rather small groups, institutions, building and manufacturing firms, and individuals.

The search for the key men in housing research and development in past years is as involved as that of a writer of detective fiction. By and large their works are buried in dusty trade-journal reports or not recorded at all. Most builders of today know little about these early men and projects that paved the way for the remarkable war production achievements of 1940-1945 and the even greater housing production boom of 1946-1950. Yet much of this is directly attributable to research carried on in the thirties.

Albert Farwell Bemis, who founded the Bemis Research Foundation in New York in the mid-twenties and nurtured its progress through the thirties, was a successful businessman/industrialist with a passion for housing investigation. Over the years he devoted much of his time and fortune to researching materials, methods, systems, and modular coordination, and testing them. He also brought in talented associates who carried on his work after he retired. Later the Foundation became associated with the Massachusetts Institute of Technology, which assisted in its programs. John E. Burchard, Professor of Architectural Engineering at MIT, later became director.

A striking insight into the Bemis Foundation work is given in a report issued in 1933, some extracts of which are given as follows:

> We have developed story-height wall units in pulp—blocks up to 20 feet high, four feet wide, and nine-and-one-half inches thick.
> "Also a self-keying partition using gypsum or transite in combination with very simple steel studs.
> We are most interested in applications of synthetic resins, in plywood, and particularly resin-bonded plywoods.
> The backbone of all our planning is the cubical modular system of design . . . which is applicable to conventional structures, but applies with particular force to all forms of prefabrication. This system is really extraordinary and will be explained in detail in Volume III of *The Evolving House*.
> We believe housing in the United States will be fostered not by three or four or 20 models of houses but by a *system of planning and design which permits every buyer to have his own plan while using standard premade parts.* Our cubical modular systems start from this premise.

Over the years Bemis Foundation carried on extensive research in house construction systems, steel and other frame and panel systems, standardized dimensions, and modular coordination. Both laboratory and field testing were carried on, including the building of some 22 test houses. *The Evolving House*, in three volumes, was published in 1934 by Technology Press of MIT and has had a definitive influence on building techniques, especially in the field of modular systems, dimensional coordination, and panelization.

A striking example of the way such housing research brought great progress is found in the life and work of F. Vaux Wilson, a top executive of the Homosote Company of Trenton, New Jersey. He studied the Bemis ideas and decided to adapt them to a simple modular system of wall panels that could be built in lumberyards.

Vaux Wilson combined technical expertise with a vigorous sales sense, and of course his *Precision Built Homes* were designed to use the excellent large-size wall panel boards made by his firm. He designed jig tables so that large wall sections could be fabricated in lumberyards. Usually they were sold to small local builders who created the houses with considerable speed.

Vaux Wilson was very well known in the industry and made much progress with his Precision Built Homes through the thirties and forties. It was a momentous occasion for him when he erected his first demonstration house in 1936—he was a tense and high-strung person who could not stand to have anything go wrong. When one of the large, cumbersome panels refused to slip into place as easily as expected, he gave vent to several highly explicit remarks, rushed over, grabbed a great sledge hammer, and with one blow put the offending piece into place—an act witnessed by this author with amusement.

The big advantage of this early prefab panel system was that it could be done locally on a small scale, and Vaux Wilson almost single-handedly launched a large, nation-wide distribution which resulted in the construction of many thousands of homes.

During the war and defense years his system proved a boon to builders seeking speed and low cost. One firm, Barrett & Hilp, broke all records by building 977 homes in three months at Vallejo, California, in 1942, and 5,000 at Portsmouth, Virginia, where it turned out 80 a day in an abandoned fertilizer factory.

U.S. Forest Products Laboratories at Madison, Wisconsin, is another of those unsung but dedicated research institutions that did wonders to advance housing. For years the labs carried on basic research in wood products and wood and plywood uses. In 1934 they made a particulary significant breakthrough by developing "stressed-skin" plywood panels which were the forerunner of many prefab and lightweight-panel building systems.

The plywood panels were modular, insulated, very strong, and very light. The lab technicians then built full-scale models demonstrating floor, wall, and roof panels that interlocked. They also developed new plywood finishes, wood flooring, and modular windows compatible with the system. Much of the low-cost war and postwar home building derived markedly from this work. Other developments included weather-resistant exterior plywood, laminated timbers and lumber, and paper honeycomb sandwich panels.

Housing Research Foundation at Purdue University was one of the first to develop prefab panel houses based on the Forest Products work. In 1936 Purdue researched and built a series of low-cost houses (under $5,000) which were subjected to detailed studies of cost, upkeep, and assembly methods. All experimented with new materials and methods intended to reduce cost. The first was a prefab panel house built by General Houses, Incorporated, based on Forest Products' ideas. It led the way to large prefab production on a national scale. Here we see an unusually clear illustration of housing progress spurred by research.

Robert L. Davison of New York became a brilliant innovator in home techniques through his work as Director of Housing Research for the John B. Pierce Foundation in the thirties and forties. He carried out meticulous studies in materials, methods, and systems. He organized standardized details and elements for baths, kitchens, partitions, exterior wall panels, and structures.

One of Davison's works was his exhaustive basic analysis of U.S. house floor plans which led to an efficient 24 × 28 foot standard plan widely used in war housing and prefab units.

Davison also invented a lightweight steel curtain-wall house with "sandwich panels" of insulation and asbestos cement or plywood. In 1941 this system was used to build 600 prefab homes in six months for war workers at the Martin Bomber plant near Baltimore.

Research and development of a somewhat different kind was also being carried on vigorously during the depression and mid-thirties: it was the work of U.S. manufacturers of building products, materials, and equipment. Again it should be pointed out that such work was done by hundreds of manufacturing firms, large and small. Their research and technical staffs were busy trying to find new products to build better, and expand their production.

It is unfortunately true that the public tends to ignore the truly important advances created by the research teams of great U.S. industries. Especially in such fields as heating, lighting, electrical, kitchen and bath equipment, their work has made the homes of America the envy of the world. A list of what were thought to be the most significant new building products on the market in 1933 follows:

- *Water-resistant plywood*, laminated with phenolic resins. A major aid in lightweight panel construction.

- *Elastic glues of latex* and or casein which could expand or contract with metal, plywood, or other materials.

- *Plywood specially treated* so it could be used and reused—as many as 15 times—in concrete forms or elsewhere.

- *Composition-board products* such as Masonite that were treated so that they could be used and reused—they produced an exceptionally smooth surface.

- *Treated, fire-resistant wood products* that could slow down or resist spread of flames.

- *Improvement in wood preservatives* and treatments to give long life and decay and rot resistance.

- *Fabricated, interlocking wood parts*, lumber, and structural members machined to exact standard sizes, precision precut to fit.

- *Blanket-type wood fiber* and mineral wool insulation—treated, efficient, easy to install.

- *Large wood fiber and composition planks*, boards, and sheets—both structural and insulating qualities.

- *Connectors for timber construction*, a whole new concept of devices that strengthened lumber structures and expanded their use.

- *New textiles*, fibers, colors, finishes, fire-resistant materials, waterproofing, latex.

This is a small sampling indeed, but indicates that progress was being made even while building activity itself was almost dormant.

Innovators of Prefabrication

The decade of the thirties was an exciting and productive one for the prefabricated-house industry. It could hardly be called an industry then, but a handful of tenacious men tried to make it so. They fought a long, uphill battle, and only a few survived. But they created a new industry that quickly caught the fancy of the American public—and the consumer and trade press.

It is a fact that the prefab firms got far more than their share of publicity, as editors rushed to write their glowing stories. All a prefab firm's president had to do was call a press conference and predict that within x days (fill in your own—it could be six months or six years) 90% of all U.S. houses would be rolling off prefab production lines. The press usually gave credulous heed—and headlines.

It is difficult to sort out the facts from the fantasies of those days. Certainly the greater promise did not materialize, but a sound beginning evolved into a substantial industry in the forties when the war gave a tremendous boost to all kinds of mass-housing production. Here are a few of the early and persistent pioneers.

E. F. Hodgson of Boston, founder of the oldest prefab firm (1892), geared up in the thirties and by 1941 had produced 100,000 units. His system employed lightweight five- and ten-foot-wide sections bolted together. Many were vacation homes and cottages.

Ivon R. Ford was a rough and tough early rural prefabricator who worked out of a nondescript muddle of buildings at McDonough, New York. He started building prefab hog houses, chicken coops, and farm buildings in 1935, but by 1940 was producing 30 good and sound houses a month. His trucks delivered a complete house package of large panels and precut materials to surrounding rural areas. He was a strong, determined outdoorsman. He developed a system of cranes mounted on trucks that put the heavy wall sections in place. His was the first prefab firm to function successfully in rural and farm areas.

The early prefabbers had a rough time working out their advanced systems and new materials. So it is not surprising that the prime movers in several projects that later proved successful were architects. One of the first was *Howard T. Fisher* of General Houses, Incorporated, of Chicago. He designed and erected his first experimental house at Winnetka, Illinois, early in 1933, and then opened an improved model at the Chicago World's Fair the same year.

The first General Houses prefabs were assembled from factory-made steel panels insulated with cork. They were lightweight and designed to fit into a modular lightweight steel frame. The all-steel houses did not sell as well as expected, and later the firm shifted to plywood-panel construction. By 1941 plant capacity had grown to 500 houses a month, and many thousands were built in the war and postwar years. Howard Fisher continued to experiment, revise, and improve his designs for years, and he contributed a host of ideas and concepts to the industry.

Robert W. McLaughlin was another architect prominent in the prefab industry in the thirties, and was one of the founders of American Houses, Incorporated, in New York, in 1932. The first model, built that year at Jeddo, Pennsylvania, had a light steel frame into which four-foot-wide asbestos cement panels were fitted. The modern design did not sell well and the firm then shifted to a more conventional precut wood and plywood-panel house with Colonial exteriors. A considerable volume of apartment work using this system later ensued. By 1942 American Houses had a plant capacity of 600 units a month, and sold some 20,000 units during the war.

George Fred Keck was also a well-known architect who did much to design new systems, components, and techniques for the prefabrication industry. His glass and steel "House of Tomorrow," which has already been described, was the center of attraction at the 1933 Chicago World Fair.

Foster Gunnison, founder and president of Gunnison Homes of New Albany, Indiana, was technically competent and also a superb salesman. In 1936 he created a furious stir by erecting a full-size prefab house in Grand Central Terminal in New York City. Gunnison pioneered the use of stressed-skin plywood panels which he built on a hot press using waterproof adhesives. His firm sold more than 5,000 war homes and expanded greatly in the postwar years.

1939 and the World of Tomorrow

It is fitting near the end of this chronicle of the thirties to include a brief comment on the New York World's Fair of 1939, which arose gloriously in the meadows and wastelands of the borough of Queens. The building press covered every facet of this huge Fair—an assignment they accepted with zeal and alacrity. There were also fringe benefits consisting of season press passes, which the editors, including this one, appreciated.

New York's 1939 Fair was the biggest, costliest, and most exciting spectacle of the decade. It was dedicated both to the blessings of democracy and to the wonders of technology—a fine combination. Again the public observed with wonder the architectural construction and engineering aspects of a breathtaking array of buildings and displays. Model houses and a galaxy of housing products, materials, building systems, and home equipment certainly gave inspiration to a rising field of architects and builders who were busily laying plans for the forties.

This editor concluded as he wrote a special issue about this fabulous Fair that it was a fitting climax to a decade that had dragged the depths of the depression, flirted with political chaos, and was now rapidly rising from it. Housing was once again on the way up—so he thought.

What Did Happen to Housing in the Thirties?

Historians have said, with some truth, that the mid-thirties was an era of political, social, and economic ferment unlike any in history. Many believe that the vigorous, innovative reforms and economic growth potential of the New Deal stopped a strong trend to socialism.

As far as housing was concerned, the record is clear. The Home Loan Bank and Home Owners' Loan Corporation stopped the housing deflation, and the Federal Housing Administration in a short time laid the base for a truly phenomenal increase in home construction. These two federal agencies and an improving financial condition permitted the nation's private builders to unleash what has aptly been called their "power to produce." The results in the number of good, livable homes have astonished the world. In many countries the restricted bureaucracy of socialistic government agencies has instead stifled home ownership and private-enterprise construction.

So what actually did happen to U.S. housing in the thirties? The combined effects of New Deal legislation and of FHA and HOLC financing aids began to show, and large-project builders began to expand their volume sharply in mid-decade. They were helped enormously by 80% FHA-insured amortized mortgages that ran for 20 years at low interest, and the number of dwellings soared.

Housing costs, although rising, were still low and were being kept within bounds by the enterprise and inventiveness of many thousand of small and large firms using new techniques and materials. These houses were also better built than pre-depression ones, having brass and copper gutters and piping, long-life roofing, more and better insulation, and improved quality lumber. They were also better equipped with oil or gas furnaces, efficient kitchens, refrigerators, electrical outlets, and modern baths.

Of course, there was also a large housing need that had built up during the low-production years of the depression, as well as a significant population increase.

The result of these factors was that private builders, both large and small, went back to work, and housing starts and sales began to accelerate rapidly in 1936. They rose to 336,000 in 1937, 406,000 in 1938, 515,000 in 1939, and 603,000 in 1940. This was certainly a striking lift from 1933's 93,000. These perhaps dry statistics do tell a human story of thousands of builders who finally found financing, buyers, and conditions favorable to *risk taking*. The dramatic increases were hard earned by mostly small businessmen who planned, schemed, took chances, dreamed, and got a remarkable volume of homes built in spite of all the problems.

During this period there was a continuing tug of war in and out of government over how housing needs and goals should be accomplished. Many New Deal advisors favored public housing, and some was built—usually at much higher costs than were achieved by the hard-nosed private builders. Before the New Deal almost all work was done by private builders, but in 1935 some 5,000 public units were built: 15,000 in 1936, 4,000 in 1937, 7,000 in 1938, and 57,000 in 1939.

For the decade as a whole, however, 97% of the 2,734,000 units were built by private builders, a striking testimonial to the enterprise system which got homes built despite depression and financial obstacles.

CHAPTER TWO

1940-1950

DEFENSE HOUSING AND POSTWAR EXPANSION

War Deeds, Daring, and Enterprise

The history of housing during the forties is punctuated by the deeds of many bold men who played a part in building desperately needed defense homes and a better-housed, postwar America. In every emergency brought on by war, materials shortages, or delays caused by confused government agencies, hard-working, inventive builders emerged to keep the production of homes alive and growing.

It is fitting to look back, take stock, and call attention to the work of those who made significant contributions to war housing. They have been largely unsung and seldom praised. Yet they set a record in the forties of which the industry is proud.

The ultimate achievement of the decade was the production of an astounding 7,443,000 homes for war veterans and other Americans, despite manifold problems. Independent builders constructed 96% of the total, which many consider a heartening affirmation of the American private-enterprise system. The decade also recorded notable ad-

vances in home design, construction techniques, research, and development.

The World War II years, 1940-1945, brought the biggest change in construction methods, materials, and techniques. In a few short years the housing industry was torn from its slow, handicraft ways and projected into a fast-paced new world of industrialized production in huge, planned projects.

The need for housing for war workers in defense plants was urgent in 1941, 1942, and 1943. Speed was of the essence, financing was available, and the bigger the project the better. For the first time, builders had an assured market and ample funds, plus a patriotic motive to get the job done quickly.

This was the combination that enabled builders such as William J. Levitt, David D. Bohannon, Barret and Hilp, Gross-Morton, Fritz B. Burns, and a thousand others to construct mass-production lines and pioneer new prefabrication and panelized systems. The results laid the groundwork for the building techniques that produced an unprecedented surge of postwar home construction. This huge outpouring was a major factor counteracting the expected depression.

New instruments of home finance were another highlight of the World War II years which spurred war housing and which were continued and expanded upon in postwar years. The major aid to private enterprise was FHA Title VI. Long-term, low-interest mortgages of 90% made home buying and building easy. Later, terms were increased to 95%.

FHA financing was available both for purchasing and for rental housing. In 1943 a new Section 608 was added to FHA Title VI that gave a tremendous stimulus to apartment building, especially garden apartments. Some 400,000 units were built under Section 608 between 1944 and 1951.

The war years also stimulated prefabricated home building as well as the greater use of fabricated parts, panels, and components. It is interesting to note that while the war fostered mass production in large projects, many of the ideas, methods, and materials were later adapted by smaller firms and became an integral part of the postwar housing boom.

Smaller firms soon adopted power equipment, site precutting, and use of panels and components. There was a greatly expanded acceptance of factory-built door and window units, prefab wall and storage units, prefab ducts and plumbing, trusses, and many other prebuilt parts and equipment that reduced on-site labor cost and erection time.

Notable technical progress was also made both during and after the war by the manufacturers of home products, equipment, and materials, and great credit must be given them for the better homes that were produced.

Builders Organize for War

A direct result of World War II was the emergence of a powerful National Association of Home Builders to carry on the battle for war and defense housing. As the war crisis grew in the early forties, it became imperative for builders to meet head on in Washington the problems of priorities, allocations, and materials shortages. It was crystal clear that strong central leadership and a spokesman for the disorganized housing industry were needed.

Most important, someone who knew the industry was needed to deal with the proliferation of government agencies, most of which were staffed with people poorly informed about the complexities and ramifications of the industry.

In 1940 there were two small national builder groups and a dozen or so state and local home builder associations. At the local level in thousands of communities there were no builder organizations at all. In effect, the huge body of building and housing interests in the United States were unrepresented in Washington.

Efforts to unify the two major groups, the Home Builders' Institute and the National Home Builders' Association, were started in 1940, but proved unproductive. The spark that finally set off action in 1941 was a proposed War Production Board order to close down private defense housing and turn all of the building work over to public housing agencies.

In response to this threat, David D. Bohannon of San Mateo, California, president of the

Home Builders' Institute, convened a historic meeting in Detroit in November 1941, which established a vigorous Home Builders' Emergency Committee, headquartered in Washington, with Hugh Potter of Houston as its chairman. At a luncheon rally led by Cyrus Crane Willmore of St. Louis, some $30,000 was raised to allow the committee to take immediate action.

And action it did provide. Potter, Bohannon, and other committee members flew to Washington the next day and soon were conferring with federal officials. Chairman Potter had excellent legal training (his friends used to call him "Judge"), and under his skilled direction HBEC became a respected voice for builders. HBEC did yeoman service in helping untangle the confusing web of priorities, rules, allocations, and restrictions that almost throttled private defense housing.

A report of the HBEC members meeting with federal officials on November 13, 1941, shows the vital needs discussed:

1. To get facts on critical materials.
2. To help work out alternative or new materials.
3. To collect local facts on the need or lack of need for public housing.
4. To bring about more realistic FHA valuation methods.
5. To study and act on allocations of materials.

Potter had strong support in HBEC from powerful building leaders such as David Bohannon, Fritz B. Burns of Los Angeles, J. C. Nichols of Kansas City, John McC. Mowbray of Baltimore, Waverly Taylor of Washington, D.C., George Miller of Detroit, Herbert U. Nelson of Chicago, George Nixon of Chicago, Ellie Stoneson of San Francisco, C. Earl Colomb of New Orleans, Robert Gerholz

of Flint, Michigan, Joseph E. Merrion of Chicago, Joseph E. Meyerhoff of Baltimore, and Harry Durbin of Detroit.

HBEC's most dramatic achievement was the rescinding of the War Production Board order stopping private defense home building, and it continued to aid the production of defense homes until 1944. In February 1942, Frank W. Cortright of Philadelphia was appointed executive secretary of both the HBEC and the Home Builders' Institute. Under the leadership of Potter, Cortright, and Bohannon, the power and influence of the Home Builders' Institute increased; and in September 1942, its name was changed to the National Association of Home Builders of the United States. A strong effort was then launched to secure merger with the rival National Home Builders' Association.

Feelings had run high between the rival builder groups. In 1941, a quiet meeting of about 30 members of the National Home Builders' Association was under way at the Ambassador Hotel in Washington when, suddenly, Dave Bohannon, the big, brawny president of the rival Home Builders' Institute, strode in, his jaw set, his eyes flashing, his fist conspicuously at his sides. "You could feel the tension mount as chairs were pushed back and builders jumped to their feet," one of those present reported. "I fully expected a fight, but Dave was too big to throw out!" Dave had one companion, Waverly Taylor, not nearly as big but just as brave. There were some tense moments, but finally Bohannon was allowed to speak. He was actually bringing a peace merger proposal, but he got nowhere. In fact, it took several more years to bring the groups together into NAHB.*

---

*Editor's note: J.B. Mason was present at this meeting.

Finally, with the "patience, tolerance, and compromise" with which the members of the committees were later credited (by Waverly Taylor in his account of the proceedings), the merger was achieved on July 1, 1943. Harry Durbin of NHBA played an important role. The first president of the new NAHB was Fritz B. Burns of Los Angeles; its executive vice president was Frank W. Cortright. This marked a turning point in the history of the U.S. housing industry.

The new organization filled a vital need and continued to provide strong national leadership both in getting defense housing built and in generating a huge postwar home program. Its rise to power and to national influence has been meteoric. With a membership in 1980 of more than 125,000, it became one of the most influential, well-managed, and constructive trade associations in the world. The growth, accomplishments, and organization of the NAHB will be discussed in subsequent sections.

Bombers, Tanks, and Defense Housing

As 1940 opened, builders, like most other Americans, were not overly concerned about the effects at home of the war in Europe. Housing was just then recovering from the shock of the depression, and starts had climbed from the 1933 low of 93,000 to a respectable 603,000 in 1940. The huge shelter shortage which accumulated during the depression years had not been made up and the builders were optimistic. They were soon due for a rude awakening.

Suddenly, German troops had overrun Europe. Italy had become our enemy, and President Roosevelt had asked for 50,000 planes and a huge armament program. By December 7, 1941—the "Day of Infamy" of Pearl Harbor—the United States was embarked on the greatest mobilization of industrial production in the history of this or any other nation.

American builders played a significant role in that production by providing urgently needed defense housing for workers in shipyards, tank and aircraft plants, and many industrial complexes such as Willow Run at Ypsilanti, Michigan. War workers, even the most patriotic, simply could not and would not work without adequate housing.

It may be true, as some insist, that the war was won on the home front. Both sides had good guns and generals, but the American production of planes, tanks, and all armaments of war was so overwhelming it finally crushed opposition. The figures are astounding: 71,000 naval ships; 300,000 aircraft; 100,000 tanks; 2.5 million trucks; 370,000 artillery pieces; 5.9 million bombs; 20 million small arms; 42 million rounds of ammunition; 5,400 cargo ships. No wonder Stalin is said to have offered a toast at the Teheran meeting with Roosevelt and Churchill "to American production, without which the war would have been lost."

Almost overnight, it seemed, the entire construction industry was caught up in a frenzy of war plant and defense construction: bomber plants, barracks, defense homes, tank plants, shipyards, industrial complexes, and a vast dispersion of army and navy projects around the world. The mammoth achievements got, and deserved, the headlines. But thousands of the "little men" of the building industry contributed, too.

Large and small builders, accustomed to working in communities near home, were asked to pull up stakes abruptly and start construction near defense industries, often far away. Army, navy, and government housing officials were urgent in their demands for defense housing, without which their production was hamstrung.

A few builders, including Dave Bohannon, got their defense housing under way before Pearl Harbor, usually with the help of a friend in the armed services. The problem was usually one of materials, manpower, and priorities. Federal officials were, at first, quick to grant high priorities to public housing projects, but very slow on private defense homes.

By 1942 it was recognized that public housing was slow, costly, and often enmeshed in production delays and bureaucratic problems. Independent builders managed to obtain enough priorities to make significant increases in defense home production. Early in that year dozens of Long Island builders, including William J. Levitt, moved to the Norfolk-Portsmouth area, and many others got into production in Brooklyn, Baltimore, Seattle, San Diego, and other defense areas.

By this time, 75% of the prewar builders were out of work, and many sought jobs in war plants, enlisted, or joined the Seabees. Those who remained had to learn mass-production techniques, prefabrication, demountable home work, and ways to build huge blocks of low-cost defense houses quickly. They had to learn to bull their way through a maze of priorities, allocations, shortages, stop orders, and bureaucratic regulations that often left them frustrated and confused.

To this housing historian it appears amazing that the nation's builders got as much done as

they did. The record is 2.3 million war and defense homes between 1940 and 1945; then 5.1 million postwar and veterans' homes built in a veritable explosion of production between 1946 and 1949.

Early impetus was given to the defense housing program in 1940 by the Lanham Act and $300 million provided for public projects by the Federal Works Administration. A defense housing coordinator, Charles F. Palmer, was appointed. FHA authorizations also were increased and terms liberalized. Later, a highly important revision of FHA Title VI authorized advance commitment to projects, which greatly speeded up large operations. An "economic soundness" provision was waived which also encouraged more builders to get into defense home work. Thus both public and private construction were encouraged.

Despite much effort by federal officials, there was widespread criticism of the confusion, conflict, bickering, and inefficiency in the defense housing setup. As a result, President Roosevelt issued a reorganization order in February 1942, placing all 16 agencies under one roof, the National Housing Agency headed by John B. Blandford. The three major constituents were the Federal Public Housing Authority (FPHA), Leon Keyserling, Administrator; the Federal Housing Agency (FHA), Abner Ferguson, Commissioner; and the Federal Home Loan Bank (FHLB), John Fahey, Administrator. The reorganizaion proved fairly effective, and defense housing in the succeeding years moved ahead much more smoothly.

During the entire decade there was constant conflict at high government levels between those who felt that housing should be built largely by public agencies and those who favored the traditional private-enterprise approach. The heat and fury of the debate often obscured results and slowed action. But the final record shows that independent builders turned out 7,153,000 of 7,443,000 housing units produced from 1940 to 1949, or 96%. The record is shown in Table 1.

Table 1
Dwelling Units Started—1940-1949

	Total	Private	Public
1940	603,000	530,000	73,000
1941	706,000	620,000	86,000
1942	356,000	301,000	55,000
1943	191,000	184,000	7,000
1944	142,000	139,000	3,000
1945	326,000	325,000	1,000
1946	1,023,000	1,015,000	8,000
1947	1,268,000	1,265,000	3,000
1948	1,362,000	1,344,000	18,000
1949	1,466,000	1,430,000	36,000
Total	7,443,000	7,153,000	290,000

The Striking Record of Home Building for War Workers

Guadalcanal, Coral Sea, Casablanca, Anzio, Teheran: these were the names emblazoned in the headlines as the U.S. war effort spread its enormous global assault. At home the builders of war housing frantically pursued their efforts to provide the houses so vital to keeping workers on the job in shipyards, bomber plants, naval bases, and industrial plants.

The scope, speed, and volume of war housing are hard to grasp, since it proceeded on a thousand scattered fronts. We can best illustrate this by describing a few of the most outstanding projects of the early forties and the men who built them.

William P. Atkinson, of Oklahoma City planned and organized the famous 6,000-home Midwest City (1943). It was the first big, well-planned, integrated community of defense homes. Sixteen builders cooperated. Excellent land planning and new neighborhood concepts were directed by Seward H. Mott, land and community planner. The project was located near strategic air force bases in the area.

Albert Balch, veteran Seattle builder, built 260 FHA Title VI homes in well laid-out Wedgewood Park Community in 1942. They were built for navy, aircraft, and shipbuilding workers. He fought to keep defense homes attractive and livable in a good neighborhood, and he employed top-level architects Thomas, Grainger and Thomas. Later Balch built 1,000 war and postwar homes in ten of Seattle's finest communities.

Barret and Hilp were large San Francisco contractors who plunged into the construction of prefab panel houses in 1942 using the "Precision Built" system developed by F. Vaux Wilson of Homosote Company in Trenton, New Jersey. They broke all previous construction records by building 977 houses in three months at Vallejo, California, then 500 more at Ft. Leonard Wood. Harry Hilp, president, then took over a 640-foot, long-abandoned fertilizer factory in Portsmouth, Virginia, installed a prefab production line, and proceeded to turn out 80 houses a day for a total of 5,000 homes for navy personnel. The panel system and production methods had a great influence on later housing.

Fritz B. Burns of Los Angeles, California, was an experienced builder of low-cost, prewar homes. Burns began defense housing in 1942 and constructed 5,000 units in the Westchester-Los Angeles area. He used advanced production-line techniques to build better and more quickly. His communities were well-planned for permanent value. After the war, he continued to build well-planned communities such as Panorama City, and later became president of Kaiser Community Homes. He was president of NAHB in 1943.

Channel Heights in San Pedro, California, was a federal public project comprising 600 low-cost permanent defense housing units built in a well-planned community. They were designed by Richard J. Neutra, architect.

The *Glenn Martin* defense homes in Middle River, Maryland, were 600 prefab "sandwich panel" homes for bomber-plant workers that were erected in six months. Called the most

significant prefab defense project of 1941, the system employed curtain walls with large insulated wall and roof panels. Robert L. Davison, research director of the John B. Pierce Foundation, developed the method. The architects were Skidmore, Owings and Merrill of New York.

Henry J. Kaiser's organization built 9,800 furnished war apartments and 100 row houses at Vanport, Oregon, near his shipyards—a complete community (dubbed Kaiserville) of 718 low-rent buildings, costing $25 million. Fast production-line techniques were used, and Kaiser went on to build many war and postwar houses.

William J. Levitt of Long Island, New York, built 800 FHA Title VI houses at Norfolk, Virginia, in 1942, to rent for less than $50. He employed new production techniques for faster, lower-cost construction, including prefab wall panels, precutting, and preassembled plumbing trees and components. He later built 1,200 more homes in the area. His new techniques set a pattern for postwar projects such as Levittown, in Long Island, and they had a strong influence on much postwar building.

George C. Miller of Detroit, Michigan, who had built 7,000 houses before the war, turned to war homes and built 1,500 brick duplex units between 1941 and 1943, alone.

Mills and Sons of Chicago, Illinois, rushed a 400-unit FHA project, Westwood, for war production workers, and completed it in less than one year.

Fred C. Trump, a Brooklyn builder, constructed 1,200 low-rent apartment units in Norfolk and Chester, Pennsylvania, in his first year (1943); another 1,000 in the second year. He later built thousands of war and postwar homes.

Valencia Gardens in San Francisco, California, was an exceptionally well planned and designed defense-home community by William W. Wurster, architect and dean of the MIT school of architecture.

David D. Bohannon of San Mateo, California, unquestionably is responsible for the most colorful capsule of defense-housing history. When he was inducted into Housing's Hall of Fame at the National Housing Center in Washington, D.C. in May 1977, the judges said of him:

"He is a giant among men. He built desperately needed war and postwar homes in well-planned communities, pioneered new and faster production methods, was a key organizer and founder of the National Association of Home Builders, and [became] its president in 1942. His work has vastly enriched the quality of American life."

There is much more to say about this brawny, six-foot four-inch rugged individualist. He was one of the first to act on the need for defense housing in 1941, and started his first project—212 defense homes at Sunnyvale, California—well before Pearl Harbor.

David B. (or Bo, as his friends call him) was also one of the few builders available, as this was written, to relate in personal, first-hand terms the war problems builders faced, which he did in a series of interviews with this author in 1978:

Q.   How and why did you get into World War II defense housing so early—before Pearl Harbor, was it not?

A.   I was called in by McDonald & Kahn in mid-1941. They wanted me to build 200 defense houses at Sunnyvale, California. They were rebuilding a huge abandoned structure there into a submarine engine plant—very hush—

hush. This was a rural chicken-ranch community with no housing, no facilities, no building labor. But the Navy said, 'We can't build submarines without housing for the workers.'

Within a week I had closed down my other jobs, loaded up my production and precutting equipment, and gone to work. We got 212 homes built fast, and I was glad to be able to show that private builders could produce war housing better, faster, and cheaper than public housing could.

Q.   You must have impressed somebody, because you went on to build a tremendous number—how many?

A.   Many, many, *thousands*. I believe we became the largest private builders of war homes. The need was urgent and we were importuned by admirals, high defense officials, and war leaders to rush production. We built 559 houses in Westwood at Napa in four months, 700 in Rollingwood at Richmond, and 1500 at San Lorenzo.

Q.   Tell us more about San Lorenzo. It has often been described as the Number 1 private U.S. war-housing job. How did it come about?

A.   The Navy came to me, said I would soon hear of *Task Force 48*—that the Alameda Naval Air Base nearby would provide total backup for the aircraft carriers in the Pacific. Admiral Friedel said, 'The need is *absolutely urgent'*—for the same reasons it was at Sunnyvale, Napa, and Richmond. What can you do?

Q.   What *did* you do?

A.   We broke all production records. At one period we were completing one house every 40 minutes. We not only produced the 1500 on schedule but built a complete planned community with curvilinear streets, a neighborhood center, recreation areas and a shopping center. It was planned by Seward Mott and has since become a highly regarded and successful residential village.

Q. That doesn't sound much like *public* war housing we've heard about.

A. No, it doesn't. We and other private builders tried to create war-housing communities that would continue [to be] livable and attractive after the war emergency. We employed the same kind of high-quality, long-range planning we had used in our prewar projects such as Hillsdale and Woodside.

Q. What gave you the inspiration for such quality community planning?

A. Through my work with the National Association of Real Estate Boards, Home Builders' Institute, and Urban Land Institute I became acquainted with such community planning giants as J. C. Nichols of Kansas City, John McC. Mowbray of Baltimore, Hugh Potter of Houston, and Duncan McDuffie of San Francisco. Their projects flourished, and when I had the opportunity, such as at Hillsdale in San Mateo, I tried to adopt and even improve on their planning concepts.

Q. How did you achieve mass production of war houses? It was a new concept then, wasn't it?

A. I studied the work of other big builders and of prefabricated-house builders—in fact, did some experimental projects that way—and I had good engineers and technicians. I came back to the principle of precise organization, pre-cutting, and streamlined site production. We brought products, components, and materials to the site and fabricated them for fast erection. We used jig tables and other aids. I still think this system is more efficient than total prefabrication in a distant factory.

Q. What about problems with material shortages, priorities, and controls?

A. It was tough! We had to fight our own constant war against bureaucrats, government delays, obstructions, and priority problems. Worst of all, private builders got only an A-1-J priority, which for scarce products was little better than a hunting license! But all *government-built* public housing got an AA-1 priority, the same as Army or Navy—tops without limitations.

Q. All those delays and confusions you've said you encountered—how did you deal with them?

A. I can only say we had to learn how to understand and take on the problem of dealing with poorly informed governmental agents who, at the same time, had great power and arrogance. There is nothing more frustrating than dealing with incompetent men, listening to them for hours on subjects they know little about, suffering long delays, waiting interminably for permission to take essential steps when projects and even lives are hanging in the balance.

Q. How did you go about getting scarce materials and labor?

A. We scoured and scavanged the country—brought labor from Texas and elsewhere, fought for nails, tubs, plywood—[and] used our influence with manufacturers, railroads, and particularly the priority people in Washington.

I would actually walk my way through a maze of bureaus, getting priorities one by one, by hard personal effort.

Q. What's that story about how you logged your own lumber?

A. Yes, we did. Due to the confusing priority and OPA pricing controls, it became almost impossible to get lumber between 1943 and 1945, and I was one of the largest lumber buyers in the country. So I went out and bought a 20,000-acre tract of virgin timber in Humboldt County, California, and plunged into logging and sawmill operations. This was a terrifying but productive move, and my success was due to several cans of undeveloped films!

Q. Undeveloped films?

A. Yes. I found that the U.S. Forest Service had cans of undeveloped film which showed through expert aerial photographs how roads and contours could be developed which would permit logging of my land. Everyone said the timber was inaccessible and could not be logged, *but the photographs showed the way.* Soon I built roads, sawmills, houses, and schools for loggers, and trucked the timber to my construction sites—took out a quarter-billion board feet.

Q. You had a big hand, I know, in organizing the building industry for war work. How did that happen?

A. The story is involved. But in early 1941 I became head of the *Home Builders' Institute* and was plunged into many war-related affairs. In May 1941, I was called to a Washington meeting where Charles Palmer, housing coordinator, made the startling statement that we were going to be at war and that the *government* would do all the home building!

Q. What happened then?

A. I was introduced to Peter Stone, an economist who had been given the job of 'putting a handle on building'—of placing war emergency controls on *all housing.* He said, 'For three weeks I have been trying to meet someone to represent house builders.' I promised to help, and shortly appointed Jack McC. Mowbray of Baltimore as chairman of a committee on materials and conservation. This later became the Home Builders' Emergency Committee which did so much to straighten out procedures and aid defense housing. I appointed Hugh Potter of Texas chairman, and he did a great job.

Q. Did other builders realize we were in imminent danger of getting into the war?

A. They were completely innocent at that time of what was being planned for them. I went to San Francisco and told a meeting of builders there that war was coming—that I was not going to put in one more foundation on my private work. Within a few months I was off and away on my first defense-home project, Sunnyvale, for workers in the submarine engine plant there.

Q. Did you continue to work on war and postwar housing problems?

A. I was, of course, very busy building defense housing, but I traveled back and forth to Washington—at my own expense—and chaired many of the HBI and Emergency Committee meetings through 1941 and 1942. I always worked hard to bring the two national builder groups together.

Q.   What happened after the war?

A.   We built many more large, planned communities and expanded and improved our efficient production systems. These made us able to build better houses for less; many in the low-priced brackets.

Q.   How do you feel about your career, in retrospect?

A.   As we look back, we see our war and postwar homes and shopping centers, all in good, planned communities which have prospered, and thousands upon thousands of families enjoying the benefits. And we have enjoyed a high degree of success in the progress.

Q.   What about today?

A.   We are in a new phase of our industry, struggling to meet housing demand in an inflation economy, but facing great environmental and other restraints and restrictions. It would have been utterly impossible to do the war and postwar housing job under these conditions.

Q.   Why do you say that?

A.   We could not have done what we did without fast processing and great cooperation from local officials, utilities, unions, and many others. And *no* interference from environmentalists!

Seabee Guts, Enterprise, and Versatility

The record of the U.S. Navy's fighting construction battalions—the Seabees—is one of the most exciting of World War II. Their contributions to victory seem never to have been fully appreciated, just as the work performed by defense home builders on the home front was never fully recognized, nor that of their counterpart, the U.S. Corps of Engineers.

In December 1941, the first Seabee regiment of 3,000 "fighting builders" was activated by Rear Admiral Ben Moreell, who has been described as the "blunt, beefy, and brilliant" chief of the Navy's Bureau of Yards and Docks. He evoked widespread interest and support from the building press, including an enthusiastic story in the *American Builder* magazine in early 1942 urging all red-blooded building men to join up.* What effect

this had cannot be ascertained, but more than 260,000 did join the Seabees and significantly helped to win the global conflict.

Quite abruptly, thousands of the construction industry's toughest and most adventurous men sailed off with the Seabees. They were of all ages, from 17 to 50: builders, architects, carpenters, bulldozer operators, electricians, plumbers, welders, steel workers, brick layers. They were mostly skilled construction men, from 59 different building trades.

Their motto was "Can Do," and they were the roughest, toughest, most resourceful crowd of gun-toting builders ever assembled anywhere. They built housing, barracks, air strips, docks, hangars, and advanced bases—often under fire—in a thousand remote and fearful spots, from the South Pacific to the Antarctic. After the war many came back to play important roles in the housing industry as builders, contractors, and entrepreneurs.

What Admiral Moreell and his hard-driving

---

*Editor's note: This story was written by J.B. Mason.

chief of operations, Captain John R. Perry, did was to mobilize and use effectively for the first time during a war the enormous construction power of the nation, as did the Corps of Engineers. U.S. builders had always led the world in the use of bulldozers, tractors, cranes, and other advanced heavy equipment to construct dams, highways, skyscrapers, and huge industrial projects. American industry had produced trucks and earth-moving equipment that could—and did—literally move mountains. Now all this know-how and equipment were thrown into fierce action to build advanced bases and airfields. At the Henderson Field on Guadalcanal, 18 inches of crushed coral was laid in a few days. Battling Seabees cut teak and mahogany timber, built a bridge over the Nalibiu River under fire, and constructed a sawmill which soon produced 100,000 feet of lumber a month. In road building, the Seabee feats were miraculous and were carried on close to battlefronts.

This two-ocean war was quite different from any other, and the Navy learned from experiences in Wake, Guam, and other locations that armed, trained construction fighters were needed to set up advance bases as the men fought from island to island. The Seabees were indispensable not only in creating but maintaining and even defending the global girdle of bases needed to fight this unique kind of war.

The work of the Seabees was bone-cracking hard, usually dangerous, and frequently heroic. One story tells of Seabee Aurelio Tassone, who elevated his bulldozer's steel blade for a shield and charged his 20-ton bulldozer directly into a Japanese pillbox in the Solomons landings, sweeping it from its base and saving many lives.

Other stories tell of Seabees dropping their tools to seize guns and repel attack. On Guadalcanal, Larry Meyer was working to rebuild Henderson Field when a Japanese Zero approached. He jumped to a machine gun and downed it in minutes.

Seabees were in the lead in the Aleutian landings: they swung on ropes while chiseling footholds in the high rock cliffs; dove in icy waters to build docks; braved sleet, snow, and gales to build barracks, warehouses, and landing strips in record time—and thought it all part of the day's work.

It is possible that the first Seabees sent overseas were not fully trained in the particular problems they were soon to be faced with, but they nevertheless were rushed into early action. The later Seabees, however, were excellently trained and equipped for the multitude of jobs they had to perform. This training included close-order drills, rifle and bayonet use, and obstacle course pursuit over dugouts, emplacements, water, and other hazards. They were taught to handle bulldozers, repair machinery, perform every conceivable kind of construction, and load and unload ships. Finally, they received advanced combat techniques, including underwater demolition.

A striking feature of the Seabee operation was that while there were many specialists, any and all would turn in to help the total operation at any given time. For example, in building a wood barracks the carpenters led the work, but other trades plunged in to help, and craft lines disappeared.

One reason the Seabees were so effective in varied and far-flung combat operations is that they were carefully organized and fully equipped at their advance training locations. Here were assembled heavy earth-moving equipment, complete machine shops, portable repair shops, power tools—everything needed to build a barracks or a complete naval base from hammer and nails to Caterpillar tractors. All of it had to be loaded on ships in logical sequence. Here the building industry's unique background in planning and logistics was found invaluable.

The tales of Seabee achievements under pressure and fire are legion. These indomitable men tackled the job of hacking flying fields out of dense island jungles with fierce vigor. They would quickly clear an area of trees and stumps with powerful saws, then level it with giant bulldozers. Coral rock was in some cases blasted to powder and laid 18 inches deep, then rolled and covered with steel strips welded together. On one day in the Solomons they landed under fire, unloaded on the beach, hauled heavy equipment to shore, built emplacements and a camp base, and finished up by bulldozing ten miles of road through mud and jungle forest.

Because of U.S. construction know-how, equipment, and Seabee guts, airfields were often completed in days instead of weeks. On Tarawa, for example, the fighting builders who landed with the first assault had the vital airstrip ready by the time the final Japanese defenders were dead. The absence of this strip had been a major threat to the U.S. fleet.

At Casablanca, Seabees were among the first to land. They cleared the way, built fuel-oil facilities, repaired docks and facilities, then moved eastward with the troops, blasting wire entanglements and locating mines and booby traps. They repaired airfields, wharves, and docks, and built housing, hospitals, and water-purification facilities.

The Seabees' greatest asset was their versatility. They could, as they claimed, do anything. They rushed into complicated repair jobs using their portable shop equipment. They could repair, improvise, and improve almost anything, especially when materials were scarce and the need was urgent. They

developed the sheet-steel pontoon to a high art for a host of uses in unloading fuel and supplies from ships and LSTs. The pontoons were plain steel boxes five-by-seven-by-five feet which could be attached or strung together. Equipped with outboard motors, pontoon barges could transport huge loads, and they were also lashed together to form causeways, as at Bizerte. Here the pontoons were attached to the fleet of LSTs and LCTs and more than 12,000 vehicles were unloaded. Seabee demolition men blasted huge barbed-wire obstacles to pave the way for the troops. At Salerno they unloaded another 12,000 pieces of equipment, blasted through obstacles, built dressing stations, and in two days cleared the beach and built a base of operations.

Somehow the Seabees created an aura of "Can Do" success. But few realize the daring and dangerous exploits of their demolition units. In every invasion they cleared the way for the advancing forces. They underwent special "toughening up" training, especially in the use of explosives. They destroyed bridges, roads, barbed wire, mine fields, docks, beaches, and emplacements. They often worked at night too—on land, and also in the depths of a cold sea.

In a more relaxed way, the Seabees contributed to the life and morale of all the services, but especially the Navy. With 1,000 architects among them, they designed and built above-average recreational and religious buildings and mess halls, as well as a few swank officers' quarters with bars and flagged terraces that were the envy of the Army.

In the Pacific the Seabee architects were famous for their use of bamboo, palm branches, and other materials to produce attractive structures, even in the most primitive jungle spots.

The work of the Seabees illustrates how a particular genius or ability of U.S. industry, when properly unleashed for a worthy purpose, can perform miracles. These men with their bulldozers, their building know-how, and their grit and pluck not only helped to win the war but returned to write new chapters in postwar housing. An equally impressive record can be stated for the U.S. Army Corps of Engineers.

War Crescendo—Postwar Home Planning Begins

On D-Day, June 6, 1944, the global war mounted to its enormous climax as thousands of paratroopers, 150,000 fighting men, and tons of war equipment were poured onto the Normandy beaches. In the Pacific, the Battle of the Phillipine Sea was being won and American troops soon landed at Leyte, then Luzon.

In February 1945, Roosevelt, Churchill, and Stalin met at Yalta to plan a better postwar world.

On April 12, President Roosevelt died at Warm Springs, Georgia, and Harry Truman became President.

On May 7, 1945, the Germans surrendered unconditionally at General Eisenhower's headquarters in Rheims.

On August 6, B-29s flew over Hiroshima and Nagasaki and destroyed them with atomic bombs. The Pacific War was won and the Japanese surrendered on September 2.

At home, the peak of war and defense home building had been reached in late 1943 and soon began to taper off. Housing production dropped to 191,000 units for 1943. Ninety-six percent of these were constructed by independent builders, while public housing almost disappeared.

During this time much attention began to be paid to postwar home planning. It was obvious that a great housing shortage had accumulated, and with war veterans soon to be returning home, the need would be even greater. NAHB expanded its Home Builders' Emergency Committee and started working on postwar plans. *American Builder* magazine researched and published a "Home for Veterans" plan to build a million postwar homes a year with FHA Title VI loans of 25-30 years and 5% down. The plan was enthusiastically endorsed by NAHB's president Fritz Burns. Later in 1943, NAHB advanced its own $2 billion postwar home program for veterans including 5% down, 25-year FHA loans at 4.5% interest.

In October 1943, Congress authorized an additional extension of FHA home financing of $400 million. It also debated new postwar legislation of the type NAHB was proposing. In November, Fritz Burns, now president of a strong and rapidly expanding NAHB, carried on a nation-wide campaign to get adequate financing for private postwar home building for veterans.

Since wartime housing starts had dwindled greatly, the urgency for a postwar plan to provide homes for millions of returning veterans grew acute. In 1944 only 141,800 houses were built. Even so, the scarcity of materials and equipment was so great that many thousands of almost completed units stood empty for lack of tubs, ranges, refrigerators, and furnaces.

Builders have related tall tales about this

great post World War II materials shortage. At one time there were 750,000 houses standing unfinished for lack of bathtubs and equipment. Builder Andy Place of South Bend, Indiana, said that in desperation he put in ten concrete bathtubs, "but the paint came off, and they were a little rough in the wrong places."

Builders drove miles to pick up a keg of nails or a few sheets of plywood. Bob Gerholz of Flint, Michigan, says, "Believe it or not, in 1944 I traded two Buick cars for two carloads of oak flooring." Frank Burns of Denver bought logs, sold them to plywood mills, then bought them back!

Joe Meyerhoff of Baltimore said, "We had an awful time getting things. So our NAHB committee, headed by Robert Gerholz, got an interview with President Truman and spelled out the problems. Soon after, many controls were lifted."

In August of 1944, Congress passed the G.I. Bill of Rights, sponsored by veteran Senator John Sparkman, which guaranteed home loans to veterans. In conjunction with FHA it was the spark that ultimately set off a vast program of postwar home construction for veterans.

In October of that year the War Production Board and National Housing Authority relaxed many housing controls. Materials were beginning to appear. *LIFE* magazine published a postwar issue with ideas for storage walls, folding partitions, built-in furniture, convertible rooms, and indoor-outdoor living. Henry Kaiser and his son Edgar announced plans for building postwar, prefab panel homes in great numbers.

Amid a burst of optimism, NAHB held its first great National Convention-Exposition and Home Show in Chicago in January 1945, attended by more than 3,000. Joseph E. Merrion, president of NAHB, appealed for a quick resumption of home building and an end to priority controls and all other housing restrictions. The Convention expressed fears that the National Housing Agency was deliberately hampering private building while still doing too much to push public housing.

Builder optimism, however, was short-lived, for 1945 proved a frustrating year. The war was still on, materials were scarce, and only 209,300 homes were built. Congress stalled over new legislation, and there was massive confusion in government agencies over the ending of priorities and controls. Worst of all, the materials shortages got worse, forcing builders to seek far and wide for scarce products. With veterans coming home at the rate of 25,000 a week and no housing available, a great hue and cry arose for homes for veterans.

By late 1945 there were 3,600,000 families lacking homes, and veterans were sleeping in trailers, Quonset huts, and temporary homes, or sharing crowded quarters with acquaintances, relatives, or their girl friends. The city of Atlanta bought 100 trailers for veterans, and in North Dakota surplus grain bins were turned into housing. Benny Goodman gave a benefit concert in Cleveland where people pledged rooms for rent to vets instead of cash. *House Beautiful* magazine suggested that for veterans' readjustment "a home should be the greatest rehabilitation center of all."

President Truman had appointed Wilson W. Wyatt, former mayor of Louisville, as housing expediter and head of the National Housing Agency. He proposed a Veterans' Emergency Housing Program calling for priority control of materials, priorities on veterans' housing, and a cutback of nonresidential construction. Builders found it most confusing; the only part they really approved of was a further extension of FHA Title VI with 90% loans.

Congress later passed and President Truman signed a Veterans' Emergency Housing Act containing most of Wyatt's proposals. Much of this program soon was bogged down in a maze of confusion. The one feature that proved helpful was the renewal of FHA Title VI with 90% loans at the "current cost" of houses. And in December 1945, most remaining war controls and restrictions were removed. Finally the nation's builders were free—or almost free—to turn loose the "power to produce" they had acquired during the war years.

1946—At Last—The Power to Produce

Americans, happy to return at last to peace after four years of war, embarked on a sensational spending spree. The predicted postwar depression did not materialize, and unemployment was at a tiny 4% with most being veterans receiving $20-a-week benefits. Employment, in fact, rose to a huge level of 54 million at good pay, and average annual income rose to $161 billion—twice that of the almost forgotten 1929. Prosperity was at hand, and that included the housing industry.

The nation's builders in 1946 were able to unleash the large-scale planning and production techniques they had developed during the war emergency years. Essentially they had learned to build faster at less cost. They had acquired a flexibility and operating efficiency that enabled them to tap huge new markets.

There were other potent reasons why the housing industry was poised for an extraordinary expansion of home building at the start of 1946:

- 10 million returning war veterans were clamoring for homes.
- A tremendous backlog of shelter needs going back to the depression of the thirties existed.
- A high accumulation of savings by the American public had been built up during the war years.

- Extremely favorable home-financing terms through FHA, VA, and conventional mortgages were available. Low down payments (5%), low interest (4.5%), and long terms of 20 and 25 years made home ownership possible for many millions of additional buyers.
- Exceptional home values due to planning and production techniques learned in war housing were offered by postwar builders.
- A large skilled-labor force was available from the ranks of the Seabees, Army engineers, and builders of war construction projects. Many had learned to boldly use new construction methods, materials, and equipment, and soon became housing entrepreneurs unafraid to launch large building enterprises.

As builders got into full production of postwar homes, they were able to draw on a great array of new or improved products, systems, power tools, and home equipment. The research and development divisions of manufacturers of home products and equipment had been busy, and the flood of new products had a major impact on the design, comfort, and efficiency of postwar homes. The extent of the new developments is indicated by the partial list that follows:

- Improved community and environmental planning.
- Large-scale engineering and project scheduling.
- Engineered house plans and designs.
- Modular coordination of house designs.
- Faster production-line methods.
- Use of power tools and heavy equipment.
- On-site fabrication of walls and partitions.
- Panelized construction using large wall, floor, and roof sections.
- Complete factory prefabrication of houses and components.
- Extraordinary truss roof systems.
- Low-cost plans and designs for garden apartments, duplexes, and row houses.
- Large panels of plywood, gypsum, insulation board, asbestos cement, and other new products.
- Prefab and packaged insulated ducts for heating and air conditioning.
- Engineered plumbing and plumbing walls, prefab plumbing trees, and simplified plumbing techniques.
- Compact floor, attic, and closet furnaces with great efficiency.
- Radiant electric heating in floors and ceilings.
- Improved heating using gas or oil, with better systems, including baseboard units.
- Factory-built kitchen cabinets, work tops, and storage units.
- Compact, built-in kitchen units with improved, easy-to-install ranges, refrigerators, and dishwashers.
- Prefab closets, storage units, and storage walls.
- Metal shower stalls, tub enclosures, and bath components.
- Metal door and window frames, prebuilt, easy to install.
- Complete packaged door and window units to reduce on-site labor.
- Aluminum siding, exterior plywood, and new composition siding.
- Asphalt floor tile with strong new adhesives.

In March of 1946, Fritz B. Burns, later president of Kaiser Community Homes, unveiled an elaborate $75,000 "Showcase" postwar model home designed by architect Welton Beckett. It was repleat with new ideas, equipment, and gadgets, and the public loved it! People were tired of war and hungry for new-home excitement.

In May of the same year Congress expanded FHA's mortgage insurance authorization by a billion dollars, which included provisions for large-scale rental housing and garden apartments. Materials were scarce and builders were complaining of confusion in the Wyatt program. Yet the pace of building accelerated swiftly, and it was probably the fastest growth in the history of housing.

Housing-starts data tell the amazing story: the 1946 total starts skyrocketed to 1,023,000 units from 1945's 326,000. Private builders constructed 1,015,000 or 98.8% of the total; public housing managed a bare 8,000 units. Builders large and small searched everywhere for men and materials; there was no problem in selling or renting. But it took great amounts of enterprise, ingenuity, and hard work to get the jobs completed. The fact that so many houses were built in 1946 and succeeding years was testimony to the resilience and effectiveness of independent builders.

People and Projects, 1946

The more spectacular projects that got under way in 1946 and later, and the men who ran them, are described here:

Franklin L. Burns of Denver, Colorado, brought new fabrication techniques to his Brentwood project, and built 1400 houses using an insulated asbestos cement panel system.

Fritz B. Burns of Kaiser Community Homes in Los Angeles got off to a fast start with low-cost veterans' homes, using panels and subassemblies built in a plant and field erected. His industrialized techniques and engineered plans produced 20 houses a day.

An outstanding example of the Kaiser-Burns projects was Westchester, in Los Angeles, a 5,000-home planned community with excellent neighborhood design and amenities.

William G. Farrington of Houston, Texas, built 175 veterans' homes to sell at $5,300. He used an integrated system of design, planning, and production. This was the first of many attractive, well-planned communities he produced.

Kimball Hill of Smith and Hill, Chicago-area builders, started the 1,200-house Oak Meadows project on Chicago's South Side. He used a site fabrication shop to build plywood panels and components, and designed a unique new counterflow heating system. His houses and communities were designed by an outstanding Chicago architectural firm, Perkins and Wills. The houses sold for $9,200. Later, Hill built Rolling Meadows near Arlington, Illinois, a well-planned residential area that set new standards in design and neighborhood amenities.

Charles E. Joern of LaGrange, Illinois,

started an attractive 366-unit apartment project, Homestead Gardens. Architect Howard T. Fisher brought good design and an engineered plan. New, fast, production-line methods got the project completed ahead of schedule. It was a landmark to good design and community planning.

Philip M. Klutznick, formerly the head of the Federal Public Housing Agency, moved to Chicago and joined forces with *Nathan Manilow,* one of Chicago's large-scale builders to form a huge private-enterprise project, American Community Builders. Together they built Park Forest, the 8,500-unit planned community, which included 3,000 apartments under FHA Section 608, renting at $65.00 a month. Carl Gardiner, the land planner, pioneered many new concepts in this large enterprise.

William J. Levitt returned to Long Island to put his war-housing techniques to work. He built 1,000 veterans' homes in 1946, and said that he did it "despite government confusion." He remarked "It was harder than building 3,000 war homes at Norfolk during the war."

Andrew S. Place of South Bend, Indiana, went into production in July 1946, on 180 veterans' single-family homes in an attractive community. A leader in housing research, Place used many advanced techniques to produce a five-room-plus-bath house for $6,650. His techniques included walls fabricated on the site, large roof sheets of plywood, a trussed roof system, power tools and heavy equipment, a prefab cutting shop, and engineered plans and scheduling. Place was active in NAHB's research foundation and institute and often tested cost-cutting ideas and systems in his own projects.

Jack Shapiro, head of M. Shapiro & Sons, a New York general contracting firm, went into home and apartment building in a big way. He built 100 New York apartments; 350 dwellings in New Britain, Connecticut; 600 brick houses in Harrisburg, Pennsylvania; and 1,000 homes in Philadelphia.

Paul Trousdale of Los Angeles started Baldwin Hills, a 600-unit rental house project. The wood-frame buildings in "California Colonial" style by architect Allen Siple were attractively clustered around courts and open spaces. It has since become a landmark of good design and community planning.

Cy Williams, builder, architect, and prefab-home producer, put up 40 contemporary ranch-style homes at Roslyn, New York. He also organized a prefab production company. He pioneered good design as well as low-cost building techniques.

William Wilson Wurster, dean of MIT's department of architecture, spearheaded a project of 100 prefab houses built by his students for resident veterans in 1946. They were prefabricated in a plant of the City Lumber Company of Bridgeport, Connecticut. In spite of strikes and materials shortages the students got 100 homes built in six months.

1947—Year of Prosperity and Housing Growth

This was the year of the Marshall Plan, a $37 billion Truman budget, and a continuing increase in prosperity and economic growth due to the expansive spending mood of the American public.

It was also the year of penicillin, home permanents ("Which twin has the Toni?"), *Best Years of Our Lives, Forever Amber*, and Milton Berle. Part of this scene was a deep-seated urge by veterans and millions of other Americans for a home they could call their own.

They had been hearing and reading about what fine homes and communities builders could produce if given a chance. Now there were the money, the know-how, and finally a free-enterprise economy that encouraged building. The results were explosive as builders embarked up on what proved to be a 1,268,000-house year.

Housing's 1947 year started with the abrupt departure of Wilson Wyatt as housing expeditor and head of the National Housing Agency.

His well-meaning Veteran's Emergency Housing program had become unhappily embroiled in controversy and red tape and was largely abandoned. It was true that Congress had failed to support parts of his program. The one big success in housing was the FHA Title VI program that was popular everywhere, that got the support of Congress, and that did get houses built. Wyatt was replaced by Frank R. Creedon, a lumberman.

The departure of Wilson Wyatt did not inhibit the meteoric rise of housing production in 1947. Builders by then were getting into the full swing of mass production. The biggest new field was in FHA Title VI Section 608 garden apartments, where liberal 90% (or greater) loans made financing easy and attractive. It was later claimed that some builders of 608s "mortgaged out," i.e. obtained mortgages that were greater than the actual cost of the project.

History shows, however, that the 608 program was a success by any objective standard.

More than 400,000 badly needed apartment units were produced in a hurry. The rents were remarkably low, ranging from $40 to $90 per month. The failures were few. The apartments on the whole were comfortable, well-equipped, and have to this day provided a good standard of living for more than a million persons.

An interesting sidelight is that the 608 program made more money for FHA than anything else it did. It became one of the few government agencies to show a profit.

The rapid growth of 608 building in 1947, encouraged by extravagant aid, initiatives, and promises by FHA and government agencies, is shown by the fact that 8,688 units were started in just four projects:

Nettleton and Baldwin, Seattle	544
Gross-Morton, Long Island	3,800
American Community Builders, Chicago	3,000
Fred Trump, Long Island	1,344

In June of 1947, FHA approved more mortgages on rental housing than ever in its history. A new Section 603 of FHA Title VI went into effect, increasing mortgages to 90% on one- to four-family homes. These and other factors boosted house production records to new highs, exceeding a million per year. The following list of men and projects gives a striking picture of the action that took place.

C. Earl Colomb of New Orleans, Louisiana, started a low-cost, 1,000-home veterans' project in a planned community, and had instant success.

Thomas P. Coogan of Florida started an 800-unit project of $6,700 houses, and 112 apartments. He used prefab wall panels built at the site. He later became an outstanding builder and mortgage banker, and was elected NAHB president in 1950.

George Gross of Gross-Morton Company, Long Island, New York, started his huge Section 608 garden-apartment complex, "Glen Oaks." This $30-million project had 3,800 units built around courts, and was designed by architect Benjamin Braunstein. They rented for $66-$90. It was well planned and well built, and it provided excellent housing at low cost.

William J. Levitt of Long Island, New York, sold his entire year's production of $18,000 houses at Strathmore in Roslyn in one week.

Metropolitan Life, in New York, New York, financed the $50-million Stuyvesant Town apartment complex which was started on 18 blocks of slum area at East River and Fourteenth Streets. Housing for 24,000 was provided in 8,759 apartments. Buildings were spaced around courts with a three-acre park and ten playgrounds. Rents were $46-$77. Gilmore B. Clark was chairman of the board of design, and Starrett Brothers & Eken was the builder. This project was followed by Riverton Houses and the famed Peter Cooper Village. Metropolitan Life and its officials have never received just appreciation for the enormous contribution they made to better housing.

J. C. Nichols of Kansas City stepped up building to a house a day in the Prairie Village section of his famous 5,000-acre Country Club District. Started in 1905, the district is considered the nation's foremost example of expert land planning and community development.

Frank W. Sharp of Houston, Texas, started his 4,700-home Oak Forest project, a skillfully planned community. His low-cost homes set new architectural standards, and were designed by Wilson, Morris & Crane, Houston architects.

Angus G. Wynne of American Home Realty Company in Dallas, Texas, began work on Wynewood, a $25-million planned community of 2,200 houses and 1,000 apartments.

1948-1949: Housing Starts Rise to Unprecedented Highs

After the U.S. returned to normalcy, a lively political contest occurred between President Truman and Republican challenger Thomas E. Dewey. Truman won by a hair and vowed to continue aid for housing and economic growth. The North Atlantic Treaty Organization (NATO) was negotiated and ratified, also.

Although there was a slight "Truman Recession" in mid-1949, the economy quickly recovered and housing, aided by favorable legislation, zoomed on to record highs.

In January 1948, FHA was given another $750-million authorization and builders were off on a record-breaking splurge. Housing starts in May set an all-time high of 97,000. A helpful contribution was the advance commitments FHA was making on an entire project. Builders could take out 100 mortgages at a time, and could move fast.

Congress spent long hours debating the Taft-Ellender-Wagner bill, which would have appropriated millions for public housing. But the bill died in committee, much to the satisfaction of the private-builder segment of the industry. They much preferred FHA building to public housing.

Congress did pass new legislation in the fall of 1948 extending rental housing loans under FHA Section 608 to 27 years at 4% interest. A new financing plan for low-cost houses extended loans to 30 years, with 5% down and 4.5% interest. The bill also expanded the secondary market for FHA and VA mortgages by establishing the new precedent-setting Federal National Mortgage Association.

In October of 1948, FHA offices were swamped with applications for Section 608 mortgages. And housing starts continued to break records each month. The 1948 total was 1,362,000, which was achieved despite rising prices, scarce materials, and a continuing confusion in government housing agencies.

Early in 1949 FNMA (Fannie Mae, as it was soon lovingly dubbed) got under way, giving enormous long-term benefits to housing industry finance. It created a strong secondary market for VA and FHA mortgages. Under the astute direction of President James Stanley Baughman for 16 years, Fannie Mae brought new liquidity to the mortgage market and greatly expanded the funds available to finance U.S. home building. During President Baughman's tenure, 30% of the existing U.S. home inventory was built. He received the President Kennedy Award for Distinguished Federal Service.

Marketing to Home-Hungry Postwar Buyers

Few people today can realize the enormous pent-up public interest in home planning and buying that was building up during the depression and war years. American families were hungry for new home ideas and designs, ways to live better, house plans, decorating, furnishings, and especially home equipment ideas.

During 1949 a new and exciting marketing vehicle for the housing industry blossomed: National Home Week, an idea that had been conceived by Edward G. Gavin, then editor of *American Builder* magazine. Home shows flourished in cities all over the land and thousands of model homes were displayed to capacity crowds.

The glittering model and demonstration homes that went on display during National Home Week gave builders their first chance to show the new designs and the colorful and beautifully equipped kitchens, bathrooms, laundries, and other amenities of postwar housing. National Home Week and its home shows helped raise housing standards, whetted the appetite of millions of buyers, and made sales. The model homes also had a strong influence on the building modernization market by giving the public ideas they soon wanted to use in old homes.

Manufacturers of kitchen, bath, laundry, heating, and a host of other new building products benefitted greatly from model and display homes. Zooming sales of many a new product were directly credited to the model-home exposure.

Another powerful marketing tool for both builders and manufacturers was the NAHB Exposition and Home Show, first opened in Chicago in 1945. The 1949 show, held in February, was jammed with a record attendance of 6,000. The enormous and colorful exhibits of home equipment and thousands of new or improved products had a stimulating effect on all home design and building. It proved a useful forum for the exchange of new ideas and for the dissemination of these to all segments of the housing industry.

The consumer and trade magazines, with

millions of the home-hungry readers, were still another powerful influence on the trend to better house design, planning, and decorating. At the close of World War II, as we have noted, public interest in house designs and plans was overwhelming. Sales of plan books of all sorts skyrocketed, and the popular consumer magazines expanded their home planning sections. Five of the editors who were active and influential in the late forties and who helped advance housing include the following:

John Normile, architect and building editor of *Better Homes and Gardens*, created house designs and plans that helped many to better living.

Mary Davis Gillies was interiors and architectural editor of *McCall's*. For many years her vivid presentation of houses, plans, and interior designs had a strong national impact.

Elizabeth Gordon, talented editor of *House Beautiful* combined traditional-style houses with contemporary elegance. She was a popular speaker at builder and dealer conventions, and crusaded for intelligent design. She researched and published important data on solar orientation and siting of houses, and gathered much original data on Japanese design and its influence on American architecture.

Joseph B. Mason was building editor of *Good Housekeeping* magazine. In 1945 he commissioned 12 outstanding architects to design moderate-price homes and had large-scale models built. These were photographed, published, and a detailed "sketch plan" sheet was offered for 25 cents. The public response was enormous: more than 100,000 plans were purchased the first year. The models were displayed at Macy's Department Store, Wanamaker's, and elsewhere, and they attracted wide attention. The architects included Edward Stone, Harwell Hamilton Harris, William W. Wurster, Julius Gregory, Bertram Weber, Clinton Gamble, and others. *Good Housekeeping* continued to publish houses by outstanding architects for the following eight years, and surely had an influence on better design.

Maxine Livingston, family home editor of *Parents' Magazine*, published many notable designs for families with children and sponsored model houses which were viewed by thousands.

Building manufacturers also got into the act. In 1947 Borg-Warner built "Ingersoll Village," a project with seven houses featuring postwar home ideas including a factory-fabricated kitchen-laundry-bath core. The houses were well designed by such architects as Alden B. Dow, George Fred Keck, Edward D. Stone, Royal Barry Wills, Hugh Stubbins, and L. Morgan Yost. The project attracted large crowds, and the model homes were published in color and in great detail in most of the large consumer and trade publications.

Another manufacturer-sponsored program was that of Revere Copper and Brass Quality House Institute in 1948. Architect John H. Callendar organized the program. Eight teams of architects were teamed with eight builders, and quality, low-cost homes were built in their projects. These, too, were seen by thousands locally, and all were viewed by millions in both consumer and trade magazines. The architects included Chiarelli and Kirk of Seattle; L. Morgan Yost of Kenilworth, Illinois; McKie and Kamrath of Houston; Kenneth Kassler of Princeton; Ralph Twitchell of Sarasota, Florida; and Samuel Glazer of Boston.

In mid-year Congress passed the bitterly contested Housing Act of 1949, providing for 810,000 public units in six years and set a goal of "a decent home for every American." It proposed $1 billion in loans and subsidies for slum clearance and set up a $1.5-billion revolving-loan fund to assist low-rent projects. Most private builders did not approve, and called it a step towards socialism.

Just three months later, however, Congress passed and President Truman signed a private-housing bill that authorized $1.5 billion for FHA Titles I, II, and VI, and extended Section 608 rental housing. It also authorized an additional $1 billion for the Federal National Mortgage Association.

So the entire housing industry, public and private, received financing encouragement that assured growth for several years. Private builders continued to expand their projects, and by year's end the industry racked up a record total of 1,466,000 starts. It was an amazing end of an amazing year.

A few of the highlights of 1949 are further revealed by the following list of men and projects:

Del E. Webb was a Phoenix, Arizona, builder. In mid-1949 he started a 3,000-home well-planned community for the elderly, Pueblo Gardens in Tucson. This was followed by his now famous Sun Cities. Del Webb began as a carpenter and rose to a builder of multi-million-dollar projects from coast to coast.

Don Scholz was a Toledo, Ohio, builder and later pioneer prefabricated home manufacturer. During 1948 and 1949 he built 250 deluxe homes in well-planned neighborhoods that displayed new design and plan concepts. His ideas had a great influence on other builders, and he later incorporated those in a successful prefab home program.

Kalman Klein of New Hyde Park, New York, a well-known builder of homes and apartments in the New York area. He constructed Lakeville Estates, providing 2,000 homes in an attractive community setting.

Irvin A. Blietz of Wilmette, Illinois, started Pine Tree Village, one of several well-planned neighborhood communities in Chicago's northern suburbs. He built homes, townhouses, and apartments, employing advanced plan and design concepts.

Maurice Fishman of Precision Housing Corporation, Parma Heights, Ohio, began an 800-home, planned neighborhood community, Ridgewood Park, on a 225-acre site. He used a large, on-site shop for precutting and fabricating components and trusses. Engineered plans and designs were employed in the $14,000 homes on large sites.

James R. Price of National Homes Corporation, Lafayette, Indiana, a fast-growing manufacturer of prefabricated homes, unveiled new models to sell for $5,720. He sold 300 in one day and started on a production program of 36 houses a day in his manufacturing plants.

Research, Development, and Industrialization Accelerate

The decade of the forties may ultimately be remembered as much for its progress in research and development of house construction techniques, planning, and design as for the building of 7,443,000 new homes. Much of the amazing burst of production from 1946 to 1950 and beyond is directly traceable to research, engineered planning and design, modular coordination, field testing, and experimental house testing. Precutting and site fabrication of parts, panels, and components, along with full prefabrication in factories, was greatly stimulated by the work of many brilliant men working in housing research.

Most of this work was carried on by many widely scattered building firms, manufacturers, trade associations, universities, and some federal agencies, just as it was in the thirties. We can mention only a few, and some of these were carried over from the earlier decades.

William A. Sheick, a Washington, D.C. architect, was a major contributor to housing research. As professor of architecture at the University of Illinois he directed the Small Homes Council which carried on research and testing and built experimental houses. The Council conducted short courses for residential builders and published bulletins and booklets on home planning, design, and construction. He later served as director of the Building Research Council of the National Academy of Science in Washington, D.C., and then went on to become executive director of the American Institute of Architects.

John E. Burchard of Cambridge, Massachusetts, was professor of architectural engineering at the Massachusetts Institute of Technology, and a major pioneer in housing research. As director of the Albert Farwell Bemis Foundation, he carried on the studies in systems and techniques, framing methods and wall panels, and test-house construction. He did original work in modular design and planning, which paved the way for the development of panel systems and standardized dimensions in design.

Forest Products Laboratory in Madison, Wisconsin, continued its major research in woods and glues which improved the quality of plywood and expanded its use in wall, floor, and roof panels in housing. It built the first stressed-skin plywood test house which sparked wide national interest and affected future building techniques.

Cotton W. Northrup, with the National Retail Lumber Dealers Association in Washington, D.C., directed and sponsored the "Industry Engineered House" which advanced the use of modular design, planning, and dimensioning in houses. Detailed small-house plans, based on modular principles, a four-inch grid, and use of stock dimension lumber, were made available to lumber dealers and builders . A comprehensive volume, *Modular Planned Homes*, was prepared by Richard Pollman, designer and engineer, and given wide national distribution by the Association.

Andrew S. Place of South Bend, Indiana, was for 24 years a member and director of NAHB's Research Foundation and Research Institute. An active builder and developer, he field tested many new cost-saving ideas and methods in his own projects. One of these was a 180-unit community of postwar veterans' homes, where his techniques included a prefab cutting shop, engineered plans, walls fabricated at the site, large wall and roof sheets of plywood, and a trussed roof system.

F. Vaux Wilson, with the Homosote Company in Trenton, New Jersey, continued his development of a prefab panel system called "Precision Built Homes," described earlier. The house was built with large wall sections fabricated on jig tables in lumberyard shops. By 1941 some 3,000 homes had been erected

by lumber dealers and their small contractor customers. It proved ideal for fast production of low cost war houses, and many thousands were built.

In 1941, the *Public Building Administration* staged a prefab, demountable home demonstration and test at Indian Head, Maryland. Eleven prefab manufacturers erected 650 units, demounted and moved them to another site, then re-erected them. There was some question as to what was learned, but the wide publicity helped advance the new techniques.

In 1942, the *Federal Public Housing Administration* researched field fabrication and assembly methods for floor, wall, and roof panels, trusses and components. Scale models of jig tables were built, and detailed plans for field construction and assembly were published. The system was based on modular design and gave impetus to wider use of field fabrication. This was a most constructive contribution, and the published detailed drawings helped many builders in their work.

In 1941, the *Tennessee Valley Authority* researched, designed, and built test models of a "sectional house," the forerunner of today's component homes. These early TVA units were box-like sections of one or more rooms which were joined at the site. In 1944, 2,000 were built by Prefab Engineering Corporation of Toledo, Oregon, and sold to the War Department. Plans and details were published, studied by builders, and were helpful in later development.

Prefabrication Progress of the Forties

The prefabricated-house manufacturing industry enjoyed a strong push from World War II. It had guaranteed orders, a huge ready market, and ample government financing. Speed, lightness, and mass production were required. The need for demountables and temporary housing stimulated use of light frame and plywood structures, ideal for the industry.

Early in 1942 the Defense Housing Division of the Federal Works Administration announced a grandiose $153-million program to build 70,000 prefabs and demountables in one year. Three months later FWA proclaimed contracts had been let as follows:

Green Lumber Company, Michigan	1500 units
National Homes Corporation, Indiana	1200
Southern Mill & Lumber, Kansas	2940
Gunnison Homes, Kentucky	750
Houston Ready Cut, Texas	900

The program soon became bogged down in delays, red tape, and government confusion, and nothing like these figures was realized. But this and other government programs did give the prefab-home industry considerable aid for growth, much of which carried over to postwar years. It is estimated that 200,000 factory prefabricated homes were built during the war years.

Like the rest of the housing industry, prefab firms benefitted from the research, techniques, and business leadership of a few enterprising men. In the list that follows we call attention to only a few who pioneered this exciting new industry.

Alladin Company of Bay City, Michigan was a pioneer in ready-cut homes. The firm had sold some 100,000 by 1941. It experimented with a "Pullman"-type mobile unit, then panel units plus pre-cutting. In 1942 the firm's plants had a capacity of 1,000 a month and sold many war and postwar houses.

Robert W. McLaughlin, an architect described earlier, founded American Homes in New York in 1932. His first units were of steel frame with asbestos panels. He later shifted to a more conventional pre-cut wood and plywood panel house with Colonial exteriors. In 1942 he had five plants operating with a capacity of 600 units per month, and sold some 20,000 units during the war.

Dawson Winn of Green Lumber Company, Laurel, Michigan, built low-cost double units (end to end) with plywood floor, wall, and roof panels. He sold thousands during the war.

Foster Gunnison of Gunnison Housing Corporation, New Albany, Indiana, described earlier, continued to develop his stressed-skin plywood panel system with waterproof plywood exteriors. He built panels on a hot press using waterproof adhesives. He sold 5,000 war homes.

Howard T. Fisher, architect and founder of General Houses, Incorporated, Chicago, Illinois, described earlier, switched to a light steel frame with plywood panels. His plants had a capacity of 500 a month at the start of the war; he built many war and postwar houses.

James Pease of Pease Woodwork Company, Cincinnati, Ohio, was an early prefab producer and industry organizer. Conventional houses were produced with large room-size panels. He developed packaged steel doors and other components. His plant capacity in 1940 was 400 homes a month.

Houston Ready-Cut House Company in Houston, Texas, was founded in 1917, and produced 10,000 ready-cut and sectional houses for the oil industry before the war. They built 4,593 tent frames for the Army in 1941. Their plant had a capacity of 300 houses a month in 1942, which was expanded to handle many war contracts.

Bertram Goldberg, an architect with Standard Homes Corporation, Chicago, Illinois, researched stressed-covered plywood panel systems for Douglas Fir Plywood Association. He built many war houses, including 57 for PBA's Indian Head project in 1941. The capacity of his plant was 800 houses a month.

Carl Strandlund of Lustron Corporation, Columbus, Ohio, conducted one of the most costly prefab experiments in history with $25 million of RFC money. His houses were factory built with steel frames and insulated panels clad in enameled steel. They were to sell at $7,000, but production, distribution, and sales cost ran far above projections. The firm went out of business after a short time.

James R. Price of National Homes Corporation, Lafayette, Indiana, turned the firm into one of the largest prefab companies in the world, with excellent national distribution. He built many thousands of war and postwar homes, and production was expanded to 750 a month. He was a leader and a trend setter.

Don Scholz of Toledo, Ohio, continued his career as a dynamic pioneer prefab manufacturer and innovator of systems and designs. He built a successful firm with large national distribution and sales, and contributed much to better design.

C. Fred Dally, with Seattle Prefab Products Company, Seattle, Washington, was an active home builder as well as a prefab manufacturer in the Northwest. He had production capacity of 400 low-cost homes a month in 1942.

Albert P. Hildebrandt, founder and president of Kingsbury Homes, Atlanta, Georgia, developed one of the first and largest regional prefab companies. His research department did much to develop new techniques, concepts, and designs, including a one-package, kitchen-bath utility core. He continued in the industry for many years.

W. Hamilton Crawford of Baton Rouge, Louisiana, was both a builder and prefab manufacturer, one of the largest in the South. He produced many war and postwar houses, and later developed the new town of Crofton in Maryland.

Architects and Designers of the Forties

A notable galaxy of architects, designers, and landscape experts contributed to improving the quality of life for the American public in the decade of the forties.

Creative leaders like Frank Lloyd Wright, Pietro Belluschi, William Wilson Wurster, and Harwell Hamilton Harris continued to make a strong impact on the home design of future decades. But there were many less-publicized men who plunged into the down-to-earth planning of building projects and contributed a great deal to the level of design of large-scale building developments.

A brief list should include such men as Carl Koch, Cambridge, Massachusetts; Anshen and Allen, San Francisco; Royal Barry Wills, Boston; Randolph Evans, New York City; Charles Goodman, Washington, D.C.; Cliff May, Los Angeles; Hugh Stubbins, Cambridge, Massachusetts; Herman York, New York City; and John Highland, Buffalo, New York.

During the war years there were few projects whose architectural design merited special mention. Two that come to mind are Richard Neutra's 600-unit, low-cost Channel

Heights project at San Pedro, California, and the even more attractive Valencia Gardens in San Francisco designed by William Wurster.

In the field of custom residential architecture, the derivative influence of the earlier work of Maybeck, Morris, and Greene seems to have evolved even further to become an important trend. The possibilities of wood, the Japanese influence, the return to a "native American architecture" blended with modern planning and the use of large glass areas.

The eclectic effects may be seen in the continuing work of Harwell Harris, Wurster, Belluschi, Gardener Dailey and—he would deny it—Frank Lloyd Wright.

All of these men did, however, contribute to a trend toward wood and natural materials, the use of large windows with protective overhangs to bring in the outdoors, and better utilization of space. They had a definite impact on the future of single family design and of builder project houses.

Frank Lloyd Wright designed many exciting and well-publicized houses in the decade of the forties. His Falling Waters, Adelman, John Pew, and Taliesin West buildings influenced hundreds of young designers. The young men who worshipped at his feet at Taliesin went out to extend his influence. One of these was a young architect and builder, David Henken, who persuaded Wright to design at least some of the woodsy homes in his Usonia Community in northern Westchester, New York. Here the wide overhangs, huge fireplaces, large windows, and use of natural cypress and stone brought a new dimension to small-home architecture.

In the field of apartment design, the most publicized impact was registered by Mies van der Rohe's Promontory Apartments on Chicago's Lake Shore Drive. The all-steel-and-glass towers with floor-to-ceiling windows

were impressive. Skidmore, Owings and Merrill also did creative work in apartments, including some in New York. But there is not much to be said, architecturally or designwise at least, for the vast outpouring of garden apartments of the war and postwar years.

Who indeed were the architects and planners who most strongly influenced housing in the forties and future years? We must look in many places. One is Princeton University, which held an august conference on the occasion of its two-hundreth birthday in 1947. The subject: Planning Man's Environment. The distinguished conferees were Frank Lloyd Wright, John E. Burchard, Howard P. Vermilya, Talbot Hamlin, Siegfried Gidion, William Wurster, George Fred Keck, Roy Jones, Kenneth Kassler, and Philip Johnson.

In 1944 the Modern Museum of Art in New York City held a "Built in USA" home exhibition. These are the architects and houses illustrated, all influential:

Frank Lloyd Wright—Falling Waters and Taliesin West.
Philip Johnson—Glass House in Connecticut.
Edward Stone—Goodyear House in Old Westbury.
Gropius-Breuer—Chamberlin House in Massachusetts.
Harwell Hamilton Harris—Fellowship Park in Los Angeles.
Carl Koch—Snake Hill Houses in Belmont, Massachusetts.

The five distinguished architects of this period who take top position for their influence on residential design are as follows:

William Wilson Wurster continued to design beautiful residences in wood and natural materials, well-planned and structured with low profiles. His San Franciso apartments were exceptional. As dean of the school of architecture and planning at MIT he became a powerful influence and advocate of restrained modern design.

Harwell Hamilton Harris of Los Angeles created a wide following with his delicate home design in natural wood and stone. Much of his early work was done in California and reflected Japanese influence and the work of early pioneers of the area. He became head of the department of architecture at The University of Texas, where he continued to influence residential building.

Richard J. Neutra of Los Angeles created a school of architecture of his own with his beautifully detailed, glass-walled residences and meticulously organized interior space. He designed one of the few architecturally attractive public war-housing projects, Channel Heights at San Pedro, California. He was the architect for more than 100 residences of notable design.

Pietro Belluschi is often associated with the "Northwest School" because of his distinguished career in Oregon. His residences reflected a deep understanding of the uses and possibilities of natural woods, plywood, glass, and stone, in a muted, contemporary style. His influence on modern residential architecture was continued while he was dean of MIT school of architecture and planning.

Royal Barry Wills, as he had done for many years, continued to have perhaps the greatest direct impact on house design of any architect of the period. His authentic Colonial houses were widely admired and copied. His influence was further extended by the plan books he prepared and by the extensive publication of his work in popular books and magazines.

In the field of landscape architecture there was considerable progress. Two men, Thomas Church of San Francisco and Garrett Eckbo of Los Angeles, illustrate the trend. Church added a great deal to the art of landscape design with his wood arbors and trellis work, patterned brick walls and terraces, and interesting surface materials. He worked on many Bay Area houses by leading architects.

Garrett Eckbo did exciting things in both landscape design and community planning. His geometric plans, textures, shapes, screens, and garden patterns were unique.

Environmental Planning and the Quality of Life

Creative land and community planning distinctly advanced the quality of life in the decade of the forties and laid the foundation for still greater strides later. The rapid growth of large, planned communities made it possible for builders to retain skilled architects, planners, and landscape designers.

An important contribution was made by the Urban Land Institute of Washington, which supported improved land development techniques through research and education. Many leading builders such as J. C. Nichols, Hugh Potter, Fritz Burns, David Bohannon, and Waverly Taylor, were members of ULI, and the high quality of their projects reflects its impact.

One of ULI's most effective means for improving community planning was to hold a clinic at which a group of ten or more developers and planners would examine and critique a project of one of the members. The exchange of ideas was productive for all, and especially for the man whose project was under fire.

A new force toward better communities was also exerted by FHA, whose land-planning division was headed by Seward H. Mott, and later by Robert O'Donnell.

As a result, the decade saw the rapid growth of such concepts as planned unit developments, community associations, cluster planning, loop streets, culs-de-sac, open space and park areas, recreational facilities, flexible zoning, and improved subdivision regulations.

Many outstanding communities were developed in the decade which today stand as high examples of creative planning. The dean of neighborhood development, J. C. Nichols, was continuing the Prairie Hills section of his famous Country Club District in Kansas City. Hugh Potter was expanding the great neighborhood design he created at River Oaks in Houston, Texas.

Joseph Beck was developing his Hidden Valley project near Sacramento, California, where he pioneered cluster and open-space concepts. And in the San Francisco area, Duncan McDuffie was carrying on the tradi-

tion of quality development established at St. Francis Wood, the earliest subdivision with park, recreational, and common property owned and maintained by a homes association. His Park Hills project, started in 1940, had curvilinear streets, three private parks, large plots, and a homes association that owned and administered the common property.

Another admirable example of creative neighborhood development must again be mentioned. John C. McC. Mowbray, president of the Roland Park Company of Baltimore, was carrying on the world-famous neighborhood design standards established by Frederick Law Olmstead. The original Roland Park area had been carefully expanded with new neighborhoods, including Guilford, Homeland, and Northwood. As it stands today, this community is a monument to creative planning and has provided inspiration to countless others.

Again mention should also be made of William P. Atkinson of Oklahoma City, who organized and developed Midwest City, the integrated, well-planned project of 6,000 homes which pioneered new community concepts in this first large subcity of war and postwar homes.

CHAPTER THREE

1950-1960

PROSPERITY AND THE RUSH TO SUBURBIA

Everything Essential Was at Hand

With the fifties came social and cultural advances, economic growth, vast highway expansion, new concepts for better living and, of course, building advances. A record 15.1 million homes were constructed, and they were markedly better built, better planned, and better equipped, were larger in size, and gave higher value than had ever been achieved in this or any other nation. And housing research, planning, and design reached new heights, paving the way for still further improvements.

After two decades of depression, war, and slow recovery, people were avidly ready, in 1950, for a better way of life. The new housing introduced inviting visions of modern living. It meant planned communities and better homes for the poor, the elderly, and racial minorities. Builders both shaped and were shaped by this flow of events.

Everything essential to a revolutionary advance in housing was at hand. Efficient systems for building with prefabricated parts instead of individual pieces had been developed during the thirties and forties. A new architec-

ture caught the imagination of the public and stimulated the long-suppressed dreams of would-be home buyers.

A substantial population increase in the forties followed by an explosive growth of 29 million in the fifties created a huge shelter need. An equally large expansion in consumer income sparked all types of spending. The poor got richer and the middle-income buyers happily sought new ways to enjoy living on a higher scale. Favorable FHA and VA financing at low cost helped make a new home the major factor in a new way of life.

As 1950 opened, housing was accelerating to the highest level it had ever known. It reached 1.95 million starts per year in 1950—a record not equalled for the next 21 years.

But then in June 1950 the Korean War broke out, and by October there was a tragic awakening as General Douglas MacArthur was thrown back by the onslaught of Chinese and North Koreans.

Housing suffered a predictable setback, declining to 1.49 million starts in 1951, 1.5 million in 1952, and 1.44 million in 1953. The most visible effect of the Korean struggle on builders was a frustrating deluge of government edicts, wage and price controls, and confusing regulations, and an acute shortage of materials. Harassed builders were forced once again, as in previous war years, to scour the country for scarce nails, lumber, plywood, and bathtubs.

A lively note during this period was introduced by Secretary of Defense Charles E. Wilson, dubbed "Engine Charlie," who was famous for his pithy, off-the-record remarks. His most quoted was: "What's good for our country is good for General Motors, and vice versa." He infuriated welfare recipients with his comment: "I've always liked bird dogs better than kennel-fed ones; [the ones] who get out and hunt for food rather than sit on their fannies and yell." He had a supremely important war production job and he let nothing stand in its way.

Builders persevered in the struggle to keep housing going in spite of war shortages and controls, and by 1954 the volume of starts rose to 1.55 million, and then to 1.65 million in 1955. However, in 1956 the volume was reduced to 1.35 million, and in 1957 it dropped to 1.22 million. That was called a "mild recession." In 1958 starts rose again to 1.38 million, and to 1.5 million in 1959. For the decade the average was 1.5 million starts a year, an astounding production under the circumstances.

Housing production tells only a part of the story of this era. The decade saw a frenetic rise in the number of backyard bomb shelters and sightings of unidentified flying objects. It recorded Martin Luther King's first bus boycott at Montgomery, Alabama; a multi-billion-dollar highway program that changed American habits; the rise of the Beat Genera-

tion; the McCarthy hearings; and a significant move to the suburbs by America's middle classes.

Last, but certainly not least, the rise of television to a dominant role in communications altered many attitudes toward living. Both Eisenhower's and Adlai E. Stevenson's nominating conventions in 1952 were televised— the first use of the powerful medium—and television sets multiplied tenfold by mid-decade. Milton Berle, Mary Martin, Edward R. Murrow, and Lucille Ball, among others, captivated millions. It is said that *I Love Lucy* had 50 million viewers—more than those who saw Ike inaugurated.

Full employment, rising incomes, and population growth all helped spark consumer spending and boom conditions. In 1955, 65 million people were employed, the steel industry was operating at 98.8% capacity, and eight million cars were sold. The gross national product was double that of 1929.

In 1958 the 3,800-foot-long Mackinac Bridge was opened—one of the world's longest suspension structures. And in 1959 the St. Lawrence Seaway connected the Great Lakes with the Atlantic Ocean, bringing new growth and trade to midwest cities.

The year 1959 brought Alaska and Hawaii into the Union as the forty-ninth and fiftieth states, and both were soon contributing mightily to the housing boom.

The fifties also ushered in great new programs of building for the elderly and retired, exotic vacation-home projects, and the rise of integrated communities called "newtowns." Late in the decade, apartment projects of a new and very attractive kind with many amenities flourished. For home builders, home buyers, and the nation as a whole, this era was truly a fabulous one.

American Life Styles Change

Home builders and real estate developers in the early fifties were the seldom praised and oft disparaged provocateurs of one of the greatest changes in American life: the rush to suburbia and exurbia. Families by the millions moved in search of clean air, green grass, space, better schools, and the amenities they thought would be found in suburban living.

New suburbs grew from raw land, or from a patch of farmland as at Long Island's Levittown, which was built on old farm acreage bought from potato growers. But mostly the suburban builder projects grew up in hundreds of smaller communities, each the result of hard work and patience by developers to get approval of zoning, planning, and building, as well as water, sewer, road, and development permits. Many town fathers furiously resisted the building projects because they resented change of any kind and did not want to construct additional schools or supply other town services.

But nothing could stop the inexorable flow to the suburbs. Teachers, doctors, lawyers, butchers, bankers—all sought a new life in the new homes and communities builders had to offer. In 1950 alone, more than one-third of the record 1.95 million new homes were built in suburbia.

Dry statistics give a still more illuminating picture of the suburban plunge. Metropolitan suburb population jumped 50% from 1950 to 1960. Suffolk County in New York gained 139%; Nassau County doubled. Metropolitan areas in Westchester County, New York, zoomed, as did those in neighboring Connecticut and New Jersey. Los Angeles, Miami, Phoenix, Atlanta, Houston, Dallas, and a hundred other cities and towns exploded beyond their earlier limits. Much of the suburban spread was aided by a vast $100-billion highway program which helped open the central cities to their surrounding areas.

American life was swept along by the suburban onslaught. An era of backyard barbecues, cocktail parties, power mowers, washers and dryers, PTA pride, and Girl Scout goings-on blossomed. Many of the new suburbanites were seeking a higher social status, and wives dreamed of sophisticated entertainment in their bright, new, fully automated and electrically equipped houses.

Suburban growth—and later suburban sprawl—had many side effects. Highways to the cities became traffic jams, and commuter trains such as the (now defunct) New Haven were overloaded, late, and a celebrated cause of complaint. School and sewage bond issues proliferated and raised local taxes. But lawn and porch furniture sales soared too, as did those of barbecue sets, hamburgers, and spare ribs. Power-mower production jumped fourfold, and the number of automatic washing machines doubled.

Other suburbiana: Bowling-alley lanes increased from 50,000 to 110,000, encyclopedia sales from 70,000 to 300,000; bicycle sales from two million to four, and the number of Girl Scouts and Brownies from 1.6 million to more than four million. Huge shopping centers sprang up to encourage more spending in glamorous settings. The builders who started all this were seldom around to see the burgeoning results, but many took pride in the communities they had created, and noted with satisfaction that with each passing decade the value and sales price of their houses had doubled, tripled, and often quadrupled. That is one of the wry facts of being what used to be called a "speculative" builder.

Government's Role in Housing

All through this decade the sharp tug of war continued between advocates of public and private housing and between more or less federal controls. The struggle culminated in 1959 when President Eisenhower twice vetoed housing bills he declared to be "extravagant, inflationary, and unfair."

Late in 1950 the now famous "Regulations X and W," issued in Washington, imposed strict credit controls intended to reduce building, and were followed by wage and price controls and a Korean Defense Housing bill that did more to confuse than aid construction.

Home builders complained bitterly of the confusion, as well as of the delays resulting from these government acts, and declared many of them the work of persons "trying to socialize housing." In truth, the regulations worked very poorly, and Korean war defense housing soon bogged down and almost disappeared under layers of overzealous federal agencies and administrators. Housing was being regulated to death.

Housing bills were the subject of protracted and acerbic debate in Congress in 1951, 1952, 1953, 1954, 1956, 1957, and 1959. Much of the debate revolved around the extent to which the federal government and our tax dollars should be involved in public housing, and also the extent to which it should increase financing aids to the private sector. Throughout the decade Congress sided largely with aid to FHA, VA, FNMA (Federal National Mortgage Association) and other private mortgage-finance assistance agencies. The resulting lower down payments, longer amortization— up to 40 years—and low interest rates were largely responsible for the enormous expansion of home building during the decade.

Monetary policies, as set by the Federal Reserve Board, also had a powerful bearing on housing finance and an unsettling effect on building. A severe tight-money crisis arose in 1952 when the FRB attempted to "pull the plug" on cheap money. FHA and VA rates were fixed by Congress, and as the FRB prime rate rose, mortgage money dried up. In 1953 the FRB reversed its policy, began pumping money into the economy, and FHA and VA mortgage funds again became plentiful.

We see the same story of Federal Reserve tight-money policies and their effect on housing repeated many times in this and later decades. When interest rates set by the Federal Reserve were low enough at market levels to make FHA and VA mortgages attractive to lenders, a boom ensued. When rates rose too high, an often disastrous cutback in housing resulted.

In mid-1952 President Truman signed into law the Veterans' Readjusted Assistance Act—the so-called "G.I. Bill of Rights"— which was helpful both to Korean war veterans and to the housing industry.

Then in mid-year Congress passed the Housing Act of 1953 which gave the President power to adjust FHA and VA interest rates, gave FNMA power to make advance commitments and raised its ceiling $500 million, added $1.5 billion for FHA mortgage insurance, and lowered down payments on FHA loans.

By the fall of 1954 Congress had readied still another bill, the Housing Act of 1954, which was signed by President Eisenhower. It included 30-year, no down payment loans for veterans, and 5% down for others. The bill reorganized the FNMA to expand its secondary market and special assistance programs, thus stimulating the flow of private capital into home building.

The 1954 Act also adopted a new concept of slum clearance, replacing it with what was called "Urban Renewal" and the idea of restoring decaying areas. Urban renewal was also aided by a new provision encouraging private builders to operate under FHA. The new FHA Sections 220 and 221 established advantageous terms for them to undertake both renewal and housing for families displaced by government action.

Another boost to housing was contained in a new tax bill in 1954 which provided for faster and more flexible depreciation for investors. Rental housing began to flourish as a result.

The 1956 Housing Act again liberalized FHA and VA terms and raised the ceiling on Section 207 Rental Housing mortgages to 90%. A severe restriction against windfall profits or "mortgaging out" was included. Public housing was again cut back in reaction to widespread voter disapproval.

In 1957 a mild recession and a decline in housing starts set up a clamor for more congressional action. As a result the "Anti-Recession" Housing Act of 1957 roared through in three weeks. It cut FHA down payments to 3%, extended VA mortgages and adjusted their rates, and gave FNMA an additional $1.5 billion authorization. It was said to have provided 200,000 more homes and 500,000 jobs, and it well may have. At least, starts rose sharply in both 1958 and 1959.

The last housing bill of the decade—the Housing Act of 1959—was finally passed and signed by Eisenhower in September after months of debate and several revisions. Since 1954, as Democratic control of Congress increased, housing proposals had become more costly and more inflationary and, as Ike said, "unfair and unwise." The 1959 bill as passed

after three tries was much watered down, especially in regard to urban renewal and public housing. It did lower some FHA down payments, provide aid to cooperative and rental housing, help the elderly, and add still more funds for FNMA.

The major effect of the various housing acts of the decade, as we have observed, was to accelerate private production to the highest levels thus far—an average of one-and-a-half million starts a year. Also, a slow but important upgrading of quality and standards took place. This was given a push by FHA Commissioner Norman Mason in 1957 with directives that permitted buyers to acquire more expensive, better quality houses with less income. In effect, cutting the income requirements tripled the number of families who could qualify for a $20,000 house.

FHA made history in 1959 by celebrating its twenty-fifth anniversary, with President Eisenhower, Senators Sparkman and Capehart, and 1300 guests on hand. Ike praised FHA's "miraculous financial record." In 25 years it had insured five million home mortgages and 22 million home-improvement loans, paid back $65 million to the U.S. treasury, built reserves of $719 million, and operated at a profit every year after 1940. No other government agency has done so much for so many at such low cost to the taxpayer.

FHA also made history of another sort in 1959 by issuing a new "construction bible"— its 300-page *Minimum Property Standards* (MPS) for one- and two-family homes. It simplified, clarified, and raised standards, and included specifications for bigger rooms, better insulation, more storage space, and longer warranties. Commissioner Norman Mason and Neil Connor, chief of FHA Architectural Standards, were justly proud of the massive technical job performed.

Urban renewal and slum clearance remained a largely unsolved problem of the fifties, as it is today. The Housing Act of 1954 provided some new tools, as did a Supreme Court decision the same year that declared it constitutional for a municipality to buy up private property, tear down the buildings, and sell the property to a private buyer or builder. This helped the programs of private builders under FHA Sections 220 and 221 in their attempts to build renewal and replacement housing.

Urban renewal also had some success in restoring city areas, as in New Haven, Connecticut, where a large business district was rebuilt. In Duluth, Minnesota, slums were replaced by an industrial park; in Birmingham, Alabama, by a medical center. In 1952 NAHB president Alan Brockbank issued a "report on the nation's slums" and urged private builders to participate in rebuilding them. A few did, such as Webb & Knapp, Renewal Development Corporation, Reynolds Metals, Lewis Kitchen, William Witt in Norfolk, Marvin Gilman in Baltimore, Joseph Singer in Philadelphia, Joseph Eichler in San Francisco, and Leon N. Weiner in Wilmington, Delaware. Public housing was helped by the ability of such firms to switch to housing displaced families and the elderly.

Highly liberal housing finance in the fifties was undoubtedly spurred by FHA and VA loans, but there were other factors. One was a huge growth in mortgage banking firms, whose loans skyrocketed from $6 billion in 1952 to $20 billion in 1955. They brought new capital, new aggressiveness, and an expanded nation-wide capability and flexibility in home finance.

At the same time, a vigorous expansion in the role of savings and loan associations took place. A surge forward was triggered in October of 1958 when the Federal Home Loan Bank Board told all federal savings and loan associations they could make 90% loans on homes of up to $18,000 value. This put them almost on the same footing as FHA, and brought keen competition. Soon conventional mortgages were available almost everywhere on more liberal terms, which further spurred an increase in building volume.

Another significant and highly important home finance development occurred in 1957. This was the first private mortgage guarantee insurance corporation—the first of many that eventually began to rival FHA in the mortgage insurance field.

The founder of this first firm was Max Karl, the dynamic and imaginative innovator who predicted that his Milwaukee-based Mortgage Guarantee Insurance Corporation (MGIC) would eventually become a bigger mortgage insurer than FHA. The books have not been closed, but over the decades MGIC has indeed become a major mortgage insurer. More than that, it paved the way for many others. FHA today has vigorous rivals, and the home building field has again benefitted by keen competition.

Builders often pay tribute to Congressman Wright Patman, who for some 50 years was a friend of the housing industry. As chairman of the House Banking Committee he fought high interest rates and monetary policies which might restrict building. He left his imprint on much important housing legislation.

Another friend of housing was Raymond M. Foley, head of the Housing and Home Finance Agency from 1947 to 1953. A capable administrator, he did his best to solve the nation's housing problems under difficult conditions.

The FHA Section 608 Apartment Building "Scandal"

A sensational scandal arose in 1954 over the FHA Section 608 apartment building program that had been started in 1946 and ended in 1950.

FHA Section 608 had been drafted by Congress in 1946 in a desperate attempt to alleviate the critical postwar housing shortage. Builders were importuned by FHA to turn out 608 rental housing in a hurry, and were offered extraordinary profit incentives to do so. Congress purposely stimulated the use of high-loan-to-value insured mortgages so that builders would participate.

The program was an astounding success and actually alleviated the critical shortage of veterans' housing. From 1946 to 1950 more than 465,000 apartment units were built in some 7,000 projects.

These apartments were on the whole well constructed and equipped, and available at low rents. In 1950 they were 98% occupied, and defaults were infinitesimal—actually 1.28%. The apartments had increased in value, mortgages were being paid off rapidly, and over the years the apartments provided sound and attractive homes for more than a million veterans and others.

Why then, in 1954, did the FHA Section 608 scandal suddenly erupt and flood the nation with sensational charges of corruption and windfall profits that blackened the reputation of the industry for years?

The answer is involved and spiced with politics. In the confusion and bad publicity, however, most Americans have lost sight of the benefits to the country that were produced by FHA Section 608 housing.

The startling news broke on April 12, 1954, when the Eisenhower administration announced it was moving against "serious irregularities and abuses" in FHA. Sherman Adams was delegated to fire the head of FHA, Guy T. O. Hollyday, which was done abruptly and without a hearing. Albert M. Cole, head of the Housing and Home Finance Agency, then seized FHA 608 and Title I files, and a series of HHFA, FBI, Justice Department, IRS, and congressional investigations started.

The most amazing fact was that President Eisenhower had made his own Republican appointee of only one year the scapegoat for a scandal that had supposedly taken place under the Democrats five years before.

Hollyday, it was clearly established, was a man of impeccable character and considerable ability. He was an "Eisenhower Democrat" who had taken the FHA job as a public service and at great personal sacrifice. He had been a past president of the Mortgage Bankers Association and in his short term had been making strenuous efforts to clean up FHA with its limited staff.

Charges of windfall profits and "mortgaging out" had been made and published as early as 1949 and 1950 and were partly responsible for ending the Section 608 program. But in 1954 charges were revived along with new claims of FHA "irregularities" in the Title I Repair Loan section. There are various explanations for the sudden administrative action, but one is that prominent Democrats were planning to make the charges, and Eisenhower—ever anxious to avoid any taint of graft or corruption—decided to move first. There may have been other factors based on politics and on the control of government housing policies and agencies. The actual charges were that:

1. Illegal or unethical actions in financing FHA 608's had given promoters of 251 projects windfall profits of $75 million, with a very small number of mortgages exceeding costs by 110% to 150%.
2. Thousands of home owners had been cheated or overcharged by high-pressure repair and remodeling salesmen who had done shoddy work.

A few FHA officials were under suspicion of accepting graft.

Hollyday was replaced by Norman P. Mason, a lumber dealer from North Chelmsford, Massachusetts, who was well qualified and brought an excellent, businesslike administration to FHA. He set about rebuilding FHA and did much to restore its tarnished image in succeeding years.

Tarnished was the most pleasant term one could use to describe what happened to FHA and to thousands of builders who worked with it. For two years a succession of congressional hearings and investigations made glaring headlines, and politicians made news by slandering many unfortunate people.

After six months, Senator Homer Capehart, chairman of the Banking and Currency Committee, ended his hearings. There had been 200 witnesses and some $143,000 had been spent, but the results were stated as "unclear." At the same time, Senator Sparkman issued a statement praising the 608 program and the 465,000 desperately needed apartments it had provided for veterans.

A grand jury investigation was finally completed in April 1956, with two minor indictments which were later dismissed. There were no convictions in the 608 affairs. Even the

case of Clyde L. Powell, the FHA administrator in charge of 608 who was the central figure in many charges, was dismissed.

There was no denying that some windfall profits had been made. One of the later FHA reports indicated that there were 70 projects which had $31 million of profit on a reported cost of $239,375,000. Yet these were only a fraction of the 7,000 projects and 465,000 units built.

Most builders explained their profits by showing how they used efficient building, buying, and production methods to bring cost below the FHA estimate. They also pointed out that they were urged to enter the 608 program with the promise of profitable operations. And they added that no one had ever said it was illegal to make a profit.

The first revelations of high profits on 608 came from the IRS, and it took several lawsuits to clear up whether such profits would be taxed as regular income or capital gains. A notable winner in the case was the Gross-Morton Company, whose mammoth Glen Oaks Village on Long Island (3,000 units) was under scrutiny. The project cost about $20 million, but 608-insured loans, made mostly by Prudential Insurance Company, had amounted to $24 million. Gross-Morton had paid capital gains tax on this $4 million profit.

The tax suit was won by Gross-Morton as the court ruled the windfall profit a capital gain, taxable at 25%, instead of regular income, which might be taxed up to 90%.

The trial brought out that no illegality was attached to the fact that the 608 program enabled Gross-Morton to show a surplus. Nobody lost under such a program: FHA had a good investment, the property appreciated in value, and the U.S. had been paid $1.5 million in capital gains taxes.

Gross-Morton also had another suit on its

hands, this one from tenants who claimed that the $4 million profit should be applied to a lower mortgage and thus reduce rentals. The tenants lost, as did others who brought similar suits against builders of 608 projects.

FHA did a great deal of barn-door closing after Norman Mason took over. It tightened rules on repair loans, did much checking and weeding out of staff, and forbade any further mortgaging out or windfall profits on apartment work. For a time it issued a blacklist of windfall recipients and refused to do any business with them. This was challenged in the courts and later withdrawn.

In later housing legislation, Congress permanently forbade any further mortgaging out or windfall profits. But it was many years before apartment construction recovered, and it has never approached the tremendous volume of the 1946-1950 Section 608 program which ended the postwar housing shortage. This was another example of Congress and the administration killing off a highly productive housing program and creating instead a regulatory confusion that stopped apartment building for many years.

Great Architecture, Exciting Homes

The most significant change in residential design in the fifties came from the teaming up of builders with talented young architects to create exciting homes and communities. Together they succeeded in sparking a new architecture of ideas and quality, and a better life style.

Big builders and big projects now produced enough income to pay higher fees. And this was enough to attract skilled architects, land planners, interior designers, and other professionals. Builders soon found that this talent more than paid its way in lower cost, higher sales, and customer esteem.

As for the architects, they found that by specializing in merchant-built homes in volume they could earn a satisfactory income and at the same time make an aesthetically desirable contribution to better home design. The new school of architects learned to work with the builder and his other professionals as a team. This meant understanding and working with the techniques of land development, planning, scheduling, production, cost saving, interior design, finance, and marketing.

It was the close team relationship of talented architects and a new breed of educated builders that produced outstanding home communities and a significant advance in quality of design.

Another powerful influence on better home design was exerted by the professional building, architectural, and consumer publications. In 1952 a new magazine, *House and Home*, appeared, whose editor and publisher Perry I. Prentice carried on a vigorous campaign for builder-architect teamwork. He conducted a series of stimulating round tables, symposiums, housing tours, and conferences that brought together leading builders, architects, government officials, manufacturers, and financiers to work for progress and improvement.

Building model and demonstration homes and displaying them in home shows throughout the country also spread the new ideas. Manufacturers frequently cooperated with builders and architects to present fascinating demonstration projects, and such models were then published in professional and consumer magazines where they were viewed by millions. Thus the appetite for better living in the fifties was whetted.

Residential architecture was also affected by the more affluent economy, the move to the suburbs, new horizon in art and education, and a greater willingness to break from established tradition.

Quality of design got a push from the Housing Act of 1954, which enabled builders to put up larger, better-equipped, better designed structures for smaller down payments. In effect, a $16,000 house could be bought with the same payments as a $12,000 one at an earlier time.

"Trading up" to better housing was another phenomenon of the era that helped produce a boom in quality. Such trading up was made possible by a sharp rise in the equity value of most houses. As a result, owners of old homes often sold them at high prices and used the cash to acquire a better, bigger, and more exciting one.

The attitude of financial institutions—the lenders that made building possible—also changed somewhat for the better. In 1954, noted housing economist Miles Colean urged lenders "to be more understanding of progress in design and construction." He declared, "Novelty that produces real advance in comfort, convenience, and eye appeal can diminish risk."

As a result of these factors an architecture of ideas and quality did blossom forth. In terms of the 15 million homes built in the decade, it was perhaps not overwhelming, but it was significant. And the relatively few architects and builders who did produce glamorous new design concepts paved the way—as always—for greater progress in succeeding decades.

What was this architecture of ideas and quality all about? First of all, it was an architecture that was *consumer oriented* to a better way of life in well-planned communities. The primary lesson the new school of architects learned was that if the houses did not sell, the project was a failure, no matter how beautiful they thought the design was. But with this reservation, they did plunge ahead with bold new concepts that were exciting and significant, and that created sales. Here are a few:

1. New geometric shapes that caught the eye and opened the houses to views and orientation.

2. A "bigger house" look created by low roof lines, horizontality, and organized fenestration.

3. Window walls and glass areas planned for the view and for good sun control, including wide roof overhangs and a feeling of bringing the outdoors indoors. Overhangs got better looking, provided shade, and kept off rain and snow.

4. Open-space plans that merged one interior area into another and took away the boxy effect of small, confined rooms.

5. Outdoor living areas created by opening the house to terraces, patios, balconies, courts, porches, and what came to be called "outdoor living rooms." Often the exteriors were planned as an extension of the interior space.

6. An indoor-outdoor look made by using interior patios, atriums, clerestories, glass enclosures, glass gable ends, window walls, and strip windows. "Patio houses" were designed by leaders such as Neutra, Breuer, Quincy Jones, Anshen & Allen, Paul Thiry, and Johansen.

7. The "natural look" induced by unfinished wood, rough textures, rugged stone, exterior timbers of massive size—a recalling of the works of Maybeck, Green & Green, and the San Francisco Bay area school of design.

8. The post, plank, and beam concept, a new building technique that made interiors more flexible, opened up the houses, and displayed the rugged support structure unashamedly. This system was usually related to wide-window wall expanses fitted into the post-and-beam structure.

9. The story-and-a-half living room grew in use and had much appeal to buyers. These rooms, when well designed, conveyed a loftier, light look, and appeared to expand interior space.

10. Split-level houses broke out like a rash all over the country in the early fifties and became the hottest, fastest-selling designs, especially on Long Island. The often ugly exteriors created consternation among the aesthetically conscious, but the house plans were popular with the public. The splits enabled builders to crowd in more living space, including use of basements and ground-level floors. They were built on two, three, or four levels. An important feature was the way they could be fitted into sloping sites, and later in the decade a few skilled architects adapted them nicely to hillside lots, with a simple, contemporary appearance.

11. The Cinderella or Disney World design fad cropped up in the mid-fifties and for a time was very popular. It was in effect a protest against plain modern exteriors. Some builders whose modern designs were not selling, loaded their models with long, sweeping gables, Hansel and Gretel motifs, diamond windows, flower boxes, scalloped fasciae, applied decorations of amazing forms, and Swiss chalet details. For a time they sold, but later the fad ended and some Cinderella builders stripped off the weird facades and went back to a simpler, modern look.

12. Family living shifted in the new designs of the fifties as living rooms were moved to the side or back where they overlooked terraces or patios. At the same time the family room grew in importance—usually available to the kitchen and opening upon an outdoor terrace. But family rooms also spread to basements, attics, and special additions.

   In split-level designs on hillside lots, the family room often became an attractive daylight room for recreation, TV viewing, study, or guest-room use, with exterior grade windows and exits. In this sense the split-level concept paid its way in usable, livable space.

These were some of the major changes in home architecture. There were equally dramatic changes in interior design, produced by many of the same factors. Builders raised their sights by employing top-flight interior designers and decorators. They displayed fully decorated and furnished model homes and brought the decorator in early to check the floor plans for furniture placement and consumer appeal.

An architect-decorator symposium in 1951 described some of the changes and influences affecting interior design and decorating:

1. New ways to treat open-space, window walls, and strip windows (usually in bedrooms).
2. Planning for storage in kitchens, baths, garage area, and living areas, and use of storage walls.
3. New ways to handle glass gable ends, dome ceiling skylights, and wide roof overhangs for sun control.
4. Use of mirrored walls to expand space.
5. New ways of handling raised fireplaces, eating bars, interior bathrooms, reflecting pools, and outdoor living areas.

A similar symposium in 1952 described the current kitchen trends as including:

1. Merger of cooking and dining areas.
2. Greater use of natural wood finishes.
3. More pass throughs, eating bars, island counters, and work space.
4. Open, decorative shelves and other storage.
5. Greater use of built-in ranges, ovens, and appliances.

Increased attention was also paid to bathroom design and equipment. A builder-designer group in 1953 spent several days discussing 39 ways to build a better bathroom. The ideas included larger, better-laid-out space, brighter colors and lighting, larger wash basins and counter areas, built-in hampers, larger medicine cabinets with mirrors, storage for towels and supplies, full-length mirrors, safety hand grips, electric exhaust fans and heaters, heated towel racks, separate large shower stalls, ample and safe electric outlets, and quiet fixtures.

Aid to home architecture was given by the 1951 Small Home Design Competition sponsored by NAHB, a building magazine, and six manufacturers who offered $57,000 in prizes. An amazing 2,700 architects and designers submitted entries.

The competition had been suggested by Thomas P. Coogan, president of NAHB in 1950, and it brought in a flood of ideas for small-house plans, kitchens, and new materials. The 63 prize-winning designs were widely published and many homes were built from them.

The distinguished jury included Pietro Belluschi, chairman; O'Neil Ford of San Antonio; Charles Goodman of Washington, D.C.; Whitney R. Smith of Pasadena; Phillip Will, Jr., of Chicago; Fritz B. Burns of Los Angeles; and Cy Williams of Port Washington, N.Y.

The first-prize winner, a 1,000-square-foot home by Bruce Walker, was displayed in numerous home shows.

The race for better housing was on.

The Trend Setters

Some indication of the change in design attitudes in the fifties was revealed by the striking exibit "Built in USA" staged by New York's Museum of Modern Art in 1953. Called "Postwar Houses of Quality and Significance" it included the following exotically depicted houses and their architects:

Plastic Roof in Tension,
        Twitchell and Rudolph

Concrete Frame and Glass,
    Richard Neutra
Meccano Set-Steel Parts,
    Charles Eames
Modular Steel and Glass,
    Raphael Soriano
Curved House Traps Sun,
    Frank Lloyd Wright
Low Profile—Two Story,
    John Johansen
Dome Roof Rotating,
    Soleri and Mills
Ship-Like Long House,
    Gregory Ain
Carpenter-Subtle Wood,
    Harwell Harris
Interior Patio or Court,
    Philip Johnson and Landis Gores

Some of the outstanding trend-setting architects described in earlier chapters continued their work and influence in the fifties. A few must be mentioned again, including Frank Lloyd Wright, William W. Wurster, Harwell Harris, Richard J. Neutra, Pietro Belluschi, and Royal Barry Wills. But there were now others, of whom we can name only a few:

Anshen and Allen, San Francisco architects, pioneered the use of exposed post-and-beam construction in contemporary homes in West Coast areas. They designed many of Joseph L. Eichler's houses and were important trend setters for builders.

Marcel Breuer of New York was described as one of the creative architects revitalizing domestic architecture. His Wolfson house in 1952 was praised for its symmetrical cantilevers and vertical wood siding—a "glass box on a stone base."

Edward H. Fickett, a Southern California architect, designed thousands of houses for merchant builders in the fifties, and was said to have added $1,000 to the value of a $14,000 house at La Habra. He brought fresh, low-profile design, color, indoor-outdoor living, window walls opening onto patios, and a contemporary California look. Large backyards were enclosed with redwood fences. Fickett was the son of a builder and had a keen understanding of building problems as well as exceptional architectural talent.

Charles M. Goodman of Washington, D.C., set high standards of good contemporary design for builder projects in the Washington area. His Hollin Hills, Hammond Hills, and Wheatoncrest communities were outstanding trend setters. He also developed exciting concepts in apartment building. In 1954 he was retained by National Homes to design a new line of contemporary prefab models that set exceptional standards for the industry.

Quincy Jones and *Fred Emmons,* California architects, designed 5,000 houses for builders. They had a contemporary style and worked closely with builders to get better design and salable plans. They had great influence on builder design.

Keyes, Smith, Satterlee, and Lethbridge of Washington, D.C., designed exceptional residential projects in contemporary style with strong emphasis on the preservation of environment. Each house was specially sited to the terrain, which was often rolling and wooded. Each lot underwent a detailed topographical study. Projects included Holmes Run and Pine Spring in Fairfax, Virginia; Kenwood Park and Flint Hill in Maryland.

Arnold Kronstadt of Bethesda, Maryland, created a national reputation for economical apartments, good site planning, and excellent design.

Vladimir Ossipoff of Honolulu created a worldwide reputation and respect for his delicately designed, wood-frame homes of Japanese influence. They were U-shaped for cross ventilation and opened onto Japanese courts and gardens. He used shoji-type doors, and windows with fine thin mullions and muntins.

I.M. Pei of New York designed outstanding modern structures, including urban renewal projects and apartments. He was the architect for New York University Bleecker Street apartments and later for the famed National Gallery of Art in Washington, D.C.

Paul Rudolph, of New Haven, Connecticut, and Florida, was a creative designer of many modern homes and apartments. His early Florida houses pioneered fresh concepts, such as his "house with screened patio living." In 1953 he researched and developed striking methods and materials for building thinner, lighter roofs such as the curved plywood vault, steel and plastic tent, and the flat-roof plank and girder mill construction.

Paul Schweikher of Glenview, Illinois, set new patterns of good modern design in his contemporary houses in Chicago's northern suburbs. His group of co-op homes in Glenview introduced wide roof overhangs, simple low profiles, natural redwood exteriors, and windows clustered with louvered vents below.

Harold R. Sleeper of New York, the well-known author of *Architectural Graphic Standards,* announced in 1953 a new series of design standards and data for builders. His reference books have been and still are widely used by architects, builders, and interior designers. He was a fellow of the American Institute of Architects, a president of the New York Architectural League, and a lecturer at the New York School of Interior Design. He worked closely with building-product manu-facturers to produce his authentic architectural details.

Edward D. Stone of New York is famous for the original concepts he brought to many residences and larger structures. His work was widely followed and published and his influence was great.

Hugh Stubbins, a Cambridge, Massachusetts, architect, was a creative designer of contemporary homes and apartments. Later he became chairman of the Harvard department of architecture.

Talbott W. Wilson of Houston, Texas, designed builder Frank W. Sharp's 4,700-unit Oak Forest project and many other exceptionally well-designed homes and apartments. He set a new standard for restrained contemporary work in the Southwest, including project houses and many large custom homes.

Ludwig Mies Van Der Rohe was justly famous for his exciting glass and steel Promontory apartments in Chicago and for many other works, but also for his much-quoted dictum, "Less is more." In 1951 Mies designed the famous Farnsworth house on the Fox River near Chicago, the classic, steel-framed "glass box" that illustrated his dictum, and it promptly attracted vast worldwide attention and publicity. But later he was criticized by his client, Dr. Edith B. Farnsworth, who complained he misled her into paying $33,000 more than the $40,000 set as the top price. The glass-box house, however, still continued to affect modern design thinking for many years.

John Yeon of Portland, Oregon, designed expertly sited, finely detailed contemporary houses of wood and glass. He employed strong roof panels, curtain walls, and modular design.

Let us now look to a few of the builders who worked closely with talented architects to produce outstanding trend-setting communities. The architecture of ideas and quality of the fifties is best illustrated by the projects of such men.

Architects' Collaborative, at Cambridge, Massachusetts, was a group of talented modernists who raised professional's eyebrows by turning to merchant building. They developed, planned, and built the Five Fields project at Lexington in 1952, and had previously built custom homes at Six Moon Hill. The group included Jean and Norman Fletcher, Walter Gropius, John and Sarah Harkness, Robert McMillan, Benjamin Thompson, and Chester Nagel.

Their styling was described as crisp, direct, simple; their houses had wide windows sited to view, sun, and breeze. Their projects had curving streets, culs-de-sac, one-third-acre plots, and a "common area" with a pond and an old barn.

Wallace "Bud" Arters of Philadelphia was known for fine communities and good design. The prize-winning community Riddlewood won praise for site planning and new split-level contemporary designs with low profiles that fit the rolling contours of the Pennsylvania countryside. *George Hay* was the architect.

Edward Bennett of Maryland was a dedicated builder of fine modern home projects such as Kenwood Park, Carderock Springs, Flint Hill, Newmark Commons, and other contemporary projects. He worked closely with such architects as Keyes, Lethbridge, Satterlee, and Condon. His houses were each carefully sited to the special rolling terrain. He employed advanced planning and management techniques and won some 30 design and planning awards, one of which was an AIA-NAHB citation for "cooperative effort to create better homes and communities."

Burke & Wyatt, Los Angeles builders, hired a distinguished Hollywood screen-star architect, *Burton A. Schutt,* to design their glamourous 190-home project in Palo Alto in 1953. These were high priced for the time— $17,000-$18,000—and beautifully executed in contemporary style with excellent landscaping, open plan, high ceilings, large glass areas, radiant-heated floors, patios, and indoor-outdoor living. They sold quickly.

An amusing sidelight was that the project was across the way from one of Joseph Eichler's, who took full-page newspaper ads to welcome his competitors, saying "the public deserves more architect-designed houses such as yours for today's way of living."

Ned Cole, an Austin, Texas, architect, builder, researcher, and manufacturer of prefab components, had wide influence on builders in the Southwest for whom he designed many projects. He pioneered new truss designs, storage walls, components, and air-conditioning systems. His restrained contemporary designs did much to raise the level of Texas builder work. He directed the NAHB Air-Conditioned Home Village project in Austin and was architect of the NAHB "Trade Secrets" house in Texas.

Thomas P. Coogan of Miami called in skilled Florida architect *Alfred Parker* in 1951 to help cut the cost of his Hialeah project while also improving the design. The houses sold for $6,800 in 1952, $1,000 less than the 1950 models. They were acclaimed the "best builder plan and design of the year" in Florida and sold extremely well. Coogan was president of NAHB in 1950, and he worked hard to improve the design quality of low-cost builder projects.

Joseph L. Eichler of San Francisco was a commanding figure in the development of contemporary home design. He jumped into prominence in 1950 when he switched from small conventionals to houses designed by such gifted firms as Anshen and Allen, Jones and Emmons, and other contemporary designers. He became one of the largest San Francisco builders in the fifties and sixties, and had an immense effect on other builders and public taste.

Eichler's Fairmeadows project was the "sensation of the area" in 1951. His projects in San Mateo, Palo Alto, Walnut Creek, and San Francisco blazed new design trails. He built more than 2,000 contemporary houses between 1950 and 1954, pioneering contemporary ideas such as:

1. The backyard used as an enclosed, landscaped living room.
2. The plank, post, and beam concept with open space plans, glass areas, and natural wood exteriors in clean, contemporary style.
3. Glass-enclosed interior courts, atriums, and living rooms that opened on to the courts.
4. The sales price to include planting by top landscape architects such as *Thomas D. Church,* as well as landscaped driveways, walks, terraces, plant boxes, benches, fences, fruit trees, a service yard, and a children's play area with sand pile.
5. Two full, glamorous baths, much all-purpose storage, fine kitchens and finishes, luxury interiors with cork floors, mahogany panels, sliding glass doors in steel frames, and high ceilings—even in low-priced homes.

George S. Goodyear of Charlotte, North Carolina, was an experienced builder who brought a sympathetic understanding of the value of good architectural design to low- and moderate-cost home building. He was president of NAHB in 1957, and fought hard for higher architectural standards.

Harry Hilp of Barrett & Hilp retained architect *Ernest Kump* to do something special in his 600-home University Village at Palo Alto in 1953. The $11,250 houses had crisp, fresh contemporary design with a modular, open-space plan, post-and-beam construction, sloped ceilings, prefab parts, and dimensional lumber.

Ray Hommes, a Los Angeles builder, set new sales and design standards in 1952 with his 1,000-home Sherman Park project at Reseda, California. The $10,000 houses were charming contemporary works by *Edward H. Fickett,* with low roof lines, a post-and-beam frame, slab floors, an open plan, high sloping ceilings, and textured wood exteriors in muted colors. All 1,000 sold quickly.

Carl Koch, the distinguished Cambridge, Massachusetts, architect and educator, turned to building and prefab production by founding Techbuilt, Incorporated. His exciting contemporary prefab designs with open-space plans and huge glass gable ends did much to stimulate public interest in colorful modern design.

Edward S. Klausner of New Jersey was the engineer and veteran builder of a pace-setting, 250-home project at Morristown in 1951. Imaginative designing was done by *George E. Nemeny* and *A.W. Geller,* architects. The houses had open-spaced planning, window walls, sloping ceilings, post-and-beam construction, modular design, on-site prefabrication of wall panels, and storage walls and components.

Albert La Pierre, a Seattle builder, worked with architect *W.A. Wollander* to produce low-cost houses of fine contemporary design and exceptional value. More than 800 were built in 1951 in the $11,500-$12,500 price range. They were said to be "the talk of the West."

Gerald and Eli Luria were builders of modern homes of fresh new design at Holmes Run, Pine Spring, and other communities in Fairfax County, Virginia. Designed by Keyes, Smith, Satterlee, and Lethbridge, these were good, small, contemporary homes, each specially sited to the rolling terrain, with good design use of brick, glass, and color. Their communities were well planned, with safe traffic lanes, segregated commercial areas, and environmental plans to save trees and terrain.

Cliff May of Los Angeles was one of the most popular designers and builders of California ranch-type homes in the fifties. Creating both low-cost merchant homes and expensive custom work, he caught the public imagination with what was described as "contemporary, ranch-style Colonial for California living." Exteriors were of rough textured boards and battens with low-pitched roofs, large-muntined windows, enclosed patios, and white board fences.

In 1953 May developed a merchant-builder package with architect *Chris Choate* which was sold to many project builders and became the fastest-selling house of the year. Cliff May was given the "Builder of the Year" award in 1963 by the California Home Builders Association for "his contribution to higher standards in housing . . . which have brought credit and renown."

James R. Price, president of National Homes Corporation, the largest prefab manufacturer in the country, retained architect *Charles Goodman* of Washington, D.C., in 1954, to design his new contemporary models with window walls, indoor-outdoor living, air conditioning, and a packaged plumbing system. The houses sold well and Price expanded production for his 500 builder customers.

Builder *E. J. Turner* made history in his Philadelphia project by engaging architect *George Hay* to design attractive split-level houses for a severely sloping site, land that was considered too steep to build on by most developers. But together Turner and Hay produced "uphill" and "downhill" models having expandable basements with family rooms at grade level. The houses had picture windows and clean contemporary lines, and made excellent use of their sloping sites, such as a panoramic view downhill or a sheltered terrace uphill.

The New Look in Apartments and Townhouses

A long-deferred apartment and townhouse revival began to make its appearance in the late fifties and was generally credited to the stimulating new ideas and designs that had been gradually developing in the preceding years.

Earlier in the decade the apartment market suffered from the devastating publicity and bad reputation of the so-called FHA-Section 608 scandals. But by 1957 much had been forgotten, and a great need for rental housing had grown up. In 1959 some 260,000 units were built, setting the pace for a program that expanded greatly in the following decade. The growth was sparked by social and economic factors:

1. Financing became easier and more plentiful as new FHA aids for low-cost rentals went into effect.
2. Tax incentives for builders investing in apartments became more favorable as new accumulated depreciation provisions were established.
3. Population change created a greater housing need in both younger and older renters.
4. New apartments in the suburbs were cheaper and more desirable than outmoded city units.
5. Low-cost rentals for the retired and elderly were in tremendous demand.
6. Small, attractive rentals for bachelors, singles, and young couples became very desirable.
7. The population shift to the suburbs created a demand for larger family units with the same amenities as single family homes.

During the apartment lull of the mid-fifties, builders and architects had been working on new concepts for better apartment living. These blossomed out in the late fifties with such ideas as:

1. Bigger, better-equipped, and colorful kitchens with built-in ranges, refrigerators, dishwashers, and laundries.
2. All the comforts, amenities, and livability of single-family houses, without the upkeep problems.
3. Terraces, patios, courts, and indoor-outdoor living ideas.
4. Exotic amenities like swimming pools, cabanas, nurseries, play areas, and green spaces. Also a planned environment with restaurants, shopping centers, ample parking, and protection from intruders.

5. Air conditioning, labor-saving devices, glass doors, and larger windows.
6. Sound conditioning; cushioned, insulated floors, walls, and ceilings: acoustic tile; quieter equipment.
7. Luxurious, colorful baths; better wiring, lighting, and electrical equipment; more storage space; and exotic interior design and decoration.

The new look in townhouse design was a significant architectural development in the late fifties. In effect the stodgy row houses of earlier years were transformed into lively townhouses and townhouse communities, often arranged in neighborhood groupings, clusters, and courts, and around culs-de-sac.

The term "townhouse" is a nebulous one as used in the building industry. It is defined in the older Webster's as "a house in town; the city residence of one having a countryseat or chief residence elsewhere."

A later definition reads, "a house occupied by a single family, usually two storied, connected by a common wall to the side of a similar house."

The townhouse builders of the late fifties, sixties, and seventies took considerable liberty with these definitions. They did draw on the lovely (and genuine) Colonial townhouses of Washington, D.C., Georgetown (in Washington, D.C.), Baltimore, Boston, Richmond, Philadelphia, and New York for inspiration. But their main purpose was to connect and group small housing units for rent or sale in an economical fashion that reduced land and construction costs.

One of the first and best examples of such modern work was Colonial Park, a 116-unit townhouse project for low-income families without subsidies, built by George Clarke Martin, president of Bollinger-Martin of Louisville, Kentucky. The skillfully designed and planned brick houses were built in the Southwick redevelopment area and sold for $8700-$11,000—probably the best housing buy in the United States at that time.

Martin was inspired by the lovely Georgetown townhouses he had admired on his many visits to Washington, D.C., to attend NAHB meetings. He later became president of NAHB.

The Colonial Park townhouses were attractively arranged in short rows or clusters and were of simple but authentic Georgetown Colonial two-story brick design. They provided a maximum amount of good living at a total monthly carrying cost of $57-$79 for two-, three-, and four-bedroom units.

This trend-setting project sold out quickly, was widely publicized, and was immediately seized upon by architects, builders, and home manufacturers across the land. It received an award from NAHB as the best low-cost housing development in the country in 1961. It had a major impact on low-cost housing and especially on townhouse design and planning.

The townhouse approach did enable builders to produce attractive single-family homes at much lower cost than houses on individual lots. They had well-designed exteriors and efficient plans, were insulated and had sound proofing between party walls, and were usually equipped with air conditioning, well-equipped kitchens, laundries, and baths. They were built as units to rent or for sale, and later they were frequently sold as condominium units.

Builders later arranged townhouses in small neighborhood groups and provided such amenities as landscaped open space, play areas, swimming pools, and other recreational facilities. They provided a new kind of private-home living in a relaxed residential environment. This concept was carried forward into the following decades.

Standardization: More House, Less Money

Progress in building techniques, systems, and products took place on many fronts during this decade. Significant leadership was provided by NAHB's Research Institute, founded in 1952, which built or sponsored a remarkably effective series of research and test houses.

The Institute made unprecedented, bold, and costly advances into the field of laboratory research on new building products and systems, testing their delivery, installation, and on-the-job use. The major thrust was to standardize dimensions so that house parts could be precut or prebuilt to fit together easily at the site.

Rapid expansion in the use of prefabricated or precut component parts was taking place, as well as improved on-site methods for putting them together.

Many builders and industry leaders helped in a wide variety of research and test house programs. NAHB was fortunate in having practical, professional builders who were willing to try out the new concepts on their jobs—the only way to check their effectiveness.

One builder who contributed impressively to research and building progress was Earl W. Smith of El Cerrito, California. "Flat Top," as everyone called him, was a third-generation home builder who started work for his father as a carpenter at age 14. He proudly carried a carpenters' union card, and always insisted on designing and laying out the plans of every house he built. During his long career this came to more than 25,000. In 1955 he became president of NAHB. He also was known as an accomplished artist, actor, and designer. He described his career, year by year, in his own words, on tape in 1978.

(1922) "I graduated from grammar school and started to work for my dad, who was a builder, as were his father, grandfather, great-grandfather. As far as I can determine, all my paternal forebears were builders.

"My dad, who, as a general contractor, built homes, apartments, stores, warehouses, etc., and always, in those days, had his own carpenter, painting, masonry, and concrete crews, had me work in all four of the above categories. As a result, I became a journeyman in each.

(1928) "The Great Depression set in. My father who had been 'well-off,' suddenly, like most builders, lost everything. I worked at anything that could produce a buck, and so we hung in during those unforgettably difficult years.

(1934) "My dad acquired a small inheritance; his father had died at age 96, in Sauk City, Wisconsin, still building at the time of his death. This money—approximately $4,000—encouraged us to start building again. I drew the plans and ran the jobs, and he handled the business end of things. We built on 'skip' lots, all over the East Bay area—small homes, priced at $3,500 to $4,500.

(1939) "Having become financially comfortable again, my dad retired and I started my own business. Being a one-man band I designed and prepared the plans for each house I built. I also laid out and cut the frames for everything I built. To this day, after building over 25,000 dwelling units (single-family, two-story apartments, small shopping centers, and mobile-home parks), I have never built anything for which I did not draw the plans.

(1945) "During the war years, forty through forty-six, I designed and built houses and some apartments for defense-industry-worker families in the East Bay area.

(1947) "I started my long career with NAHB as a director. I made the motion which started the NAHB technical department and hired Carl Lans as staff director. Because of my involvement with many public meetings, dealing with the need for good, low-cost homes for returning veterans, I became aware that something should be done to reduce the cost of housing and came up with what was well known as Smith's flat tops (hence the nickname which was hung on me for a lot of years).

"With the advent of my flat-top house, everything changed. I couldn't find enough skip lots to keep up with my presale orders—all referred by previous buyers, no advertising necessary. So I bought my first subdivision, approximately 65 lots, and began to increase production. Then there began a most amazing amount of local publicity in newspapers and magazines.

(1948) "Meanwhile, I was heavily involved in helping build a first-rate technical department with NAHB. To Carl Lans and Eloise Fisher we added other good staff people. I had insisted, when gaining approval from the board of directors in 1947, that we had a responsibility to aid our builder-members in becoming even better builders.

(1950) "Carl Lans, having left NAHB to join my staff, was replaced by Leonard Haeger as director of all NAHB technical departments and service. Len and I made a good team, in-

asmuch as we shared much the same philosophy regarding NAHB's responsibility in improving the service of builders to home buyers.

(1951) "Bill Atkinson was president of NAHB and had been instrumental in setting up 'Operation Trade Secrets,' using all of us active in the technical committees to work in and develop the program. About this time (mid-1951), Haeger and I began to think out the beginnings of the NAHB Research Institute. Our conviction was that the manufacturers of housing parts needed some guidance in their ongoing research programs. Using the minds of our technical people, and doing a hell of a lot of researching, we gradually put the idea in final shape.

(1952) "By then, Alan Brockbank was president. We took the package through the NAHB mill to gain approval and proper funding. Finally—all appropriate NAHB committees having given our Research Institute their approval—I presented it and the Research Institute was approved by the Board of Directors.

"Alan Brockbank, as president, thought the Research Institute so important that he named immediate past president Bill Atkinson as the first chairman. Later, I was officially given the title, which I held until 1955, when suddenly I became president of NAHB.

"In the meantime, back home, my organization had greatly expanded. We were building some 2,000 to 2,500 flat-top homes per year, all over northern California. Even then, every house that was built originated on my own, old drawing board—which I still have and still use!

(1955) "During my year as president, I never lost my abiding interest in the technical services and the Research Institute. If anything, we gave increased emphasis to all of

these activities and endeavors. We continued, as we had for several years, to provide good copy for a host of consumer papers, magazines, radio and television shows.

(1978) "In closing, I'm still building. My sons are also builders (in our organization), although our operations are today largely in the management and maintenance of our rental properties. We do build two or three homes a month on land we've long held, just to keep our hand in. I still practice what I've always preached: 'Take good care of your customers, and they'll take good care of you!' "

In all of these comments, Earl Smith neglected to say that the enormous success of his flat-top houses was due to cost-saving techniques, careful planning and scheduling, and effective modern design. In 1950 his 1,009-square-foot houses sold for $6,000. He claimed he saved $1,000 a house by his building methods.

"It would be easy to build a better house at more money," he remarked, "but my aim is to build a *good* house for *less* money."

Throughout the fifties, sixties and later, a quiet, soft-spoken builder from Royal Oak, Michigan, Edward W. Pratt, was active in many areas encouraging and promoting better research and improved building techniques to assist fellow builders in producing a better product for less money. Among his contributions in the fifties was the work of a task force which he spearheaded to develop recommendations for presentation to the FHA simplifying and clarifying existing and conflicting property standards. The work of this task force lead the way to the issuance of a new construction book by the FHA entitled Minimum Property Standards (MPS) for one- and two-family housing.

Research Houses and Programs:
The Trend Toward Industrialized Building

NAHB's Research Institute got off to a good start in the early fifties with its well-qualified architect-engineer director, Leonard G. Haeger. He held a master's degree in architecture, and had previously been in charge of technical research at FHA and HHFA. By 1953 he had 40 builders doing field testing, and 110 manufacturers cooperating. The aim was to bridge the gap between manufacturers, research labs, and on-the-job builders.

The series of NAHB research houses were built in various locations in cooperation with builders, manufacturers, research groups, or associations, all exploring new and better ways to build. The 1957 "NAHB Research Home of the Year," for example, was built with the technical assistance of the Lumber Dealers' Research Council. It was constructed of coordinated parts, pieces, and components, all presized to fit. Some 24 new ideas were tried, including large wall panels, new-type trusses, screw-on windows, plastic-covered roof panels, vented soffits for large roof overhangs, hollow-core panel partitions, thin wood floor strips laid in mastic, and above-floor plumbing.

The 1958 and 1959 houses created wide interest with stressed-skin panels, wall-hung toilets, plastic plumbing, base board wiring, surface-mounted hardware, and new-type floor panels. All of the test houses were viewed by builders from many areas, and were widely publicized by NAHB and the press.

Another ambitious NAHB project was the Air Conditioned Research Village built in Austin, Texas, in 1956, directed by architect

builder Ned Cole. Here 22 small homes were built by 18 local builders with the cooperation of 22 air-conditioning equipment and insulation manufacturers. They were small homes of 1200-1500 square feet. Extensive field testing checked such ideas as extra-heavy insulation, vented gables, light-colored roofs, forced attic ventilation, window shading, extended roof overhangs, vapor barriers, ground-moisture barriers, new locations for cooling units in attics, garages, or closets, perimeter heating and cooling, overhead diffusers, crawl-space cooling, zoned systems, and furred-down ducts in hallways. The findings were later checked and analyzed by University of Texas specialists.

Air conditioning made rapid advances in the early fifties and was the highlight of exhibits at the 1953 NAHB convention in Chicago. A host of new units and systems blossomed, including smaller, more efficient units requiring less space, easy-to-service equipment, heating and cooling in one package, and hermetically sealed compressors, all at lower prices.

Among major firms then active were Carrier, General Electric, Servel, Frigidaire, Bryant, Lennox, Coleman, Chrysler, and Mueller.

Later in the decade a new but slow to develop giant appeared—the heat pump. It was more than a decade before this new marvel came into general use.

In 1954 the Lumber Dealers' Research Council of the Washington-based National Association of Lumber Dealers embarked on an ambitious panel-system program called Lu-

Re-Co. They retained the University of Illinois Small Homes Council to develop and field test the system, and it made great progress.

Essentially Lu-Re-Co was a locally prefabricated component system in which all parts, pieces, trusses, and components were built in the local lumberyard and assembled at the site by a local builder or contractor. NAHB cooperated by building a test house.

By 1956, many thousands of Lu-Re-Co homes had been built, and one of the converts to this system was a small-volume builder in Knoxville, Tennessee, Martin L. Bartling, Jr. His house employed large components, modular panels, and roof trusses. But it also included integral insulated decking, preassembled gable ends, and window walls in modular sizes supplied by his local lumber dealer.

Bartling had a long and interesting career in the building industry, starting at age 21, and he was always concerned with trying out new ideas. He built four research houses during his career, and because some of them were too advanced, he ended up living in them. "That's the story of our life," his wife Catherine ruefully remarked. "We have lived in nine houses, but it's been fun."

Bartling's interest in technology led him to active leadership in NAHB's early research endeavors, and he was a founder and trustee of the NAHB Research Institute. He was chairman of NAHB's Trade Secrets Committee in 1952, and traveled the country tracking down new ideas and techniques. In 1960 he became president of NAHB and threw the full power of that office to expand research programs. When elected he said, "I want more emphasis on building research, more cooperation between builders, manufacturers, designers, engineering schools, and FHA. We must supply manufacturers with the basic data from which they can develop interchangeable parts for industrialized building."

Industry Innovators Trade Secrets

"Operation Trade Secrets" was aptly described as the "best NAHB idea of 1951." It was conceived by the then president of NAHB, W. P. "Bill" Atkinson of Oklahoma City, and it contributed greatly to building progress in the fifties, as well as in later decades.

Atkinson's idea was a simple one: bring together the best and smartest builders, researchers, and technicians and have them trade secrets about their jobs. "There are few problems that some smart builder somewhere has not solved," he insisted. He held the first session at his own famous Midwest City project in Oklahoma. The trade secrets flew fast and furiously and the ideas spread like wildfire. Soon there were Trade Secrets conferences in cities all over the country, including a big one in Washington, D.C.; and in 1952 a huge "Trade Secrets Show" was staged at the NAHB convention in Chicago. In this program 37 top builders and technical persons traded ideas on how to bring buyers more house for the money.

The ideas generated at the Trade Secrets sessions were recorded and passed on to other builders. Then many of the country's biggest firms proceeded to build a Trade Secrets model home; 23 were built in 1952 and were viewed by thousands.

As a result, a wide range of planning, designing, and cost-saving methods and marketing improvements were suggested. A few ideas from the Washington session included rearranged floor plans, better storage space, shorter lot sizes, warranties, cost analyses, new plumbing techniques, engineered concrete slabs, improved insulation, low-voltage wiring, superblocks, and larger panels with prefitted doors and windows.

Operation Trade Secrets was a huge success because it uncovered practical, down-to-earth methods or innovative procedures that had already been tried and tested by builders on their own jobs. It also succeeded because of the experienced men on its committee, headed by Martin Bartling, and such research-minded scholar-builders as Andrew W. Place of South Bend, Indiana; Ned Cole of Austin, Texas; Dave Slipher of Los Angeles; and others.

A great variety of tested ideas and techniques was contributed by Andy Place, who had long been active in practical on-the-job research. A few of these included:

- Site protection with inflated plastic tents.
- Materials scheduled and mechanized.
- Grade beams to replace footings.
- Use of earth compactors and concrete vibrators.
- Steel forms for concrete slabs.
- Warm-air perimeter heating in slab, with a 14 inch fan.
- Plumbing trees and new grouping of pipes.
- New trusses with a span of 32 feet.
- A machine to fit doors, hinges, and locks quickly.
- Surface-mounted bath fixtures.
- Spray painted interiors.
- Truss roofs and double 2-by-6 beams at top of framing, creating one big room.

- Double-glazed windows with extra insulation.
- Wide roof overhangs with 28-inch minimum.
- Efficient wiring and more circuits, a 100-amp panel box, circuit breakers, and a 220-volt system.

Another innovative, active builder who put new ideas to work was Clayton Powell of Savannah, Georgia. An 80-house-a-year builder, Powell developed a semi-prefab system using large wall panels or components, delivered to the site with doors and windows installed. In 1958 he was described as the "fastest U.S. builder," and he was regularly completing a finished house in only 14 working days. Powell achieved such speed by careful planning and scheduling, and by the use of prebuilt parts and components constructed on a four-inch module. His houses were of simple southern contemporary style that lent themselves to fast erection.

In Austin, Texas, research-minded Ned Cole, was an architect, builder, designer, and manufacturer of prefab storage walls, components, and roof trusses. He took part in the Trade Secrets program, was member of the Research Institute Board, and designed many of the Trade Secrets and Air Conditioned Research Village houses. He built many low-cost houses after testing new ideas and concepts. He also supplied a unique plan service for Texas builders: houses of contemporary design and studied for efficient erection.

Cole carried out much excellent research on, and development of, storage walls and components as well as air conditioning. His influence was widely felt.

Perhaps as a result of NAHB's research house programs, a few large manufacturers got into the act. In 1954 the U.S. Gypsum

Company built its Research Village at Great Barrington, Illinois. Here six well-known house architects were teamed with six outstanding builders to demonstrate the latest ideas in design and construction. Among the ideas explored were metal and gypsum decking, lift slabs, steel studding, metal joists, solid-gypsum partitions, and a new system to eliminate drywall taping.

These houses were opened to the public and viewed by thousands. They were also widely publicized in both trade and consumer magazines, where they were seen by millions. Thus were new ideas and concepts spread nationwide.

Researchers and New Building Products

We have seen in earlier chapters how researchers from the thirties and forties pioneered the way for new building techniques and products. Many continued to work in the fifties and were joined by others of equal talent and dedication. One was James T. Lendrum, director of the Small Homes Council of the University of Illinois.

In 1952, SHC erected a 1,000-square-foot test house financed by an HHFA grant. Extensive time and materials studies were made to check new cost-saving techniques, including truss roofs, nonbearing partitions, and a combination laundry-bath.

Also in 1952, SHC published details for building stronger, better, and less-expensive storage wall components. Later it published details and instructions for building a new W-Truss, a flexible, easy-to-make truss, spanning up to 32 feet. This was followed by an expansion attic truss, providing a clear span from wall to wall without interior support.

Lendrum made research history in 1953 with his document, "Ten Ways to Cut Costs." These included:

1. Build on an interior module.
2. Precut all framing material, using engineered drawings and cutting schedules.
3. Use tilt-up exterior walls, and build them flat on the slab; it is much faster.
4. Use a modern, long-span roof truss; it can be erected quickly.
5. Apply wallboard on ceiling and side walls before partitioning; this saves time and labor.
6. Lay entire finished floor before partitioning so that you don't have to work around small, irregular spaces.
7. Place windows at top of exterior walls.
8. Make all ceiling heights exactly 8 feet $3/8$ inches; this is the most efficient way.
9. Use prebuilt storage walls and use them as closet and interior partitions.
10. Use a double wall around plumbing, as it eliminates cutting and fitting. Have a plumber install pipes before the carpenter builds the walls.

Lendrum's SHC research also included a significant study of warm-air heating by perimeter ducts embedded in concrete floor slabs. The tests were jointly sponsored in 1953 by the National Warm-Air Heating Association, and led to improved heating of basementless houses built on a concrete slab. Detailed installation instructions on perimeter heating were later published, and these helped builders work more efficiently.

Lendrum left SHC in 1954 to become chief architect of FHA, and he later became head of the department of architecture at the University of Florida.

A new outpost of housing research came into the limelight in the early fifties with the forming of the Southwest Research Institute of San Antonio, which was directed by C. W. "Bill" Smith. Its work was firmly grounded in practical builder methods and in the use of test houses. In 1953 Smith published a document entitled "New Frontiers for Home Builders," based on three years' work. His advice to builders was:

- Don't hire a cheap architect.
- Avoid "apple crapple" design.
- Strive for quality, not variety.
- Get the best site planners.
- Use open kitchens and open-space plans.
- Have the best in air conditioning.
- Get away from last year's model.
- Don't let yourself be limited by FHA as to good design and livability.

In 1952, Southwest Research Institute granted a special award to Joseph L. Eichler of San Francisco for outstanding design and construction of 500 contemporary houses in four tracts, priced at $15,000-$25,000. Eichler's plank-and-beam system, wide overhangs, glass walls, interior space concepts, and excellent modern design were cited.

Still another housing researcher of distinction in the fifties was Glenn H. Beyer, professor of housing and design and director of Cornell University's Housing Research Center. In 1953 he published the results of a six-year study of kitchen planning and design. It was the combined effort of engineers, architects, home economists, psychologists, and kitchen equipment manufacturers. The study did much to focus attention on the basics of good kitchen planning and was widely published and studied.

Later Beyer and Cornell published a study on what people want in a home. One important fact revealed was that 64% enjoyed eating in the kitchen, and the study urged builders to provide adequate and attractive space for it.

Purdue University Research Foundation also carried on important studies in the early fifties under the direction of Carl F. Boester. One of the most fascinating was the development of a new three-wire electric system for homes. It received wide industry endorsement. It could be installed faster, and it saved time drilling holes, used less wire, made 220 volts available everywhere at low cost, was extra safe, and used individual five-amp fuses and pressure-lock terminals.

Sound conditioning and noise control were also major research and product developments of the fifties. A host of new acoustic tiles, insulating, and sound-deadening products appeared. Manufacturers also brought out quieter laundry, bath, and kitchen equipment, and they developed installation methods to isolate the sounds, especially in apartments. Noise control brought out sound-deadening wall partitions and ceilings, double walls, floating ceilings, and wall and floor coverings that absorbed sound. Notable was a huge increase in carpeting in both houses for sale and apartments for rent. In fact, builders found that luxurious carpeting was both an excellent sound absorber and a good sales attraction. It became even more attractive to them when FHA ruled that carpeting could be included as a building cost under an insured mortgage.

Product improvements took place on many fronts. An important one was the insulated, weatherstripped, double-paned, packaged window unit. This was factory built on a four-inch module and delivered to the job fully glazed and easy to slip into place. Removable plastic or wood muntin bars were provided which snapped into place and were easy to remove for window washing.

Later the same prefabrication and packaging of both interior and exterior doors took place. Doors were then delivered to the site in a package, complete with surrounding trim and hinges, locks and door knobs in place. Such packaged units could be slipped into position with a minimum of on-site labor.

In 1956, U.S. manufacturers brought to the market what has been described as "the most wanted building tool." This was a light-weight, portable pneumatic nailer. It had a thousand uses in home construction, from nailing shingles to applying wall board and building paper, and later for nailing flooring, siding, and sheathing. The early models could shoot 60 nails a minute into the jobs, and later the pneumatic nailers became, as predicted, the most important tools in industrialized production.

Late in the decade the aluminum industry entered the housing field with a multi-million-dollar research and marketing program. Soon builders began using aluminum windows, gutters, storm doors, siding, roofing, prefab panels, soffits, structural members, and much else. Aluminum panels were produced in new colors, finishes, and textures, and these were very well liked and contributed a great deal to prefab use.

Another significant product of the late fifties were the prefabricated fireplace and chimney, which almost put the old brick construction out of business. These fireplaces and chimneys were sturdily built, heavily insulated, and scientifically designed for a good

draft, which was more than could be said of the older hand-built brick units. The prefab units could be set in place in minutes and cost much less than brick.

Plastics and plastic building products, backed by millions of dollars in research and product development by leading manufacturers, also moved strongly into the construction market in the mid-fifties. The major products were counter tops, vinyl floorings, plastic wall tiles, paneling, shower stalls, luminous ceilings, moldings, skylights, and plastic panels for a variety of uses, including carport enclosures.

Research in concrete and its many uses in housing also blossomed. In 1951 some 600 architects, engineers, contractors, and researchers met in a conference at the Massachusetts Institute of Technology to explore new dimensions in prestressed concrete. Notable progress in producing stronger, lighter, safer concrete components and structures followed the discussions and discoveries.

The ceramic tile industry, aided by extensive research in adhesives, made striking advances in mid-decade in new, lower cost techniques. Outstanding was the use of thinner tiles applied with strong, fast-setting adhesives. The tiles were packaged to be easily and quickly applied with adhesive over gypsum board or other surfaces. The tiles were lighter, thinner, and could be applied much faster, and this revitalized the industry despite the opposition of labor unions.

A major contribution to housing progress was made in the mid-fifties by a series of seven round-table conferences conducted by Perry I. Prentice, publisher of *House and Home* magazine. The topic was standardization of building parts and components, and the object was to develop basic standard dimensions for builders' houses and dimensional standards for components, including door and window sizes. The conferees included leading architects, engineers, builders, lumber dealers, home manufacturers, government officials, and research men. The published findings did much to further the development of workable, industry-wide dimensional standards.

Without any doubt the decade of the fifties introduced striking advances in building products. *House and Home* declared in 1959 that "more new building products have hit the market in the last ten years than in the previous fifty." The editors added, "Today's new houses can be built better and tighter . . . can be cooled and heated for less . . . can have more baths and better plumbing . . . better storage . . . acoustic ceilings . . . and indoor-outdoor living with more glass.

"Today there is a new and better product, a new and better tool, or a new and better method to do almost everything."

Industrialization Moves Ahead

Prefabrication was the key word that described the home building industry's first approach to an industrialized housing revolution in the fifties. We use the word "approach" because it took many more years for complete industrialization to take hold in the far-flung reaches of this vastly dispersed field.

Certainly the organized prefabricated home manufacturing industry made great progress in the fifties. But even more important was the effect it had on thousands of smaller builders by showing the advantages of building with parts or components instead of individual pieces.

Let us first describe what the organized prefab home manufacturing industry did: it increased prefab house production and sales moderately from 55,000 a year at the start of the decade, to 90,000 a year in 1959, still less than 8% of the total single-family-home market.

But its impact was far greater than these sparse data indicate. The industrialized techniques spread far and wide, with builders like Levitt of Long Island, John Long, Phoenix,

Fischer & Frichtel of St. Louis, and many others building their own local prefab production shops or plants.

Production methods of the larger prefab home manufacturers were also adopted and adapted in various degrees by thousands of small firms who developed on-site cutting and prefab techniques in their own small shops.

By 1954 a new breed of builder-prefabricators began to emerge—men who started out with precutting and on-site fabrication for their own large projects and then began selling prefab packages to other builders. They expanded rapidly.

This in turn led the larger prefab home manufacturers to develop a policy of selling packaged home components and parts to builders—a wide range that enabled the builder to select the parts or components most suitable to his job.

The organized prefab home manufacturers went through a series of mergers in the late fifties, one of the most notable being that of National Homes Corporation, which absorbed seven leading competitors: American Homes, Knox, Thyer, Lester, Fairhill, Best, and

Western Pacific. The result was that in 1959, National built 45,000 homes, or about 56% of the prefab market.

Realizing its vast growth potential, the Prefabricated Home Manufacturers Institute in 1957 was restaffed and reorganized into the Home Manufacturers Association. Its staff was headed by Conrad "Pat" Harness, then a past president of the National Association of Real Estate Editors and NAHB's ex-public relations director. For the next several years HMA played an important role in showing builders the many advantages of using house packages manufactured by HMA members.

The larger prefab manufacturers took many steps in the late fifties to increase their sales and services to homebuilders. These included market research, financial aids, land and site planning, landscaping, color coordination, FHA and VA processing, accounting systems, scheduling and planning, subcontracting assistance, model home promotions, decorating, marketing, and merchandising help. Top-level architects were retained to provide a wide range of consumer-tested floor plans.

While prefab manufacturers were expanding their services, the techniques of industrialization were spreading even faster to other elements of the housing industry. The use of components such as wall panels, roof trusses, and door and window units increased rapidly. But by 1957, U.S. industry had gotten forcibly into the picture by producing packaged heating-cooling systems, prebuilt plumbing walls, and complete kitchen units. Large manufacturers such as Johns-Manville, U.S. Gypsum, National Gypsum, Masonite, and Koppers began marketing stressed-skin wall panels, sandwich panels with polystyrene cores, and other factory-built components.

But the most significant boost to industrialization on a large scale was given by the perfecting of industry-wide dimensional standards so that panels, doors, windows, cabinets, flooring, and components of all types, built in uniform modules, could be used without cutting or fitting.

Near the end of the decade the ultimate in industrialization began to take form: the complete factory-built house, built in sections and trucked to the site, usually in two or three completely finished units. It took a few more years, but this new outgrowth of the mobile home became an important factor in the industrialized housing industry progress of the seventies.

The $100-Billion Highway Program and Its Effect on Housing

Perhaps nothing in the decade of the fifties had a greater impact on the lives, living habits, and housing of Americans than the huge highway-building programs that were spawned by a beneficent Congress with 90% grants, financed by higher gas taxes.

Highway programs began to grow in the early fifties, but a "giant step forward" was engineered by the Highway Act of 1956, a $33 billion program with $27 billion in subsidies which were later increased. This was the start of what ultimately became, or was described as, a $100 billion program—certainly the greatest highway spending spree in the history of this or any other country.

It is difficult to assess and comprehend the

enormous ramifications of this huge national interstate program which brought thousands of miles of roads, expressways, thruways, and urban and suburban development to towns and cities in every corner of the land. It was a major stimulant to building projects in cities, suburbs, and outlying areas. It spawned thousands of new home communities, shopping centers, motels, and vacation-home projects.

The program transformed thousands of square miles of farm and other rural land into valuable residential sites and communities and, unfortunately, hastened the decline of the central business cores of many cities. It accelerated the demise of railroads and rapid transit lines, displaced and moved millions of persons who had to be rehoused.

Many commentators say, with good reason, that the planning was bad. But it is also clear that the creation of one national, centrally designed system had many benefits and ultimately did result in coordinated city, state, and regional planning.

The effect of the multi-billion-dollar program on metropolitan areas was dramatic, drastic, and frequently damaging. One city-planning expert declared that the impact on the form, growth, character, and structure of metropolitan areas was greater than all the work done by city planners for decades.

While the new expressways, thruways, interchanges, and fast traffic systems cleared the way for quick entrance to and exit from the cities, many local urban patterns were disrupted. The problems and plans of urban renewal programs were soon becoming entangled, with more than half of the federal aid funds for expressways going into urban areas. Eventually the federal highway planners, urban renewal experts, HHFA, and state and local agencies worked out a modus vivendi to get the work done. But many of the problems of the central cores of cities still remain.

More pleasing to contemplate is the development of newtowns and planned residential communities that the highway programs encouraged. Vast suburban and rural areas, once considered too remote, were brought within minutes of town and city centers and became coveted building sites. The large new-home communities were, on the whole, better planned and more inviting to buyers anxious to flee the noise, dirt, and deterioration of sections of the central cities. The resulting move to suburbia and exurbia was one of the greatest changes in American life in the decade of the fifties and later.

As a natural consequence of this mobility, great commercial and industrial changes also occurred. One was the migration of industry to the rural fringes of the suburbs, providing new jobs and housing markets. Another was the building of large, better-planned commercial and shopping centers in the far-away suburbs. The new industrial parks also brought greatly improved planning and architectural concepts to a backward field.

The American urge to be on the move got an impressive push from the new highways. Due to the extensive building of motels, hotels, filling stations, roadside stands, garages, drive-in movies, and restaurants to drive through or sit in, the tourist trade flourished.

It would be difficult to assess the full impact on the building industry of all this activity, but one very significant area was the motel-hotel business.

On the 41,000 miles of new highways there developed an almost unlimited market for motels. Some 3,000 a year were being built in 1958, and the market was expanding. U.S. population was up, the number of automobiles had increased astronomically, 90% of vacationers were going by automobile, and more than 70% of business travel was by car.

The new hotel-motel explosion was not a mom-and-pop affair. By the late fifties the huge chains were building deluxe 100-300 unit structures with air conditioning, swimming pools, and plush carpeted interiors. They had developed sophisticated planning, design, and financing techniques. Most of all, they quickly closed in on the 4,000 or so interchange sites that held golden promise for tourist trade.

"Location," the motel experts said, "is 75% of the success story." It was a highly speculative affair, but some of the rules included:

1. Find a site drivers can see 1,000 feet in advance.
2. Have at least 200 feet of frontage.
3. Locate in a residential area, away from noisy locations.
4. Locate where there are movies nearby and where there are local patrons for the motel restaurant.
5. Set the motel back from traffic and do a good job of landscaping.

Certainly the motel investments (aided by double-rate, declining-balance tax depreciation) must have proved profitable, for the business continued to expand immeasureably in the following decades.

Most glamorous of the results of the highway building spree was the effect on recreational, vacation, travel, and resort building. The new rapid escape ways from the cities and towns enabled millions of mobile Americans to fulfill their long-pent-up vacation or camping dreams.

The fast highways brought exotic mountain, lake, forest, ocean, bay, and rural campsites into easy reach. Builders in Florida, California, Arizona, Nevada, Georgia, and Vermont expanded their projects. Exotic ski resorts blossomed, and projects in such places as Aspen, Tahoe, Sun Valley, the Adirondacks, and New Hampshire flourished.

The vacation-home program was often combined with second-home building. Many resorts in ski areas or near lakes or mountains began selling year-round recreation homes, which became a flourishing business. The architecture of such resorts also took on exotic new forms, such as the Swiss chalet, rustic modern, and log cabin cottage designs. The builders, architects, and buyers all seemed to feel freer to express their personalities, and the results were often bizarre.

Hard figures are not easy to come by, but by 1960 it is estimated that 100,000 vacation and resort homes were being built, which was double the 1950 figure. This was really only the beginning, and in later decades the volume expanded even more.

This massive highway-building program of the fifties created one of the most explosive inflations of land prices in the nation's history. The expressways and the interchanges have been described as "the most efficient devices for exploiting and reshuffling land values ever invented."

The mere mention of a new highway or an interchange brought skyrocketing prices. Canny farmers often reaped huge profits, as did other land owners fortunate enough to be in what were considered "hot" locations. These, of course, were usually on the access roads or local streets adjacent to the intechanges. It took extensive study to determine where the best locations were.

In some areas, politicians with an inside track were able to dump fortunes into the laps of lucky landowners. However, there were also less-fortunate owners whose holdings were by-passed and their value ruined by loss of traffic and customers directed away from them.

Sophisticated Management Teams Up with the Housing Industry

As though signaling the end of the "hammer and saw" era of building operations, a new breed of managers began to take over in the late fifties. These were builders who adopted sophisticated corporate organization, planning and business methods, and controls.

They studied and employed many of the Harvard Business School's concepts of corporate management, applying them to the rapidly expanding housing field. This was no longer a small-time game. The building and development operations of this period called for expert financial and capital handling, large-scale land acquisition, and advanced corporate-management ideas new to builders. One declared that "Management is the art of employing and rewarding other men's talents."

The new breed of builders also introduced another idea—the "team concept." Old-time builders were often lone individualists who tried to do everything themselves. But the team concept made the builder the captain of a group of specialists, each highly capable in his field, but working in coordination under an overall management plan. Such professionals in a large building-development operation would work only in one area: financing, feasibility studies, marketing, consumer research, accounting, computer controls, land and site planning, engineering, architecture, production systems, model home design, or promotion.

The big-builder operations that emerged in the late fifties accented five major keys to success:

1. Management means good men. Invest in the best, get the best.
2. Capital for growth is essential; be sure to have it. Undercapitalization is the greatest danger.
3. Land is essential for growth. Have a safe inventory available.
4. Be ready to move to other areas as opportunities arise. Be willing to diversify to shopping centers, mobile-home parks, industrial parks, or other related fields.
5. Adopt advanced production systems to cut costs, control quality, and increase volume.
6. Train salesman to become specialists in demonstrating the value of home ownership.

A few of the large builders of the fifties who employed many of the techniques include the following:

John Long of Phoenix, Arizona, who built 2500 houses in 1958, was a pioneer in good design and factory production methods that brought high value at low cost. He sold a well-equipped, 1570-square-feet house in 1958 for $11,995.

Frank Mackle, president of Mackle Brothers of Miami, was one of the largest and best Florida developers of recreation areas. He sold 2,500 houses in 1958.

Tom Lively, with Centex Corporation in Dallas, built large projects in Texas, Illinois, and Hawaii, of good value and with advanced techniques. He sold 2,300 houses in 1958.

Ross Cortese of Los Angeles was a pioneer in well-planned adult leisure communities. His Rossmoore project near Long Beach sold out quickly. In 1958 he built 910 houses.

Chris McKeon of San Francisco was known as the "fourplex" king. He pioneered new low-cost plans for duplex and fourplex homes, and sold 740 in 1958.

Hamilton Crawford of Baton Rouge, Louisiana, built high-value homes in well-planned communities using new factory production techniques. His Gently Woods sold 700 homes in four weeks. Later he developed the newtown of Crofton, Maryland.

Al Branden of San Jose, California, sold 800 homes in one month at Tropicana Village in 1958. He used advanced prefab techniques to provide houses from $11,500 to $14,900.

Other large builders of the late fifties included Dale Bellamah, Alberquerque; Ray A. Watt, Los Angeles; Bollenbacher & Kelton, San Diego; William J. Levitt, New York; Bert L. Smokler, Detroit; Larwin Company, Los Angeles; Fox & Jacobs, Dallas; Kettler Brothers, Washington, D.C.; and William P. Atkinson, Oklahoma City.

The First Great Newtowns

During 1951-1952 a bold and thoroughly American phenomenon loomed great on the housing horizon: the first mammoth, self-contained satellite cities, or newtowns.

These were to be planned communities containing homes, apartments, shopping centers, industrial areas, schools, parks, and recreational facilities. They were usually located in areas of industrial expansion and close to large population centers, and they dramatized to a high degree a converging of powerful social and economic forces. They reflected, to some extent, the development of city-planning patterns laid down 20 years before by Henry Wright and Clarence Stein in Radburn in New Jersey, Sunnyside Gardens in New York, and Baldwin Hills in California.

The two most prominent newtowns of the early fifties were U.S. Steel's Fairless Hills and William J. Levitt's Pennsylvania Levittown, both located near Morrisville, Pennsylvania.

The economic trends and conditions were right for the growth of these and the many other newtowns that followed. An affluent public was eager to move to homes in a safe, well-planned environment. Large-scale builders such as Levitt had the capital, skills, and mass-production techniques to undertake such huge projects. Prices, down payments, and interest costs were low. New highways were encouraging the population shift out of cities and into outlying areas, and big-city department stores as well as corporate offices and industries were inspired to join the exodus.

The home buyers of this era were also intrigued by the new amenities and luxuries of these communities, which were planned by a galaxy of skilled professionals. They liked the curvilinear, traffic-safe streets, the culs-de-sac, greenbelts, open space, parks, playgrounds, swimming pools, and community clubs, as well as all the other conveniences of a complete, well-designed community.

U.S. Steel announced its Fairless Hills project in mid-1951. The director was John W. Galbreath, who retained land-planning consultant Seward H. Mott. The original area was 2,000 acres, including a lake, parks, and much green space. Some 15,000 prefab homes and apartments were included. Prices were low: $11,000 for a three-bedroom house on a 60-foot lot.

William J. Levitt's Levittown, Pa., was even larger. It was hailed by him as "the biggest new city in the U.S.," and it may well have been. It covered 5,000 acres and had 17,000 homes to house 60,000 people. Levitt said, "We planned every foot of it!—every store, filling station, school, house, apartment, church, color, tree, and shrub."

He brought all his wartime know-how and his Levittown, Long Island and other experience to bear, and it was formidable. He threw himself and his large trained staff into the job with ferocious zeal, and was soon selling homes at the rate of 1,000 a month.

The prices were appropriately low, ranging from $8,990 to $16,000, with 5% down and nothing down for veterans. The $8,990 "Rancher," which had two bedrooms and a two-bedroom expansion attic, cost only $57 a month to carry with a long-term mortgage.

The significance of the Pennsylvania Levittown lay not only in the fact that it was successful, but that it was visited, studied, and copied by builders from all over the world. It had a road layout that detoured through traffic, and provided safe, quiet, local streets. Its long-range blueprint introduced the concept of neighborhood areas or "villages" within the overall plan.

The land and site planning did much to make the community inviting, including extensive landscaping and provision of parks, playgrounds, swimming pools, community clubs, and green space. A variety of well-conceived architectural designs and plans were included at popular sizes and prices.

Important also in this newtown was the handling of shopping and parking. There were several large, central shopping areas, but those were supported by many smaller neighborhood stores scattered through the project. The planning included segregated sections for commercial and industrial use, thus providing many jobs within walking distance of the workers' homes.

Levittown, Pennsylvania, sold out quickly and was followed by a series of others in New Jersey, Washington, D.C., and elswhere. In 1958 Levitt opened Levittown #3 at Willingboro, New Jersey, a project of 15,000 homes. Again the planning was good and the sales gratifying. Prices ranged from $12,000 to $15,000, with low down payments and low interest. For many years Levitt continued to develop such communities, both at home and in France, Spain, Puerto Rico, and, most recently, Florida.

The Home Marketing Revolution

At the start of the decade, few builders understood the need for aggressive, scientific marketing methods—they had been enjoying a sellers' market. But by 1952, NAHB's president was warning builders that changes in buyers' demands would force drastic improvements to be made in their sales methods. Soon there were NAHB seminars and marketing clinics aimed at new markets—people who already owned homes, the "trade-in" market, second-time buyers, and buyers looking for the new and the exotic. Yes, in a way, it was a revolution.

Merchandising was the sell-out theme of many of NAHB's heavily attended convention-expositions in Chicago in the fifties. One meeting was so popular there were 200 standees spilling over into the corridors. The marketing themes included taking old houses in trade, cashing in on manufacturer promotions, hiring consultants, making in-depth surveys, and, above all, showing exciting new model and demonstration homes.

The old idea of a circus approach—of stringing up banners and hiring a cowboy movie star—was discarded. Instead, the new approach was to base all sales appeals on a better product, a better environment, and a more livable, lovable home. One marketing expert declared: "You must start your selling plan even before you close on the land or design the house. You must have a viable selling theme based on the overall quality or appeal of the project."

The revolution in selling of the early fifties certainly must be credited for a good part of the surge in building that followed. The order taking of the previous years was replaced quite dramatically by new techniques for marketing, merchandising, and selling.

As builders became bigger and adopted new management concepts, they also inevitably embraced a wide range of new marketing techniques. They retained professional marketing consultants and hired skilled advertising persons, real estate sales specialists, buyer analysts, consumer researchers, and specialists in interior design and promotion of model homes.

Perhaps the most important change was to dramatize and exploit the neighborhood or community the builder was creating. He learned that people were interested in environment, architecture, and landscaping—a planned and protected area.

By 1957 a new term, "curb appeal," began to appear. One builder remarked, "I want a model house that looks so good that when people drive by they jam on the brakes and say, 'WOW! we've got to see that!' "

Curb appeal meant exciting design, clearly visible from the street. It meant landscaping, fences, planting boxes, and bold decorator colors. It meant strong textures such as those provided by old brick, stone, wide siding, or heavy shakes.

After curb appeal, the marketing experts, who were trained in special schools and clinics, talked about location, schools, shopping centers, churches, recreation, transportation, utilities, and police and fire protection. Identity was an important element—creating a feeling of pride in the mind of the buyer in the social quality and high character of his home and community. This kind of marketing and selling was a far cry from the razzle-dazzle of earlier periods.

Model and demonstration home projects were highly appealing to consumers. The larger builders hired interior decorators who were also specialists in marketing. The homes were furnished skillfully, based on a consumer study of the likes, tastes, and needs of expected buyers. They introduced many new ideas in color, design, wallpaper, draperies, furniture, and decorative amenities that had a considerable effect on consumer taste. Many persons who visited the builders' model homes often went back and remodeled or redecorated their own homes—an unexpected plus for the overall advance of home improvement.

Progress in marketing techniques was certainly aided by the NAHB, which inaugurated a series of seminars, training schools, and clinics that helped usher in the new level of professionalism in the merchandising field. Among the leaders were Milton Kettler of Bethesda, Maryland; Steve Yeonas of Washington, D.C., and William Underwood of Jackson, Mississippi. NAHB's long-time and beloved marketing director, William A. "Billie" Molster, contributed brilliantly.

A builder and marketing expert who did much to further this effort was Dave Fox of Dallas, Texas, who for many years was chairman of the NAHB Marketing Committee. In his own building operations he was an out-standing and imaginative leader and brought a host of new marketing concepts into practical use. He as one of the top builders and marketing men of the sixties and seventies, and his business continued to expand. In 1977 he sold more than 6,500 houses.

Marketing and merchandising of homes in the fifties were also strongly advanced by manufacturers, the trade press, and consumer publications. One of the most effective concepts was the "Idea Home of the Year" in 1954, sponsored by *Better Homes and Gardens* and its building editor, John Normile. Some 92 model homes were built in 37 states in cooperation with leading architects, builders, and manufacturers. The houses were seen by two million visitors plus four million magazine readers.

These were truly "idea homes" to stimulate the interest of home buyers, and included large family rooms, post-and-beam construction, exotic kitchens and baths, paneled walls, free-standing fireplaces, open-space plans, fenced patios, large glass area walls, and indoor-outdoor living concepts. Certainly the acceptance of such ideas by American consumers was furthered by model homes such as these and others that succeeded them.

This modern California-style house, built by Nels G. Severin in 1961 near San Diego, won an award as "Best Home for the Money." Edward Fickett was the architect. (Photo courtesy George Lyons.)

This prefab modular home of the mid-sixties was priced at $18,950 and marketed by Scholz Homes. The house was shipped in two completely finished sections which were attached at the site.

Exciting modern design by architect Barry Berkus made this house in Valencia Hills, California, a rousing success. High ceilings and post-and-beam construction helped create open space. Built by M.J. Brock and Associates in 1968.

Marina City in Chicago, twin 40-story towers built in 1960, housed 896 families and included balconies, swimming pools, 24 shops, a skating rink, theater, bowling alleys, a park, and a marina for 700 boats. Bertrand Goldberg was the architect.

Heritage Village, in Connecticut, under construction in January, 1973. Advanced techniques kept work going during freezing weather. (Photo courtesy J. B. Mason.)

Promontory Point incorporated 520 luxury units arranged in 5 horseshoe-shaped clusters on a bluff overlooking the harbor at Newport Beach, California. The architect was Fisher Friedman Associates; the builder was the Irvine Company. (Photo courtesy David Ross.)

Small apartments nestle among landscaped areas and face a free-form pool at Brookside Village, Redondo Beach, California.

Woodbury Place condominiums, built by Carl Jalbert at Woodbury, Connecticut, in 1979. Patricia Easterbrook Roberts was the landscape designer, and Drexel Yeager the architect. (Photo courtesy Frederick E. Paton.)

Heritage Tower, a mid-rise apartment project in White Plains by Heritage Development Corporation, was converted to condominiums in 1979.

Harbortown at San Mateo, California, clusters small townhouses along a man-made lagoon. The architect was Fisher Friedman; the builder was Vintage Properties of Menlo Park. (Photo courtesy Charles Callister.)

Mission Viejo, California, was one of the best planned and most successful communities in the United States in the sixties and seventies. Shown here is a cluster of its Madrid del Lago models.

Sun Tronic solar house at Greenwich, Connecticut, demonstrates both active and passive solar enegy systems, including a 150-square-foot photovoltaic array. Built by Copper Development Association.

A New England style solar house designed by Acorn Structures of Concord, Massachusets. It incorporates a full complement of passive and active solar features. (Photo courtesy Barth Falkenberg.)

Beam ceilings and natural wood contributed to the interiors of Amherst Fields houses. Warren Callister was the architect. (Photo courtesy Ezra Stoller.)

Soaring ceiling lends impressive space to small attached house at Morningside Woods. (Photo courtesy Mark V. Branjinikoff.)

Interior of Pond Place home. The architect was William Callister; Otto Paparazzo was the builder.

Exotic interiors illustrate design advances in project houses of the seventies. This Homestead model was built by Ponderosa Homes at Walnut Creek, California. Interior design was by Color Design Art. (Photo courtesy Leland Lee.)

Striking interior of Woodridge Gables home built by Irvine Pacific at Irvine, California. Interior design by Color Design Art. (Photo courtesy Leland V. Lee.)

Interior of the Hillsborough model at Turtle Rock Ridge. Irvine Pacific was the builder. (Photo courtesy Garcia-Carmer.)

This 1977 zero lot line house at Crow Canyon has terrace at rear, sideyard walkways, atriums, and patios. Morris and Lohrbach were the architects. (Photo courtesy Jeremiah Bragstad.)

Yankee Barn country house developed by Emil Hanslin the sixties and seventies. It was first built at Hanslin's New Seabury on Cape Cod, and later sold as a pre-engineered, precut house package.

Montecito model at Turtle Rock Ridge, one of the largest of the single-family homes. Design reflects influence of the Bay Area School, MLA Architects. (Photo courtesy Garcia-Carmer.)

These clusters of attached single-family homes, designed for "empty nesters," sold for $100,000 in 1979. Morningside Woods was built at Escondido, California, by Zellner Communities. (Photo courtesy Mark V. Branjinikoff.)

Pond Place in Avon, Connecticut. These single-family homes are sited on heavily wooded land and clustered around small courts. Warren Callister was architect; Otto Paparazzo was builder; Patricia Easterbrook Roberts was landscape designer. (Photo courtesy Martin Tornallyay.)

CHAPTER FOUR

1960-1970

REVOLUTION IN MANAGEMENT, MARKETING, AND DESIGN

"Give a Damn"—the Crusading Spirit

It was a decade of hope and violence, of progress and despair, of riots, assassinations, and antiwar demonstrations. Some called it "the angry decade." Yet it was a time of remarkable housing growth, and it saw more than 14.42 million homes provided by American builders.

Vigorous, young President John F. Kennedy brought optimism and a crusading spirit with his New Frontier dream of help for the old, the sick, and the needy, and with plans for expanding housing and urban development. "Give a Damn" was the slogan of the time.

"Never has a decade started with greater expectations," proclaimed Perry Prentice, editor and publisher of *House & Home* magazine. "Technology is at high levels, pocketbooks are bulging, [and] new frontiers in space and energy lie before us."

There were indeed reasons for optimism in the housing industry at the opening of the decade. Population growth was at an all-time high of 13.4% per decade. Housing vacancies were low, financing was available in ample supply at low interest, and building costs were stable. Most important, a higher level of competence engendered by new planning and construction techniques was bringing better home values to consumers.

Offsetting these conditions were the Bay of Pigs fiasco, the Russian confrontation, the shocking assassinations of John and Robert Kennedy and Martin Luther King, and later the race riots and violent anti-Vietnam demonstrations verging on anarchy. Housing, along with all progress, suffered.

Each of the three U.S. presidents of this decade took office on a wave of political promises to aid housing and urban development. Lyndon B. Johnson's Great Society brought ambitious new programs for health, education, housing, urban development, clean air and water, and expanded medical care. Medicare and Medicaid helped the sick and the elderly.

The cold statistics, however, show that the greatest housing advances of the decade came in the private sector. Of the 14.42 million total starts, only 357,000 were in public housing—less than 3%. The dream of great urban development and redevelopment to restore the decaying central cores of the cities simply did not materialize. Undoubtedly, spending $21 billion a year to conduct the Vietnam War contributed to the failure of such programs; during the decades that followed, redevelopment still remained one of the great unsolved problems of American life.

Housing in this period was also strongly affected both by the population growth and by change. From 1950 to 1960 the population increase was an astounding 29 million, creating an enormous shelter need. From 1960 to 1970 the U.S. census count rose 13.4% from 183,285,000 to 207,999,824. Here indeed was the fuel that fired the continuing growth of housing.

Yet even more significant were the changes in the location of home buyers. Suburban-area living jumped 48%, and continuing U.S. highway-building programs opened thousands of new residential communities, shopping centers, recreational areas, trailer parks, new-towns, and industrial parks. Metropolitan areas expanded greatly.

The impact of population change was felt in many ways. The greatest growth came among the youngsters—age 18 to 24—and among those 65 or older. They both brought new housing requirements—and change. Higher incomes in the middle classes also brought on new demands for a different—and better—type of home and life style.

Another change had taken place by 1960: the close of a decade of huge production of more than 15 million houses had brought an end to the acute shelter need. Builders now found they had to build better and sell harder, and they did.

The decade of sixties may well be remembered for the rise of talented leaders in finance, industrial management, planning, production, and design. They pushed private house building to new highs, reaching 1.64 million starts in 1963, and averaging 1.4 million per year. The era must also be credited for daring new concepts in condominiums, retirement housing, apartment and townhouse design, and exotic vacation communities.

In spite of the social and economic problems, the housing industry in the sixties rose to new heights of design, value, environmental planning, and community development, and found new approaches to the American dream of better living.

The Managerial Revolution and the Emergence of Housing Giants

"A few years ago the financial community thought homebuilders all wore overalls and went bankrupt regularly," declared Eli Broad in 1968 at a glittering breakfast with 70 top Wall Street analysts at Shepard's in New York.

"Now you know this industry is studded

with capable businessmen and a limitless future. The way is well paved for heavier Wall Street investments in home building."

The speaker was head of Kaufman & Broad of Los Angeles, one of the largest U.S. builders. The occasion was the founding of a new organization of building firms, the Council of Housing Producers. Its objective was to act as think tank and image maker, and to attract attention and money from government, the stock market, and large investors.

The timing was right, for housing and finance were running full tilt into an enticing period of expansion. The early and mid-sixties produced a multi-billion-dollar growth of giant builders, shelter conglomerates, and housing finance institutions. Financing the large-scale operations of these goliaths called for vast amounts of front money, equity capital, and mortgage funds. The story of how these needs were met is one of the most striking of the decade.

The force that propelled the growth of housing's powerhouse of builders was the infusion of fresh new pools of capital from many sources. Builders, who had always suffered from undercapitalization and periods of tight money, were now happily able to draw on the stock market, investment firms, banks, insurance companies, U.S. corporations, mortgage guarantee firms, mortgage-backed securities, mortgage investment trusts, and the exotic real estate investment trusts for ever increasing sums.

The billions of dollars of capital raised for housing ventures in the sixties put to shame the gin and jazz era of the twenties with its mortgage bonds, unamortized loans, and junior financing, all of which collapsed during the depression. Some doubts were expressed, but the flow of funds continued as Wall Street and investment firms took delight in the high profits. It was not until 1973 that the weaknesses of many of the investment devices surfaced in another huge liquidation period that again brought losses in the billions.

We shall not attempt now to assess the reasons for the later losses, but for the decade of the sixties it is clear that these infusions of capital brought many gains in the form of better planned communities and well-designed homes. The new giants bought land ahead, hired costly teams of architects and planners, and invested in computer-oriented systems of design, construction, and marketing. The objective was a creditable rise in the quality of design, planning, and environment, and an increase in the volume of good housing.

Some have described the emergence of the big firms with their sophisticated systems as a managerial revolution, which it may well have been. It did bring a much needed increase in the use of new techniques of management and building. It certainly was responsible for the millions of Americans getting better built and better planned houses during the decade.

The adoption of improved management methods by builders was indicated by a 1964 survey which showed that 43% owned calculators, 30% intercoms, 14% two-way radios, and 34% photocopiers, and that many had computers for cost analysis, research, accounting, and cost control.

Still others were adopting and putting to use effectively the critical path technique for job control developed earlier for heavy construction. By the mid-sixties many home builders had plugged computers into their CPM systems to bring about an astounding improvement in management control. The CPM systems diagrammed the exact interrelation and timing of every job operation, action, and subcontract, showing the date or hour each must be completed to be on schedule.

The sophisticated management methods were vitally essential to large-scale operations, but they were also critical to the process of going public, or to raising equity capital. The first requirement of underwriters was for expertise, and that was what the so-called managerial revolution was all about.

Go Broke, or Go Public

Of the new sources of finance that fueled the growth of housing in the sixties, and that also sparked a managerial revolution and the rise of giant builders, the most dazzling was the stock market and its untiring coterie of underwriters, brokers, analysts, and promoters.

Early in the sixties a few large, well-respected building firms stepped gingerly into the Wall Street maelstrom. They were principally seeking new equity capital to finance expansion, and included such firms as Levitt & Sons, Eichler Homes, Crawford Corporation, Kaufman & Broad, Laguna Niguel, Arvida, and others with creditable track records. Within a few years the rush to Wall Street included hundreds of other building firms as well as land-development firms, investment trusts, mortgage insurers, and mobile-home giants.

As housing starts climbed, the lure of profits in stock market offerings grew. Housing stocks became hot issues, and investors pumped millions into the industry, hoping to cash in on a housing boom. One headline in 1969 read, "Housing Stocks Become Wall Street's Sweethearts," and prices skyrocketed to new highs. More than a billion dollars in public offerings was made. We regret to say that this euphoria came to a sad slowdown in the seventies, but while it lasted, it brought vast sums into the housing industry which aided the production of homes.

There were, of course, sound reasons builders, developers, and housing finance firms should go public. The first, as we have indicated, was the constant need for the equity capital for stability or growth. The industry was (and is) notorious for its vulnerability to undercapitalization and periods of tight

money. Many firms used the proceeds of stock sales to retire debt, boost working capital, or buy land. But mostly this infusion of fresh funds was regarded as a recipe for survival. As one builder put it, "Go broke, or go public."

Another reason why many of the entreprenurial giants went public was to protect their personal fortunes. They felt uncomfortable with all their eggs in one basket. By going public and selling, say, 25%, they could reinvest the proceeds in a wider selection of securities. Estate and inheritance problems were simplified, they could protect their inheritors much better with publicly held stock or securities.

A third reason for going public was that builders could use a stock issue as a springboard to later financial moves which could be even more important. Once they had gone public and established a good track record, they could go back into the market for much less costly financing—medium-term debentures, preferred stocks, convertible bonds, warrants, options, and other equity producers.

In effect, going public helped many firms create their own currency—a marketable security with which they could do many things. One was to offer stock options to attract top-flight executives. Another was to arrange tax-free exchanges to buy or merge with other firms. As we shall see, this became an alluring feature in later corporate development.

By late 1969 the headlines were reading, "Big Builders Team Up with Wall Street for a Ride on the Boom." It was a year of optimism, and rising housing-stock prices helped everyone. Some of the larger firms' stock quotations included Kaufman & Broad, 71;

Arvida, 17; Deltona, 50; Laguna Niguel, 10; City Investing, 68; Rouse Company, 51; Tishman, 77; Presidential Realty, 23; U.S. Homes, 24; Jim Walter, 34; Del Webb, 14; Ryan Homes, 38; Canavaral, 10; General Development, 27; Sunasco, 32; Champion Homes, 44; Fleetwood, 40; Redmond, 96; National Homes, 27; and Scholz Homes, 40.

The type of building firm and its operation that appealed to Wall Street is revealed by the 1970 report of the Council of Housing Producers, which had been formed in 1968 and had grown to 13 giant firms. Council members had produced 41,729 units in 1969, an increase of 30% over 1968 and far ahead of the industry as a whole. "We have dispelled the widely held myth that the housing industry is devoid of modern management and techniques," the Council declared.

Success was attributed to "professional structure, quality management, intensive business experience, and a high degree of educational background." Member firms, it was stated, "were staffed by people with degrees in such disciplines as accounting, business administration, engineering, economics, law, and psychology. They include experts in computer technology, finance, marketing, and systems engineering.

"The Council has proved that broad-based, well-capitalized firms with sophisticated management are best able to cope with the periodic downtrend cycles in the industry."

To fulfill its goal of leadership and project an image that would appeal to investors the Council held briefings in 1969 with 1,000 financial analysts, bankers, and members of the press in New York, Chicago, Houston, and Los Angeles. The report concluded, "Despite talk of tight money and its negative effect, Council members, primarily because of the size of their operations, have been able to ob-

tain large-scale financing well in advance of their needs. This, plus the efficiency of their operations, enabled them to move into profitable new markets quickly to profit from the latest population trends and opportunities."

A striking picture of the workings of one of the largest publicly held companies, Kaufman & Broad, Inc., is given in that report. In 1969 the firm had 42 major, widely distributed housing developments under way, and its sales had increased 39% during 1968 to $100,460,000, with net income of $4,611,000. Five reasons given for its growth:

1. Land is treated as a raw material and is not purchased far ahead of need.
2. Homes are sold through models with 95% sold prior to completion.
3. Operations are financed from working capital, commercial paper sales, or unsecured bank borrowings rather than costly construction loans.
4. FHA and VA mortgage loans are secured in advance at committed prices for their customers.
5. Multimarket operations protect the firm from poor conditions in any one location.

Kaufman & Broad had raised $30 million of capital funds in 1969 through a $16-million public offering of 250,000 common shares, 500,000 warrants, and a $15-million private placement of 5%, 25-year convertible debentures. It became a prime-rated issuer of commercial paper and had $25 million outstanding by January 15, 1970. Thus did a publicly held firm illustrate ways to bring new funds into the housing industry.

Members of the Council of Housing Producers in January, 1970, included:

- Alcan Design Homes Limited, a subsidiary of Alcan Aluminium, Limited, Montreal, Quebec, Canada.
- Boise Cascade Building Company, a subsidiary of Boise Cascade Corporation, Los Angeles, California.
- Centex Corporation, Dallas, Texas.
- Kaufman and Broad, Inc., Los Angeles, California.
- The Klingbeil Company, Columbus, Ohio.
- The Larwin Group, Inc., a subsidiary of CNA Financial Corporation, Beverly Hills, California.
- Levitt and Sons, Inc., a subsidiary of ITT, Lake Success, New York.
- Lewers & Cooke, Inc., a subsidiary of U.S. Plywood-Champion Papers, Honolulu, Hawaii.
- William Lyon Development Company, Inc., a subsidiary of American Standard, Inc., Newport Beach, California.
- National Homes Construction Corporation, a subsidiary of National Homes Corporation, Lafayette, Indiana.

- Occidental Petroleum Land & Development Corporation, a subsidiary of Occidental Petroleum Corporation, Newport Beach, California.
- The Perl-Mack Companies, Denver, Colorado.
- Bert L. Smokler & Company, a subsidiary of Dreyfus Development Corporation, Detroit, Michigan.

This list of Council members is not necessarily indicative of the wide field of building and finance firms that went public. Many—in fact most—were smaller, but the total of their offerings swelled into the billions of dollars.

Other events were complicating the finance picture, such as the entrance of billion-dollar firms into housing and the frenetic growth of mergers, acquisitions, joint ventures, and new vehicles such as investment trusts. All were heavily involved in the stock market boom. It will require a special section to sort out these developments.

Mergers, Acquisitions, and Joint Ventures

Nothing in the housing picture of the sixties was more dramatic than the bold intervention into housing of billion-dollar corporate giants and insurance and financial firms. Their moves sparked an explosion of mergers, acquisitions, and joint ventures that changed the face—or at least the financial face—of building.

One of the first was the acquisition of giant Levitt & Sons by the multi-billion-dollar International Telephone and Telegraph conglomerate. It proved a stormy and unprofitable marriage, for the choleric, individualistic

Bill Levitt could never agree with nor adjust to ITT corporate manners, nor could his successors. ITT also acquired other firms, including United Homes Corporation of Tacoma, headed by Herman Sarkowsky, also an individualist. These firms were outstanding and profitable, but the top executives, like Bill Levitt, soon became disenchanted with their positions and left. The ITT housing volume declined, and ultimately the parts and pieces were sold off.

The moral, if any is to be drawn, is that men like Levitt and Sarkowsky were accustomed to running their own jobs and making quick decisions, and they were not given to long corporate conferences, filing reports, or consulting with third vice-presidents. They, like many other builders who had constructed their own empires, universally declared that the building business is a different breed of cat from large corporate enterprise, and they wanted none of it. Their departure was often a blow to the continued growth of the building empires they had built. Even worse, most of their successors seemed to have the same complaints, and many of the projects, sooner or later, lapsed into decline.

The Levitt-ITT merger caught the headlines, but the subsequent stampede of corporate and financial giants into land and housing brought such a bizarre era of mergers, partial acquisitions, 50-50 deals, leasebacks, salesbacks, and intricate financing schemes that it defies a full account. We can only touch the fringes of this period. One observer remarked in 1969, "Not since the Cherokee Strip has there been such a stampede into land and housing. Muddy-shoed builders are openmouthed in astonishment at their colorful new bedfellows." He referred to Exquisite Form Industries (brassieres and girdles) which had bought into two North Carolina mobile-home firms; aerospace conglomerate Lear Siegler, Inc., who had paid $20 million for the Trousdale Construction Company of Los Angeles; and Grolier, Inc., the New York encyclopedia publisher who planned to enter subdivision development in Vermont, Connecticut, and Texas.

The major entrants into the housing field in the sixties were U.S. corporations with an interest in building products, industrial conglomerates with large land holdings, and giant insurance, financial, or investment firms. Each approached the housing industry in its own way with outright offers of purchase,

joint-venture deals, and financial help based on participation in profits. Most of the arrangements tried to keep the original builder or entrepreneur in the picture; sometimes it worked, but more often it did not. However, the infusion of great amounts of capital into the building companies undoubtedly contributed considerably to the expansion of building volume.

There were, however, unfortunate aftereffects on investors that arose in the seventies, but these must be detailed later.

An early and very vigorous corporate entrant into building was the *Boise Cascade Company,* a lumber products producer of Boise, Idaho. By 1968 it had produced 6,000 factory-built homes, 3,000 conventional homes, and 18,000 mobile units. It had acquired large tracts of land in Nevada, California, Illinois, and New Jersey, and was engaged in developing recreational areas, mobile-home parks, shopping centers, and industrial parks. Its Kingsberry Homes division was an important producer of prefab houses. It acquired or merged with many building firms, and engaged in a variety of joint ventures with others.

Leading the parade (for a time) of giant firms with an interest in building products was Aluminum Company of America, which combined altruism with a search for increased sales. Early in the sixties Alcoa bought into 11 large urban-renewal projects in joint ventures with builders or land developers, projects involving layouts of close to a billion dollars. A few included:

- *Golden Gateway,* San Francisco, an $85-million joint venture with Perini Land Development Company.
- *Century City,* Los Angeles, a $500-million joint venture with Zeckendorf Property Corporation.

• *United Nations Plaza,* New York, a $40-million joint venture with Zeckendorf Property Corporation.

Whatever Alcoa's purposes, their results were apparently far from satisfactory. Later, in a revealing talk to Chicago mortgage bankers, Leon F. Hickman, executive vice president said, "We have seen enough to know we have had it!

"We have unlearned any faith we might have had in the seed-money concept of financing, that with 3%, 4%, or 5% the promoter is off and running. But construction delays, proximity to slums, long rent-up periods, and a host of other unanticipated costs can upset the plans."

Plywood manufacturers also plunged into the housing spectrum, sometimes to their sorrow. U.S. Plywood Company got into the building in the early sixties and soon was building, joint venturing, and financing. In 1965 it bought Lewers & Cooke, a 188-year-old building supply and land development firm in Honolulu, for $10 million. Both Lewers & Cooke and USP soon expanded in many joint ventures with builders. One of the most notable joint ventures was Crystal Shores, at Lake Tahoe, that won wide attention.

Other mammoth firms entering building included Westinghouse, which brought James S. Hunt's Florida Coral Ridge properties, and General Electric, which joint ventured many projects and took over the Red Rock Hill project in San Francisco. Also active were U.S. Steel, Weyerhauser, Reynolds Aluminum, American Standard, and National Gypsum, which acquired the Behring Properties of Fort Lauderdale.

A striking joint venture of 1969 was the teaming up of California builder Jerome Snyder with New York's Loew's Corporation, a large holder of hotels, theatres, and land, headed by Laurence Tisch. Snyder was able then to embark on an extensive building program of houses and apartments in San Francisco, Los Angeles, and Staten Island, New York.

A second major group entering the housing market was made up of industrial conglomerates, oil companies, auto giants, and even railroads, most of which had large holdings they hoped could be profitably developed.

The Pennsylvania Railroad led the way in mid-decade with purchases of Great Southwest Corporation of Texas, Macco of California, and Arvida Corporation of Florida, investments in the multi-millions. Arvida owned 100,000 acres from the estate of Florida tycoon Arthur Vining Davis, which included the Boca Raton Hotel and other choice properties in Dade, Broward, and Palm Beach counties.

By 1969 the merged companies were producing thousands of homes a year and were engaged in extensive land development and joint-venture operations with builders in California, Texas, Florida, and elsewhere.

An early and flamboyant oil company entrant to housing in 1960 was Sunset International Petroleum headed by J. D. Sterling. In three years he converted the oil gas producer to a giant land and community developer. Observers said the 27% depletion allowance for oil companies was a helpful factor.

Whatever the reasons, Sunset Petroleum embarked on an expansive program that made it one of the largest home building and development firms of the sixties. Its first move, in 1960, was a merger with Carlos Tavares Development Company to acquire 4,600 acres in San Carlos, California. Then it embarked on such huge projects as the 12,000-acre Sunset City near Sacramento, the 8,000-home San Carlos project, and the 2,000-home Sunset

Hills Community north of Los Angeles. The firm continued to expand its operations through mergers, acquisitions, and joint ventures, became "Sunasco," and later merged into Canaveral International Corporation of Miami.

Many other oil companies leaped onto the housing bandwagon. One of the largest was Gulf Oil, which first loaned $17 million to Robert E. Simon, Jr., for developing Reston, the exotic newtown 18 miles from Washington. Later Gulf took over the project and dispensed with Simon rather unceremoniously. Humble Oil also got into housing by financing and joint venturing Clear Lake City, near Houston, and other large projects. Occidental Petroleum joint ventured many large projects.

Other firms joined in the merger acquisition whirl. Avco Corporation, a conglomerate listed on the New York Stock Exchange, acquired 51% of Rancho Bernardo, a 6,000-acre newtown near San Diego. Uris Corporation of New York teamed up with Multicon Corporation of Columbus to build a $24-million garden-apartment project in Atlanta. And Deltona Corporation of Miami, the famed Florida development firm headed by Frank Mackle, entered a joint venture with Barron Collier, Jr., to raise capital for his huge Marco Island project near Naples, Florida.

The merger-go-around also included City Investing Company of New York, which through expansion, mergers, and aggressive management became widely involved in many projects. One of it subsidiaries, Guerdon Homes of Louisville, a leader in mobile and modular-home production, entered into merger plans with Ryan Homes, Incorporated, of Pittsburgh, which were to merge mobile-home and on-site building work in an interesting fashion.

Late in the decade, as the mobile-home boom and mobile-park expansion grew, the merger-go-round reached new circles. Arthur Decio, president of Skyline Corporation, predicted a merging of traditional home builders and the new modular mobile-home producers. "We manufacturers know how to produce houses on assembly lines," he declared, "and builders know how to subdivide land."

Mergers soon began to blur the line between builders and "mobies." Redman Industries purchased Kansas Quality Home Construction, Boise Cascade bought Divco Wayne, and Eli Broad went shopping for mobile-home firms. Builders also chimed in by saying they would be glad to expand into planned, modular mobile-home developments.

The charisma of the merger-acquisition era was further brightened by Alodex, a Memphis conglomerate closely related to Holiday Inns of America, headed by Wallace Johnson. The firm arranged a merger with Iowa builder Lloyd Clarke's firms and planned immediate expansion through an industrialized housing division. Clarke was a past president of NAHB. John Hancock and U.S. Gypsum agreed to aid in the expansion.

Two big auto companies got into housing in the late sixties, largely as a result of their realty holdings and activities. Chrysler had a lively realty company which developed plans for a 1,600-home, 2,200-townhouse project in Troy, Michigan. It also planned residential projects in Bloomfield Hills; Fort Lauderdale; Ann Arbor; Tempe, Arizona; and Riverside, California. The company worked largely through joint ventures with local builders.

Ford Motor Company also announced plans in 1969 to develop housing projects and bought into a modular operation, Concept Environment, Incorporated. General Motors reported no plans to get into housing.

The third group that helped pour vast new sums into housing was made up of life insurance and financial giants. Leading the parade was the $23-billion-strong Metropolitan Life Insurance Company. In 1967 it stepped briskly into a series of lending innovations of great consequence—this in addition to its current mortgage buying rate of a billion dollars a year.

Metropolitan boldly started making loans for land purchases and improvements on large developments. It also began promoting joint ventures, issuing takeout commitments, and doing a big volume of participation lending. It also helped organize new corporations of building-materials producers to make 90% conventional builder loans nation-wide and agreed to take part in the financing.

Prudential Insurance Company, with $25 billion in assets, also plunged into an innovative program of joint venturing, financing, and building in 1968. One of its first was a $20-million Hawaiian Hotel complex with Del Webb. Through various subsidiaries, Prudential was soon involved in large building and development projects nation-wide.

Prudential and Metropolitan led a parade of other insurance companies into joint venturing, financing, and equity participation in housing. These included John Hancock, Connecticut General, Travelers, Aetna, Fidelity of Philadelphia, and a host of others. The impact on housing growth was tremendous. Undoubtedly a strong underlying motive for the financing charges was a need for equity participation as a hedge against inflation. It became, and still is, a powerful influence no investor can ignore.

A much talked about deal of 1969 was the acquisition of the Larwin Company of California, a diversified home builder, by giant CNA Financial Corporation. The builders got $200 million in CNA stock and what they called "relaxed long-term capital." They then embarked on a vigorous expansion which doubled their volume. Scholz Homes of Toledo, a pioneer prefab-home manufacturer, also caught merger fever and joined Inland Steel Corporation in an $85-million stock exchange.

Perhaps the most striking growth story was that of City Investing Company, which became a multi-faceted shelter conglomerate through its acquisitions, mergers, buy-ins, and investments. By 1969 it owned all or part of Sterling Forest, General Development, Southern California Financial, Motel 6, Rheem Manufacturing, Guerdon Industries, and many smaller development firms. Its annual revenue had risen from $8 million in 1966 to more than $1 billion in 1969. It continued to expand in the next decade.

After having said all this about housing giants and mergers, it must be said that 95% of all housing built in the sixties was still produced with the same techniques and the same design and marketing concepts which marked the success of the fifties. The bulk was built by many thousands of small-volume builders.

The major exception, of course, was in the growing rental-housing market and in the introduction in the late sixties of a new lender-investor into housing development, the real estate investment trust.

New Pools of Capital:
REITs, Mortgage Trusts, and Mortgage-Backed Securities

Billions of dollars in fresh capital were poured into housing and land development in the sixties by spectacular changes and innovations in mortgage finance. One of the first was the growth of real estate investment trusts, authorized by the Congress Act of 1960. The REITs flourished, but ran into severe difficulties later in the seventies. They did, however, pump vast sums into housing and were well accepted and financed on Wall Street.

By 1968, mortgage investment trusts were attracting feverish attention in the stock market, and new issues in the hundreds of millions were being offered. The new trusts invested in construction and land development loans secured by first mortgages and were able to show high yields—often 13% or more. Equity trusts also flourished as investors sought increasing protection against inflation. They became involved in joint ventures, land banking, sale and leasebacks, and extensive equity participation in large projects.

Mortgage banking and lending practices underwent striking change near the decade's end as "piece of the action" fever swept the industry. Lenders had become convinced that inflation was here to stay, and they evolved a complicated and often bizarre series of formulas for participation in equities and for the income of properties they financed. Banks, insurance firms, mortgage companies, and nearly all the large lenders used some or all of the following devices:

1. *The joint venture.* It could well be called the "front-money" deal. The lender supplies the money, the developer the land and know-how. It can be a partnership or corporation.
2. *Sale and leaseback.* This is a common equity device using prepaid interest.
3. *Sale and leaseback of land, and leasehold mortgage.* Under this device only the land under a building is sold, which is then leased back to the developer.
4. *Sale and buy back.* This refinement of (3) could be called an installment sales contract; it permits the vendee to take depreciation.
5. *Contingent interest deal.* This variable-interest arrangement sets the rate in two parts: a fixed rate and an extra based on the property's performance. The add-on could be 4% of gross, 15% of improvement in gross, or a percentage of net.
6. *Purchase of mortgaged land.* Lender buys the land and leases it back. Ground rent is 10% or more, subject to possible additional rent increases.
7. *Wraparound mortgage.* A complicated deal that leaves old mortgages with encumbrances untouched, but includes their total.
8. *Basket clause and kickers.* These were special provisions that permit share of profit, contingent interest, second mortgages, and other variations not otherwise allowed under state insurance laws.

A prophetic picture of the mortgage banker of the seventies facing inflation, competition, and change was made in 1969 by Robert H. Pease, president of Mortgage Bankers Association. He declared, "He will be a combination real estate man, partner in real estate dealing, investment underwriter, and mortgage banker. He will run a completely integrated corporation that will operate in realty, bonds, and mortgages simultaneously." That was the picture of mortgage bankers at the beginning of the decade of the seventies.

Still another aid to housing was the growth of private mortgage guarantee insurance companies. Their advance was so strong that they threatened to overtake FHA (and later did). The leader in the field was Mortgage Guarantee Insurance Company of Milwaukee, founded in 1957 by Max H. Karl. By the end of 1969 MGIC was insuring at the rate of $10 billion a year, and still growing. Numerous others joined in, and many floated large public stock offerings that swelled the flow of funds to housing.

By late 1969 the first start at tapping the investment markets with pass-through securities guaranteed by the new Government National Mortgage Association began. GNMA had been made possible by the Housing and Urban Development Act of 1968. The new guaranteed mortgage-backed securities paved the way for vast new investments by pension funds, trusts, insurance companies, and private investors. It was a major advance in housing finance which had great repercussions in the following decade.

The New Glamour Communities

Now, at last, the precepts of famed early land planners and architects Clarence Stein, Henry Wright, Frederick Olmstead, Seward Mott, and others flowered in an outpouring of fine environmentally planned communities.

The new glamour projects of the sixties were sophisticated, colorful, and in some cases unbelievably lush, such as the Bluffs at Newport Beach, Rancho Bernardo at San Diego, Casas Capistrano at San Juan, and Westlake, near Los Angeles.

The architecture was stimulating, and showed the skill of intelligent designers who worked closely with land planners, builders and marketing experts.

Very significant was the fact that the best projects were totally planned to include mixed housing types in a broad range of sizes and prices—apartments, townhouses and single-family and patio units—as well as shopping and recreational facilities. The new breed of architects and planners was as good as any in the world, and they brought deep concern for such matters as street patterns, siting, culs-de-sac, clusters, open space, recreational areas, parks, and green areas.

They also developed more efficient land use—zero-lot line, patio homes on narrow lots, PUDs (planned unit developments), clusters of townhouses, four-plexes, or small apartments with open space and recreational facilities.

Progress in the communities and newtowns of the sixties was greatly enhanced by a new type of specialized architect or industrial designer who provided a complete design package for large PUDs and other projects. An early leader in this field was Richard Leitch of Newport Beach, who started with the raw land, envisioned an overall scheme, designed the houses and their pricing, planned the siting, grades, and landscaping, designed the model homes, interiors, and model-home areas, and then developed a merchandising plan. He and his firm worked for many outstanding builders and land developers and had a strong impact on design and community planning.

Both the glamour communities and the newtowns of the sixties were made possible by the emergence of giant firms that were backed by sufficient capital and that had astute management. The giants had the money and the discernment to pay for top-flight architects, planners, landscapers, engineers, interior designers, and environmental experts, and their example was often followed by smaller firms. The result was housing that opened a sensational new world of enriched living. Here are some of the trends that brought this vision to reality:

1. New patterns of land use combined public and private open space, green areas, and parking space.
2. Close cooperation between builder, developer, architect, land planner, and local zoning/planning bodies was achieved by changes in local zoning which made possible the new planning concepts.
3. Traffic-safe street patterns were designed with loops, culs-de-sac, pedestrian walks, and intimate neighborhood enclaves or villages as part of the total project. Thus ample shopping and community facilities and schools were provided within easy reach.
4. Planned outdoor living space, both public and private, was established for each family.
5. Recreational facilities such as golf, tennis, swimming, club houses, and social centers were provided.

6. Each house was sited to preserve the trees and natural land contours. Ample landscaping of sites and common areas became commonplace. Large trees were planted or transplanted.
7. Varied setbacks from the street and designs to avoid monotony were introduced. Studied relationships and control of housing shapes, patterns, and colors for aesthetic value were essential.
8. High project standards were established to control the quality of design, construction, landscaping, color, and environment.

As in previous decades, the Washington-based Urban Land Institute continued its excellent work in community planning through research, workshops, round-table discussions, and publications. In 1961 its Technical Bulletin #40, "New Ideas for Better Land Use," was produced. Harmon, O'Donnell, and Henninger of Denver were technical consultants who brought new insights on flexible zoning, double-frontage layouts, patio/townhouse concepts, cluster plans, and PUDs. Another valuable ULI technical bulletin was "Open Space Communities in the Market Place," by Carl Norcross and Sanford R. Goodkin, which appeared in 1967.

It is noteworthy that residential builders became more keenly aware of the sales appeal of good design. In 1961 a group listed their most popular home sales features as "baths that look luxurious . . . kitchens to entertain in . . . separate dining area for gracious eating . . . wide, attractive entryways . . . a second living area such as a family room . . . master bedroom suite with bath and dressing room, sitting area, walk-in closets . . . spacious, gracious rooms—large fireplace, ample storage . . . private outdoor living areas . . . garages screened from street."

A few of the gifted architects, land, landscape, and environmental planners, interior designers, and consultants who brought the new look and uplift to housing are described here.

Harwell Hamilton Harris revitalized the California style of Maybeck and Greene & Greene. His influence is seen through the wood and "natural look" houses that builders put up throughout the sixties and seventies.

Charles Warren Callister blazed new trails at Walnut Creek, California, and Heritage Village, Connecticut, with his natural wood and angular contemporary shapes, as well as with his unprecedented siting and overall planning.

Richard Leitch created a new and exciting concept with his package approach to planning, design, siting, landscaping, decorating, and marketing of large PUDs.

Barry A. Berkus of Santa Barbara, California, became a national figure with his colorful, popular designs for patio homes, duplexes, and small apartments, including those at Huntington Harbor. His work was carried on in 22 states and many foreign countries.

Robert E. Jones of La Jolla, California, created new design excitement with his zerolot line and patio-home concepts, including those used at Casas Capistrano, Westlake Village, and Laguna Niguel.

Victor Gruen brought new dimensions to community design and planning with such projects as El Dorado Hills and Conejo Village.

Bertrand Goldberg stirred the design world in the early sixties with his astounding twin-towered Marina City in Chicago.

A score of others contributed to residential design progress, including Walter J. Richardson, Claude Miquelle, Henry D. Norris, Cliff May, Welton Beckett, Anshen & Allen, Francis D. Lethbridge, Pietro Belluschi, William Wurster, Arnold Kronstadt, and many others.

High Life Style for Apartment and Townhouse Dwellers

Apartment construction climbed rapidly in the sixties, continuing the rise begun in the late fifties. By 1969 it accounted for half the market, and in some cities much more. In Houston, for example, apartments and townhouses took 80% of the total starts.

The multi-family increase came largely in the fast-growing suburban areas. But the major cause was the flight from downtown urban centers and the appeal of the new designs, amenities, environment, and way of life offered by builders.

The apartment and townhouse builders of the sixties not only built individual projects,

but made much of their work a part of large, planned communities and newtowns. They contributed an improved concept of what apartment life could be by introducing bigger and better floor plans, air conditioning, noise control, window views, park-like settings, patios, terraces, open space, landscaping, swimming pools, clubs, parking and recreational facilities—in short, many of the advantages enjoyed by single-home occupants.

By mid-decade, the cooperative and condominium methods of owning apartments came into widespread use and soon were a great stimulant to sales. Builders liked the condominium idea because, among other reasons, every sale meant a reduction in the front-money cost of carrying the land and development.

Another boost in apartment volume was given by the entrance of former single-family home giants such as Levitt, Kaufman & Broad, Larwin, Kassuba, and Macco into multi-family work. In their new role they became "all-product" builders; they started many apartment/townhouse jobs and entered into joint ventures on others.

By 1965, apartment builders began planning for specific groups or classes of renters, or—if they were building a condominium—for buyers. Their thinking and planning are illustrated by the following somewhat frivolous list of possible future occupants:

- *Young swingers,* unmarried, who want fun and frolic.
- *Young sophisticates,* looking for luxurious small units in a good setting.
- *Newlyweds,* wanting small, smart quarters at low cost.
- *Home and family,* looking for medium-size units for two children, with emphasis on good schools and community.
- *Exurban type,* seeking luxury units in safe environment, close in.
- *Large-home oriented,* ex-owners of large houses, who want big, well-appointed apartments with all the amenities of suburban life.
- *Job oriented,* wanting modern, easy-care apartments near jobs, but with good suburban accouterments.

While most apartment building of this period was suburban oriented, some large, well-designed projects were built in the cities. By far the most exotic and publicized was Marina

City, on the river side in the heart of Chicago. Architect Bertrand Goldberg called it a "total environment, created vertically, for high-density living and greater leisure." The 40-story twin towers housed 896 families, and included balconies, swimming pools, skating rinks, 24 shops, a theater, park, bowling alleys, and a marina for 700 boats. It was sponsored by the Building Service Employees' International Union.

Hand in hand with apartment growth came a continuing and truly striking development of a new kind of community life of clusters, or other groupings, of townhouses, duplexes, four-plexes, and zero-lot line and patio homes.

High land costs were, of course, a strong motivating factor. But a few brilliant architects and planners devised improved ways to group small, lower-cost houses on narrow sites or smaller acreage while still providing green space, amenities, and an attractive environment. Such skillful high-density planning reduced land and development costs substantially.

It seemed that high land costs were making the price of single-family homes almost impossible. But the new ways of clustering and designing for narrow lots brought the cost down and opened suburban living of a high order to millions of families. This was a trend of the late sixties that increased and multiplied in the seventies as land and other costs continued to skyrocket. We shall later describe a few of the outstanding projects of this type.

Noise and sound control for all types of multi-family structures became more sophisticated and effective as the builders hired skilled acoustical experts to work from the early planning stage. Acoustical buffering was often achieved by staggering the placement of buildings or by extensive tree plant-

ing, and sometimes by placing all parking underground. Other acoustical devices included
floating floors that deadened sound; pipes and
fixtures that were isolated to cut vibration;
flexible couplings on pumps and equipment;
staggered and heavily insulated party walls;
metal ducts that were muffled as well as insulated; cushioned waste and vent lines; avoid-
ance of back-to-back placement; discontinua-
tion of through-floor wiring; baffles and
absorbent lining placed in return-air plenums;
fiber ducts; and laundry and kitchen equipment mounted on pads and springs.

Noisy equipment was placed at outside
walls and mounted on floating slabs; double-
pane windows were used to keep out sound;
there were tight fitting, acoustical exterior and
interior doors; fans were oversized and slow
moving; sound-absorbent furnace areas had a
quiet fan; quiet garbage disposers and dishwashers were provided; there were acoustical
ceilings in kitchens, baths, and bedrooms; and
carpeting, sound absorbent walls, and silent
electrical switches were commonly expected
luxuries.

The Lure of Recreation for Leisure Time

Builders called it the greatest sales asset
they had. Buyers were universally seeking an
active recreational, leisure-oriented environment with a sociable way of life. Old and
young, apartment dwellers or house owners,
city, suburban, or vacation-home buyers—all
sought a diversity of recreational amenities.

These took many forms, from exotic swimming and beach clubs to million-dollar golf
courses, marinas, riding trails, and tennis and
community clubs. Americans in the sixties
had both money and the leisure time to enjoy
it. As the decade progressed, the recreational
facilities of the glamourous home communities, the large apartment/townhouse complexes, the newtowns, the retirement projects,
and the vacation resort places all became
more opulent. They brought, indeed, a new
way of leisure life for millions of people.

Emil Hanslin, the talented builder, developer, and environmentalist who created New
Seabury on Cape Cod, summed it up by saying, "Recreation is one aspect of the public's
need for self-expression. The time will come

when it will be the core of a large cultural center, the focal point of the whole community."

Swimming pools were by far the most popular facility, and they were designed to fit a
variety of uses, depending on the nature of
each project. Usually a bathhouse or club was
provided. By mid-decade many of the large
apartment or community projects were providing both indoor and outdoor pools. At waterside projects such as Huntington Harbour, a
2,500-home community south of Los
Angeles, the beach club was a major attraction. "It's the most important sales tool we've
ever had," the builder said.

Water sports were a close second to the
pools, and docks, waterside facilities, and
marinas proved extremely popular. Large-
and small-boat owners and sailboat devotees
from Maine to Florida and from Seattle to San
Diego helped swell the sales of homes and
apartments. Prices of housing close to water
brought premium prices, but apparently it
was worth it, as values have skyrocketed over
the years.

Builders soon discovered new ways to expand waterfront sites by building lagoons, canals, and waterways. A notable example was Marco Island in Florida, developed by the Mackle Brothers. Here, miles of waterfront and thousands of water sites were created by dredging, cutting, and filling to make an elaborate system of canals. Almost every home buyer could thus have a dock in his backyard—and a boat if he could afford it after paying for the house.

Another boost to recreational fun was given by man-made lakes and ponds. Often a builder would make the most of a low or marshy area by excavating and creating such bodies of water—and at the same time creating premium-priced waterside lots.

Many other activities were encouraged by builders. Horseback riding appealed to affluent buyers, and soon developers used it as a helpful sales appeal. At New Seabury, Hanslin cleared 5.5 miles of riding trails and built a stable, corral, and show ring. One of his areas was especially oriented to the "horsy set," and it is said that Hanslin surreptitiously scattered a judicious amount of horse droppings around the model homes to create the right atmosphere.

Community centers were another source of entry by new home residents into the "active and sociable life" so greatly desired. They ranged from a modest meeting house with kitchen facilities to million-dollar, full-scale recreational complexes. They provided a great variety of hobby activities and many kinds of sport, including shuffleboard, ping pong, and bowling, rooms for bridge, club, and social meetings, lounges, saunas, billiards and pool rooms, exercise facilities, and in some cases a bottle club.

The ancient and honorable game of golf had an enormous growth in popularity in the six-

ties, and builders quickly seized on it as a major attraction. Golf was a prime symbol of prestige and attracted not just golfers but all who liked open space and green vistas. Houses along the course, naturally, brought premium prices, so one of the first objectives of planners was to squeeze in as many sites as possible with a view of the course.

Golf facilities ranged all the way from a short nine-hole pitch and putt course to elaborate country clubs with two or three 18-hole layouts. In some cases, such as Charles Fraser's Sea Pines Plantation on Hilton Head Island in South Carolina, the golf clubs became the nucleus of an inn and cottage complex which included cocktail lounges and other entertainment facilities.

Some of the golf courses were able to show a profit, but many did not. The problem to the developers was that golf facilities were extremely costly, often running into the millions, and seriously affected the amount of front money required to finance the whole project as well as the later carrying costs. Many projects ran into financial difficulties later because of overextension on golf and country club costs.

Nevertheless, golf continued to be an important adjunct, and most of the large-project developers of the sixties and seventies built courses. They retained top-flight golf course designers who skillfully wove the inviting fairways and greens through miles of home and apartment sites. Later we will describe a few of the more notable ones.

The lure of leisure/recreational activities also kept strong the vacation/second-home market described in the decade of the fifties. The multi-billion-dollar U.S. highway program also helped dramatically as engineers bored through the Rockies, and threw wide roads across New England, the South, and the

West. Millions of acres of new vacation spots were opened in parks, forests, and mountains, and by lakes, waterways, and the seas.

American families had become more mobile, often had two cars, and had longer vacations and a great itch to enjoy life in a home away from home. By 1966 the vacation, resort, and second-home market had grown to 125,000 a year (admittedly a ballpark figure, since accurate statistics are hard to come by).

The mushrooming market was aided by more liberal financing and eye-catching designs such as the A-frame and Swiss chalets, and by often exotic new patterns in log, timber, and natural wood structures. Prefab manufacturers got into the act and were able to sell attractive small units which were trucked to the site and erected with a minimum of hard-to-get local labor.

Builders and developers seized on the strong recreational appeals of skiing, swim-ming, water sports, and golf, and built around them. Exciting new resort communities grew up in such areas as Aspen, Tahoe, Cape Cod, Hilton Head, and Marco Island, as well as in choice spots in Vermont, New Hampshire, Maryland, Oregon, and California.

The vacation-home projects first began to grow into vacation/second-home communities and then slowly shifted into year-round and retirement living. The combination of all these appeals brought expanded building volume, and also increased the quality of the homes built. The development of resort communities became big business. An example was Incline Village on Lake Tahoe, which turned 9,000 acres into a haven for 25,000 vacation-homes, second-home and permanent-home buyers, and which included apartments, condominiums, hotels, and entertainment facilities. Later we shall describe some of these communities.

Newtowns: the $75-Billion Dream

Certainly the planning, development, and problems of newtowns frame a fascinating picture of housing progress and frustration in the sixties. With high hopes, some 75 projects, each of 1,000 acres or more and capable of housing six million people, were under way by 1965. If they had all been completed, their value would have been more than $75 billion (at 1965 prices).

But this was a dream that failed to materialize. Only a handful survived the decade, and in the late seventies the Department of Housing and Urban Development (HUD) brought what was then called the New Communities Program to a screeching halt when losses exceeded $140 million. "It's a sad, painful, and expensive experience," a HUD spokesman said.

He pointed out that newtown developers had suffered from huge front end costs: buying, holding, and developing land, building sewers and roads, and creating costly amenities to serve people of all incomes with residential, commercial, and industrial facilities.

Under the New Communities Development Program inaugurated by the Johnson administration in the late sixties, the government was to support newtown developers by guaranteeing their loans and by coordinating federal aid for basic community needs such as housing, sewers, and land. But most of the builders ran out of money before they could sell enough property to keep going.

HUD was eventually forced to pay off the loans and foreclose on many projects. Some of the more prominent were Jonathan, Minnesota, Park Forest South in Chicago, Cedar-Riverside in Minneapolis, Flower Mound near Dallas, and Riverton and Gananda near Rochester. "Our real estate portfolio will continue to be a large one for years to come," concluded the HUD spokesman in what must have been one of the more impressive understatements of the year.

The newtown record, however, is not all bad. As we have previously reported, such earlier projects as William Levitt's Pennsylvania Levittown and U.S. Steel's Fairless Hills were most successful. But the projects of the sixties and seventies became progressively bigger, more costly, and more difficult to finance. For this discussion we shall define a newtown as a large, self-sustaining community that offers both employment and a wide range of housing types for people of all economic levels. It also is expected to bring "green space," good environmental concepts, and extensive recreational facilities and community services such as schools and shopping and community centers.

Newtowns were the somewhat idealistic answer to the problems of urban sprawl. They were planned for a greatly improved living-working-playing environment. Future historians will surely credit the planners and developers with advancing many worthy ends. But their greatest problem was bigness itself; they simply became too huge, costly, and slow moving to survive the financial pressures they generated. As one observer declared, "No one has that much money." Later, when the U.S. government became involved, even it could not support the enormous costs.

Other problems trapped the well-intentioned newtown developers. One was location. To acquire large tracts—often of 6,000 acres or more—meant going far out and building costly connecting highways. People often balked at the distances. Front-end financing was another problem: the builders had to spend millions—even $100 million or more—before they sold a single piece of property. Sales were a third and perplexing problem. The builder's cash-flow needs called for immediate large sales; but in the early stages, lack of schools, shops, and the industrial facilities to produce jobs made sales extremely slow. A fourth obstacle came from local governments which often held up projects for months—or years—with zoning, codes, and red tape. The costs of such delays were enormous and killed many a good start.

We shall discuss the problems and successes of just a few, beginning with the best known, *Reston* in Fairfax County, Virginia, 18 miles from Washington, D.C., which for a long time represented a newtown ideal. The original developer, Robert E. Simon, Jr., was a millionaire with high cultural and social ideals. He hired top-flight architects and planners to create an ideal city of 7,000 acres and 75,000 residents. The plan called for green belts winding through seven villages, and included parks, lakes, exotic shopping centers, and two industrial centers. It provided townhouses, high-rise apartments, and single-family homes in a wide range of prices. But sales were painfully slow and the financial burden great. Eventually Simon sold out to Gulf Oil, which spent additional millions to develop sales. Even so it took many years to finish, and in the meantime Simon and others lost large investments.

Columbia, Maryland, proved to be one of the most successful newtowns, although it too had its share of delays and financial problems. The developer was James W. Rouse, a perceptive builder, mortgage banker, and creator of shopping centers. He brought together an amazing team of architects, planners, and behavioral scientists to design an integrated community to fit the social and economic needs of many people. His new city held 14,000 acres, was located mid-way between Baltimore and Washington, and was planned for a population of 110,000. It had village areas for different social and economic levels as well as a broad housing mix. It included recreational, shopping, and community facilities as well as a large industrial area.

Columbia took many years to plan and still longer to build. It ultimately became one of the few successful newtowns and a monument to the creativity of James Rouse, but it was not a large financial success to the investors.

Perhaps newtown is not the proper term to describe the famous *Irvine Ranch* in Orange County, California, about 40 miles south of Los Angeles. The Irvine Company described it as the "nation's largest master-planned urban environment," and that would seem as good a definition as any. Whatever you call it, this is the giant among giants in California's land and community developments. It was started in the early sixties when the Irvine Company began transforming the 193,000-acre Irvine ranch into "a total urban complex." The long-range plans by architect-planner William Pereira called for planned communities of houses and apartments, shopping centers, recreational areas, a research park, industrial parks, a 1000-acre campus for the University of California, and much else.

The remarkable growth and success of Irvine Ranch can largely be attributed to its excellent environmental and development plans which were largely followed through the years.

By the late seventies some 7,000 acres had been built up and included six marinas, the University of California, ten shopping centers, six golf courses, 11 apartment complexes, office buildings, huge industrial parks, many villages, and the incorporated newtown of Irvine.

As a measure of its financial success it can be noted that when the Irvine Company changed hands in a spectacular corporate battle in 1978, the price was $337 million. But the true value of the fine communities and good living it created far exceeded this figure.

Among the giant newtowns, El Dorado Hills near Sacramento was considered to have the brightest prospects. It had strong financial backing, and its developer, A. H. Lindsey, knew the ropes. He put a team of big-name men to work: Victor Gruen on site planning, Anshen & Allen as home architects, Douglas Bayliss as landscape architect, and Robert Trent Jones as golf course designer.

The 10,000 acres were well laid out and called for green belts, a lake, small villages, recreational sites, a golf course, shopping centers, and industrial parks.

But in spite of this careful planning, sales and development were very slow. After four years of hard work, fewer than 400 houses had been sold. One reason was that many people felt 25 miles was too far to commute. In 1969 the John Hancock Insurance Company, which was heavily invested, took over. New infusions of capital, new model homes, and expanded sales efforts helped, but growth did not live up to the early expectations of developer Lindsey.

One of the smaller and more successful newtowns was Crofton in Ann Arundel county, Maryland, opened in 1964. The developer, W. Hamilton Crawford, was a builder and prefab manufacturer of wide experience and he retained Mott & Hayden as planners. The 1,300-acre project was built around a delightful, brick-paved Colonial shopping center called the Village Green, and a 210-acre golf course. It had a balanced mix of housing types, schools, churches, recreation, office and research parks, plus an area for light industry. The houses and townhouses were skillfully clustered around open-space areas. Most of them were built by outside building firms, but under the strict design standards of the community.

The Easy-Care Life: Retirement and Condominium Living

The signal that a new way of living for the elderly and retired was blossoming was given by builder Del E. Webb in January, 1960, when he opened his famed Sun City near Phoenix, Arizona. In less than a year he sold 1,300 single-family homes and 250 garden-apartment units. On his 10,000-acre site he built swimming pools, motels, shopping centers, extensive clubs and recreational facilities, and fine golf courses. Everything was built—at a cost of millions—before a single house was sold. The big theme: "An adult community for active retirement living."

Everything was go for retirement housing. In January, 1961, a White House conference on the aging put the spotlight this way:

"Earlier generations were satisfied merely to wait out their remaining years.

"But today's shorter work week, increased leisure, and longer retirement period reveal the need for ways to occupy one's time, and an environment in which to enjoy them."

A prototype retirement home was opened near the White House, sponsored by the American Association of Retired Persons and the Douglas Fir Plywood Association. It was loaded with ideas to make retirees' living easier, more pleasant, and less costly. It was viewed by thousands and widely published.

Social security, Medicare, and swelling pensions made retirement easier. Older people also had large equities in houses that often paid the cost of a retirement home.

Del Webb is said to have spent four years of extensive research before he built Sun City. Other builders, such as California's Ross Cor-tese of Leisure World fame spent even more, and improved on Webb's ideas.

Cortese may well be credited with the best planning and development of the decade for his Rossmore Leisure World project at Laguna Hills near Los Angeles and his Walnut Creek near Oakland, both enormously successful and attractive. Walnut Creek was the work of architect Charles Warren Callister and planners Mott and Hayden.

Cortese's Leisure World projects—there were many extending into later decades—provided community, club, and recreational facilities, hobby shops, golf and tennis, swimming pools, health clubs, and shopping centers. Callister's contemporary designs in natural wood were carefully sited to fit the contours of the land. At Walnut Creek he created an architectural style that has since been widely admired and copied all over the world.

From Arizona, California, and Washington the "adult leisure community" idea spread—to Florida, Texas, the Carolinas, Illinois, New York, New Jersey, Connecticut, and nationwide. Then in the mid-sixties the condominium way of buying retirement homes began to enter the picture. In 1967, for example, one of the most newsworthy projects of the decade emerged at Southbury, Connecticut, called Heritage Village, a 2,600-unit adult leisure community that was also a condominium. This wedding of retirement and condominium features was to have a great impact on the building on succeeding years.

"Housing's greatest innovation of the decade" was the phrase used to describe the condominium idea—a form of ownership that dated back to Roman times. It had been used in Europe and Latin America, but did not begin to make serious headway in the United States until 1961, when Congress authorized FHA to insure such work.

By 1967 a condominium boom was in the making, as builders, buyers, and financial institutions took enthusiastically to the "easy-care way of living." By that time nearly every state in the union had adopted condominium statutes, and FHA had insured 3,000 units.

In the early years, builders had a problem with the word condominium. One declared: "My worst difficulty is trying to explain what the heck it is!" A recent Webster's definition reads: *condominium*—a residential building consisting of multiple units, each under individual ownership, but subject to certain joint agreements and regulations." Also, "one unit in such a building." As a rule the condo buyer got a deed giving him full ownership of his unit plus an undivided interest in all common property of the project.

There were many reasons why the condo idea spread so rapidly in the late sixties and on through the seventies. The first was that it made home ownership easier, cheaper, and available with increased amenities. It particularly fitted into the growing planned unit development (PUD) concept which provided open space and recreational and community facilities. It nicely accommodated the trend toward cluster plans of townhouses and patio-home units, with common property managed by a homeowners' association. For apartment dwellers it paved the way to becoming an owner, with all the economic and tax advantages of conventional home ownership.

In a condominium the owner may usually sell, lease, or rent as he sees fit, although often there is a stipulation giving the condomin-

ium association the right of first refusal. He is responsible only for his own home and a share of the common property upkeep—known as the condominium fee.

The trend toward care-free condominium life came at a time when two large new markets were emerging: vacation homes and retirement housing. Condominiums were uniquely suited to people seeking a wider range of recreation and leisure-time activities.

But more than any other reason, the lure of the condominium lay in its easy-care and maintenance-free living features. Most of the chores of home ownership were removed. For a modest fee, paid to the home owners' or condominium association, lawn mowing, snow shoveling, leaf raking, and window washing were taken care of. Usually the fee also covered exterior upkeep and maintenance as well as care of common property, walks and driveways, and recreational facilities. This is certainly one reason why condos have been so popular with older buyers.

By the late sixties the condominium ideas had spread across the land and were used in many projects. Luxury high-rise projects rose in Boca Raton, Miami, Houston, Chicago, and New York. Garden-apartment condos sold briskly in suburbs of Washington, Dallas, and other cities. Townhouse projects were popular in Phoenix and New Haven, and duplex and four-plex clusters proliferated in California.

Elderly buyers retired in increasing numbers in condominium communities such as the Leisure Villages of Robert Schmertz at Lakewood, New Jersey, and Heritage Village at Southbury, Connecticut. We shall describe Heritage Village in detail because of the amazing national influence it had on later condominium development.

Heritage Village was the product of a family of builder brothers, the Paparazzos: Henry, trained in management and finance; Otto, a talented designer and graduate of the Rhode Island School of Design; and Frank, a rugged construction man. Together they made a good team, and in the late sixties they assembled large parcels of rolling, wooded land, laced with streams and ponds in rural Southbury, some 80 miles from New York City.

Ultimately the property rose to 1,100 acres and included the old estate of Victor Borge and several historic Colonial structures. The ambitious plans called for transforming the buildings to a meeting house, a leisure-activities center, a men's club, a women's club and various arts and crafts shops for painting, ceramics, and woodworking. Also provided were 27 holes of golf, four swimming pools, and tennis and paddle courts.

The first big hurdle was the local Southbury zoning and planning boards which were worried about such a large project. When it was announced as an adult community for persons older than 50 with no school children, much opposition vanished. Then the attractive PUD plan was unveiled, which took all the burdens of roads, sewer, water, and maintenance off the shoulders of Southbury. It skillfully wove the one- and two-story condo units around the golf courses, open green space, and community buildings without destroying the trees or natural terrain. Eventually the project was approved.

But then the second great hurdle arose: financing. The Paparazzos were experienced builders, but had never been through a project as costly as this with its huge front-end money requirements. All of the recreational amenities and buildings had to be completed—at a cost of millions—before the first home was sold. A million-dollar water and sewer system had to be completed as well as the $200,000

sales building and a cluster of nine fully decorated model homes. After many precarious delays and dealings, a solution was reached: a 50-50 joint-venture partnership with Fidelity Mutual Life Insurance of Philadelphia.

Under this arrangement there was a careful division of responsibility and authority. The Paparazzos handled planning, design, construction, and selling. Fidelity arranged both temporary and permanent financing fitted to the production schedule. The builders were relieved of the dangers and difficulties of tight money—but also, it may be presumed, of a goodly share of the profits from their industry, imagination, and skills.

Another aspect of the project was an attractive shopping-center area, the Village Green, which included a unique, 900-foot-long bazaar, banks, commercial buildings, a luxurious inn, and much else. Fidelity became a partner in financing these as well.

From this point, Heritage Village moved swiftly, and the project opened with the nine model homes in early 1967. Some 200 units were sold the first year, and in the succeeding ten years the entire project of 2,600 units was completed and turned over to the Heritage Village Master Association, which from there on managed its affairs.

Many observers have speculated about the reason for the success of this community in an obscure village in Connecticut, far from any city. Most conclude that an *ambiance* was established early—a quiet, country environment of hills and woods in an historic setting with its Pomperaug river, fine inns, and a socially and culturally attractive milieu. The architecture was low key—a restrained, woodsy, contemporary style with forms and shapes reminiscent of old New England. The model homes were decorated in a comfortable but luxurious lived-in, traditional way to appeal to middle-aged, middle-income, but well-off, buyers.

Great credit, of course, must go to architect Charles Warren Callister whose successes and reputation in California caught the attention of design-conscious Otto Paparazzo. Callister's work at Ross Cortese's Walnut Creek project won wide acclaim. His work at Heritage Village reflected his interest in strong, bold shapes, wooded exteriors, and a remarkable ability to fit the siting of houses to the rolling terrain of Connecticut.

Callister devised a "garden court" design approach that was extremely popular. He clustered small groups of units around a charming court, but at the same time faced their living areas with large glass expanses to overlook the golf courses, lakes, and wooded terrain.

Garages, under his plans, were clustered away from the homes so that the "asphalt jungle" was well removed from the living areas. Some buyers objected to walking a short ways from the garage to their homes, but for the most part the advantages of the quiet, car-free garden-court concept won buyer approval.

To this day, however, the most appealing feature of Heritage Village is the way the houses were sited to fit the land, and the way the trees and landscape were preserved. "Here is a project where the builder has refrained from taking a bulldozer to nature," is a common comment. When roads were laid out they were carefully walked and studied to avoid harming the topography or trees, and house placement was equally studied.

At the opening in 1967 the nine models were priced from $18,900 to $31,000. They had all tripled in price by 1979. But they did represent a broad mix of plans including one-, two-, and three-bedroom models of one and two stories in townhouse-like clusters.

No one knows the alchemy that brought buyers to Southbury in 1967-1978. But come they did, from Scarsdale and Bronxville, New York; Westport and Darien, Connecticut; Madison and Chatham, New Jersey; Hempstead and Great Neck in Long Island; Dobbs Ferry and Hastings in Westchester; and many more distant points in New England.

The community that evolved was one of affluence and culture. There are writers, artists, professors, musicians, retired bankers, semi-retired corporate executives, and a wide range of professionals such as doctors, lawyers, sociologists, and psychiatrists.

Another ingredient of sucess was the careful fashion in which 24 condominium associations were established and then united in a master association which manages the project. Well-organized committees supervise upkeep and maintenance and operation of the recreational facilities, which are extensively used.

An abbreviated list of a typical week's activities includes badminton, four days; bowling clubs (scheduled in nearby towns), three days; Bridge Club and classes, seven sessions; Camera Club; Chess Club and clinic, two days; Choral Society; dancing, round and square, three days; great books class; health insurance and service committees, two days; humane education; investment clubs, four days; knitting and crochet; language clubs (French, German, Hebrew) four days; lapidary workshop; opera appreciation group; painting, nine classes and workshops; pewter and silver class, four days; physical fitness class; piano ensemble group; ping pong; poetry class; quilting class; radio electronics workshop; Record and Tape Club; rug hooking; sculpture class; Shakespeare discussion group; skating group; Singles Club; Stamp Club; Photo Darkroom Club; theater guild group; Travel Club; Women's Club; yoga; gymnasium, five days; and the Heritage Village Library Association. Frequent bus tours and trips are conducted to New York, New Haven, and Hartford for shopping, theater, opera, and museum visits. Golf and tennis are actively pursued, and in season the four large swimming pools are crowded. The Heritage Villagers lead an active and, it would seem, an enjoyable retirement life.

One report states that 60 percent of the residents have full- or part-time jobs, some paid and some volunteer work. But another source claims that a more accurate statistic would be that 95 percent are workers in some field or other.

A notable pioneer in the luxury high-rise condominium field was the legendary *Janis Risbergs,* head of General Builders Corp. His 16-story Sky Harbor in Fort Lauderdale was the eye-catching wonder of the waterfront in 1963, and was designed and sold in luxury suites to vacationers and year-round residents. Risbergs built many outstanding projects, and

his rags-to-riches rise to housing giant is one of the remarkable tales of the industry.

Risbergs arrived in the United States in 1947, a near penniless refugee from Latvia; in fact, he later related, he had but $3.00 in his pocket. He managed to get a job as a carpenter, worked 18 hours a day, often far into the night, on interior finishing, using a flashlight.

Soon he became a carpenter subcontractor, using four other six-foot, newly arrived Latvian friends, then a tract builder, and ultimately head of giant General Builders which, by 1965, was doing a $15-million business. He stoutly proclaims that his story illustrates the greatness of the American private-enterprise system. He has educated his sons to succeed him in the building business. Along the way he has provided many thousands of low- and moderate- cost homes and apartments, as well as luxury condominiums such as Sky Harbor.

Notable Planned Communities of the Sixties

In the preceding sections we described the emergence of the new glamour communities, newtowns, leisure-vacation projects, and retirement and condominium communities of the sixties. All were the result of new forces at work, particularly talented architects and land planners, forward-looking builders and venturesome financiers. Let us now look briefly at some of the notable and often outstanding projects that resulted.

Aubin PUD Homes in Amherst, Massachusetts, was one of the first small (23 acres) Planned Unit Development projects. Builder William E. Aubin and land planner Per Nylen clustered houses, townhouses, condominiums, and apartments around green-space

areas and provided recreational amentities and services. Aubin developed a unique slide presentation for the Amherst Planning Board to convince them of the advantages of the PUD concept.

The Bluffs in Irvine, California, is an exotic community of high-rise towers, townhouses, and single-family and duplex units in a well-conceived environmental plan. This was one of the first projects to be built on leased land of the Irvine Ranch in Orange county. The builder was George M. Holstein & Sons and the architect/land planner was Richard Leitch.

Carderock Springs in Bethesda, Maryland, is a skillfully planned community of homes and apartments with shopping and recreational facilities, excellent design, and fine environmental planning by Keyes, Lethbridge and Condon. The builder was Edward Bennett, who also built in Kenwood Park and Newmark Commons and won some 30 design and planning awards.

Carmel Valley Manor in Carmel, California, is a non-profit, church-sponsored, life-care village. The 170 one-story apartment units in Spanish style are clustered around attractive open space, with rear patios facing wide lawns. Facilities included a clinic, pool, library, church, community hall, and recreation areas. The architects were Skidmore, Owings & Merrill, and the builders Williams & Burroughs.

Crofton, Maryland is the 1300-acre, small but successful newtown developed by W. Hamilton Crawford (described earlier this chapter).

Carriage Hill in Glenview, Illinois, is an elegant, well-designed cluster project of 126 luxury rental townhouses around landscaped gardens. The builders, Irvin and Bruce Blietz, coined a new name for them: Studio Garden Homes.

Carrollwood in Tampa, Florida, is a 600-home project built around Lake Carroll, with marinas, a golf course, a community center, and a nursery school. The fine environmental plan won a top award in 1963. The developer was Matt Jetton, president of Sunstate Builders, and planning was by Ernest L. Greene.

Columbia, Maryland is one of the most successful newtowns: 14,000 acres developed by James W. Rouse (described earlier in this chapter).

Conejo Village in Ventura County, California was one of the first big, well-planned newtowns, with 11,000 acres, and plans for 80,000 people. The original builders, the Janss Corp., headed by Edwin E. Janss, Jr.,

retained famed architect/planners Welton Beckett and Victor Gruen. A variety of housing was planned as well as extensive recreational areas, a country club, and a 1,000-acre light-manufacturing and research area. Golf courses, riding trails, and green-space areas contributed to its appeal.

Golden Gateway in San Francisco, is a spectacular project of eight 22-story towers. An area of townhouses provided more than 2,000 rental units. It was located in an urban-renewal area and included extensive shopping and recreational facilities as well as offices. It was designed by architects Wurster, Bernardi & Evans and Pietro Belluschi. The builder was Lou Perini of Boston.

Hawaii Kai in Honolulu, is a fantastic 5,700-acre project by Henry Kaiser and Fritz B. Burns, and is composed of homes, apartments, hotels, and shopping and recreational centers.

Heritage Village in Southbury Connecticut, is an adult leisure community of 2,600 condominium units built by Paparazzo Development Corp., with houses designed by architect Charles W. Callister (described earlier in this chapter).

Incline Village in Lake Tahoe, is a huge 9,000-acre resort/vacation/second-home project. It has golf, swimming, shopping, hotels, and recreation centers in 14 planned neighborhoods. The developer was Crystal Bay Co., the planner was Raymond Smith.

Irvine Ranch in Orange County, California, is the nation's "largest master-planned urban complex" (described earlier in this chapter).

Laguna Niguel in Orange County, California, is an early planned newtown of 7,000 acres with an expected 10,000 houses and apartments of various types. It had a careful master plan by Victor Gruen which called for high- and low-rise apartments, motels, hotels, shopping areas, extensive recreational facilities, and a park for light industry. The original moving force was the Laguna Niguel Corp. formed by Cabot, Cabot & Forbes of Boston, of which Gerald W. Blakeley, Jr., was president.

Lakeridge in Matawan, New Jersey, is one of William J. Levitt's small but excellently planned projects of the mid-decade which he called a "country club community." The 207 acres includes a lake with promenade, and a wooded greenbelt surrounding the 400 houses. Recreation includes boating, skating, tennis, volleyball, swimming, and a picnic area. It sold out quickly.

The Landings in Fort Lauderdale, Florida, is a lush, opulent 200-home project of expensive homes built by Burt Haft and Jack Gaines. The baths, kitchens, and decor set a new high for glamorous interiors. The builders called this the "customized approach to production building." They later did the equally opulent Imperial Point and Royal Oak Hills in Boca Raton.

Leisure Village in Lakewood, New Jersey, is a pioneer adult leisure project of condominium townhouses in clusters that set new planning standards as well as sales records in the mid-sixties. It included a lake, golf course, and much open space as well as swimming pools, craft and hobby shops, recreational areas, and an auditorium. The builder was Robert J. Schmertz.

Leisure World in Walnut Creek, California, was undoubtedly the outstanding, trend-setting retirement community of the decade. Builder Ross W. Cortese transformed the 2,100-acre Stanely Dollar Ranch near Oakland into a breathtaking setting of golf courses, swimming pools, roque and tennis courts, community buildings, shopping centers, and a hospital. Architect Charles Warren Callister and land planners Mott and Hayden worked closely to make the most of the spec-

tacular site. The 10,000 units consisted largely of contemporary one- and two-story cooperative apartments with ample open space and landscaping. Medical service for buyers was a part of the extensive services provided.

Meadow Lake in Memphis, Tennessee, was built by Irving Evans on 42 acres of low, marshy land, which he transformed into a lakeside project of 616 apartments and 122 townhouses. He created a 30-acre landscaped lake with bridges, retaining walls, and recreational areas. It rented quickly.

Mission Viejo in Orange County, California, is a large, well-planned home community (11,000 acres) with fine golf courses, swimming pools, recreational areas, a clubhouse, and shopping centers. It has outstanding houses, design, and community planning.

New Seabury in Waquoit, Cape Cod, is easily the outstanding recreation/second-home project of the sixties. Developer Emil Hanslin divided the 3,000 acres into 14 distinct villages oriented to specific activities such as sailing, horseback riding, golf, and beach and marina life. The names were intriguing: *High Wood*, large houses with barns and corrals; *Nor' East* for those who like boating; *Fells Pond*, for hunters and fishermen; *Tide Run* on a cove, for sailors and kids; *Summer Sea*, clusters for retirees; *Triton Sound*, luxury homes on estate sites. The environmental planning was excellent.

Northglen in Denver, Colorado, is a well-conceived residential project by Harmon, O'Donnell & Henninger on an 1800-acre tract started in 1960. It has excellent recreational, shopping, and environmental features. The builders, Samuel Primack and Jordon Perlmutter of Perl-Mack Companies, later developed many fine award-winning communities. Advanced construction techniques brought costs within reach of low-income buyers. "We try," said Primack, "to offer Cadillac values at Chevy prices."

Rancho Bernardo in San Diego, California, is a 5,400-acre project begun early in the sixties by builders W. R. Hawn and Harry Summers and later sold to Avco Corp. It provided a broad mix of housing units—many built along its fine golf courses—and a wide range of recreational and social amenities. It also included a park for light industry.

Reston in Fairfax County, Virginia, was the "ideal newtown" of the early sixties. It had its problems, but still remains a landmark of good early planning (described earlier in this chapter).

Sea Pines Plantation on Hilton Head Is-

land South Carolina, is a glamorous vacation resort and second-home project on 5,200 acres near the ocean. Its luxury houses, townhouses, apartments, motor hotel, large clubhouse, golf courses, swimming pools, beaches, and riding stables made it exceptional. Open space and cluster plans were part of a fine environmental layout. The developer was Charles Fraser; the planners Sasaki, Dawson, DeMay Associates.

Sterling Forest in Rockland County, New York, is a fine planned community of 23,000 acres with mixed housing types, shopping, recreational areas, and light industrial. It was started in early sixties by City Investing Co., Robert Dowling, president.

Toward Industrialization: Techniques, Mechanization, Research

How shall we describe the technological progress in housing during the sixties? It was certainly not the industrial revolution most of the experts were predicting. Nor was it a nono, or do-nothing, decade. What developed was a bit-by-bit continuation of better methods, techniques, products, and systems well begun in the fifties. NAHB's Research Foundation under the direction of Ralph J. Johnson did much to help.

This progressive evolution was carried on, as before, on a thousand fronts. It included the perfecting and increased use of larger components, roof trusses, stressed-skin and foamcore panels, wall, floor, and roof systems, utility cores, plumbing trees, packaged door and window units, modular units, steel and aluminum systems, compact packaged heating and air-conditioning systems, large bath

components, and more efficient kitchen/laundry appliances. And above all, it included dimensional standardization of the parts and pieces of a building to permit easier installation.

Progress was again aided by dedicated researchers such as those at the U.S. Forest Products Laboratory at Madison, Wisconsin—a unique combination of chemists, engineers, biologists and structural experts—who celebrated their fiftieth year of notable work in plywood, lumber laminates, and building systems.

Major progress was also achieved by the nation-wide series of test, research, and demonstration houses sponsored by NAHB and by plywood, lumber, and brick manufacturers, as well as by the aluminum, plastic, gypsum, and air-conditioning industries. Many individual builders carried on their own programs to reduce costs and build a better house for less. The mobile and prefab home producers made spectacular news with their advances in modular and sectional home systems—a new concept of truly low-cost building.

Each of these developments in a way aided the others. The success of each group—of researchers, builders, home manufacturers, and product manufacturers—was interrelated. For the first time, industry groups worked together, and this may explain why the sixties produced the greatest technological housing advances in U.S. history.

One of the first research approaches to the industrial revolution got under way early in 1960. This was a test house jointly sponsored by NAHB and Michigan State University and erected at Lansing. The consultants and advisors included Koppers Company, Andy Place, Ralph Johnson, Martin Bartling, and Robert Schmitt, who was chairman of NAHB's Research Institute.

This was a far-out project, and many of the ideas *seemed* far out at the time. Yet they helped progress. They included:

1. Insulated floor panels of asbestos cement and polystyrene laid on the ground in winter.
2. Foam-core sandwich panels used in a balloon framing system for a two-story house.
3. Roof panels, 16 feet long, prefinished on both sides.
4. Wiring run through vinyl baseboards.
5. Long ceramic-tile areas laid with synthetic rubber backing over plywood.

In 1961 a dramatic demonstration to show that private builders could put up better low-cost houses than were being built by the federal public housing agencies was staged by the San Antonio, Texas, builders' association. The project, called SARAH, was sparked by Jim Burke, then president of NAHB, and builder Quincy Lee, president of the San Antonio association. The 26 houses, each built by a different builder, were priced at $5,950 to $7,000, and would cost the buyers an average of $50 a month. The city modified its codes to permit new ideas for reducing costs. Manufacturers of materials and equipment cooperated, as did FHA, and a host of new cost-saving ideas were widely publicized and certainly had a helpful effect on costs.

By 1962, the industry was ready for what has been called "the most significant technological event, the most important research project" in home building history. This was TAMAP—the Time, Methods, Analysis Program of NAHB's Research Institute—conducted in cooperation with the industrial engineering department of Stanley Works and builder Robert Schmitt of Berea, Ohio. It was directed by Ralph Johnson, Research Director of NAHB.

Under TAMAP a team of industrial engineers made a two-year observation of the process of building one of Schmitt's houses. A minute, detailed study of every operation was made, using time-lapse photography, stopwatch recording work movements, flow process, design and material analysis. One of the first reports showed the need for a quick-draw nail pouch and a better organized toolbox for workers, as well as the need for an engineered heating duct system, less time-consuming crating of furnaces, and less make-ready and cleanup time. In its summary of advice to building-product manufacturers, TAMAP made the following suggestions:

1. Ascertain what new products builders really need and design to fit that need.

2. Redesign many products to secure simpler installation and less waste.
3. Package products for greater convenience and easy use. Provide better installation instructions.
4. Clearly identify the unique advantages of a product to the builder and the consumer.
5. Give the complete installed cost.

Robert "Bob" Schmitt, builder, adopted and improved on many of the significant research findings which pertained especially to production management techniques such as modular dimensioning, designing for production as well as for sale, work planning, scheduling, purchasing, crew size, supervision, and materials handling. The importance of these production management principles was the key finding of TAMAP. Builders by the thousands adopted many of these principles and used them to produce better-value housing.

In 1963 a different and costly problem of home construction was boldly tackled by NAHB's Research Institute: winter building. The fifth of NAHB's research houses, built by W. Evans Buchanan, demonstrated how to build in winter, with a striking display of new techniques and products. These included:

1. A steel-frame foundation laid on frozen ground.
2. A prefinished roof built in large, ten-foot sections.
3. Large-section, tilt-up frame walls.
4. A tough combination sheathing-siding guaranteed for 15 years.
5. Lightweight steel interior framing.
6. Interior walls with prefinished surfaces, long lasting and easy to clean.
7. Non-warping, prehung doors.
8. Plastic water and plumbing lines.

9. Large molded-plastic bathroom sections or components.
10. Easy-to-install, surface-mounted wiring.
11. Luminous ceilings in kitchen, bath, hall, and family room.

The sixth NAHB research house, built in 1966, was a well-publicized showcase of home-building innovations that could improve on existing techniques, but which were held back by archaic codes. NAHB's Research Institute and its Research Foundation made maximum use of new glues, adhesives, laminates, and plastics, and designed wood and plywood components for greater capacities.

The technological progress of the industry had far outrun the building codes of the country. The new products and systems were lightyears ahead of local codes. The sixth NAHB research house not only dramatized the technological advance in products, but projected systems that a small builder of 6-10 homes a year could use—if codes would permit.

No one today can say exactly what the total effects of the sixth research house were, but industry-wide, they must have been great. It showed that new techniques and new products made amazing advances in construction possible, if only the codes would permit.

We shall attempt to encapsulate what Research House No. 6 tried to demonstrate (some observers said it tried to do too much too soon):

● A roof system framed by two-by-four trusses on four-foot centers. They were spanned by ⅝-inch nailed and glued plywood.

- A floor system of wide-spaced, two-by-six floor joists, aided by glue-nailed members for added strength.
- Glue-nailed plywood skins that helped compensate for lighter, wider-spaced framing.
- Plywood, trusses, and other components, tested under extreme conditions at the NAHB Research Foundations's testing and research labs, Rockville, Maryland, that could be easily handled and installed by a small builder crew.
- End-glued joints and framing, laminated beams, and glue-nailed splice plates and gussetts that added to the strength of members.
- New adhesives for producing laminated, double-faced gypsum-board interior wall and ceiling panels.
- Wood sash and frames of windows and sliding doors that were clad with factory-applied white vinyl material, impervious to rot.
- A neoprene gasket for sealing the joints in the cast iron and waste vent pipes, saving time and effort.
- Low-cost aluminum flashing, fascia, and gutters designed in cooperation with Reynolds Metals that cut installation costs.
- A roof vent system any small builder could use.
- Textured cedar siding flash sheathing to practically eliminate upkeep.

Unlike much of the industrial revolution of the sixties, NAHB Research House No. 6 was planned to help the smaller builders of the country do a better job. Its success was unmeasurable, but it was widely publicized and observed and undoubtedly stimulated thousands of small builders from Oshkosh to Os-

caloosa to think about new ways to build better—the basic way progress takes place in this far-flung industry.

Again in 1968, NAHB's Research Institute and Research Foundation brought their efforts to bear on a very tough problem: housing for the hard-core slum areas of the nation. No one yet has solved this problem. NAHB's idea was that rugged, fire-resistant precast concrete townhouses might be the answer.

So in 1968 the NAHB research house was dedicated in Washington, D.C., to a solution of inner-city housing problems. A cluster of precast concrete townhouses of modest size was designed. They were built around a court, using heavy-stock, precast panels for walls, floors, and roofs. The panels were large but built of lightweight aggregate, and each panel included preinstalled windows and doors. A huge crane hoisted each wall panel into place—and it was not easy. These were intended to be safe, secure, low-cost units for inner-city building. Again, it is hard to say what the total effect was, but in this area of urban work, very little has been accomplished due to such an overwhelming series of problems, and to this day no one has arrived with an answer.

We now come to the near-end of the decade, the spring of 1969. It was an expansive year, and this may account for the fact that one of the biggest, most expensive, and most exhaustive test/demonstration house projects of the decade flourished in Austin, Texas. It was sponsored by The University of Texas at Austin, financed by a $360,000 grant from HUD, and supported by building-product manufacturers and a host of small builders.

The project was Austin Oaks: ten small, low-cost houses built by small local firms with the backing of research groups, industrial giants, and HUD grants. The advance publicity said that a team of engineers, architects, and social scientists from The University of Texas would analyze each house. They were to be sized up for their design, acoustics, comfort, and cost—and also for their psychological and sociological impact.

The local builders—mostly very small operators—were overwhelmed by the national publicity by giant corporations, psychologists, government researchers, and many others. These ten houses threw much light on how small local building firms could do something to build a better low-cost house:

1. *Wood-frame panels* with aluminum facing formed the walls of a 768-square-foot house. Bathroom and kitchen walls were covered with laminated plastic.

2. *Prefinished stressed-skin modules.* $12'' \times 45\frac{1}{2}''$, were the components of a 1,080-square-foot home.

3. *Aluminum-skin panels* with honeycomb cores were used for walls and roofs of this 784-square-foot house. Kitchen and bath plumbing were prefabricated.

4. *A mobile home that expanded* with a pitched roof was trucked to the site in two sections to produce a 717-square-foot house (built by Magnolia Homes of Vicksburg).

5. *Concrete sacks were used.* An imaginative builder, Dickson Stack of Dallas, used 50-pound sacks of concrete for the walls.

6. *Precast concrete set in aluminum frames.* The Lockheed Aircraft Service Corporation provided the system for this 718-square-foot house. The four-by-eight-by-two-foot panels were cast at the site in aluminum channels.

7. *Precast frame with curtain walls* comprised a component-system house of 654 square feet for fast erection, low cost.

8. *Asbestos cement* extrusions for walls made one of the lowest-cost units, with only 591 square feet. The Certain-Teed wall system consisted of panels of asbestos cement set between posts.

9. *Concrete block walls.* This was a conventional 720-square-foot house of concrete blocks by the Chanen Construction Company. It was built in 21 days and priced at $6,350.

10. *Modified mobile* on concrete piers. This 672-square-foot unit by National Homes Corporation was set in place with a large crane. It was completely equipped and decorated at the factory.

Individual builders were also hard at work at new industrialized techniques—many complementing the industry efforts. John Long of Phoenix built a 100,000-square-foot shop with power saws and advanced equipment to produce large components, foam-core partitions, trusses, and gable ends. Trusses were built on jig tables at the rate of one a minute, all interior partitions for one house were built in 20 minutes, kitchen counters were built in 20 minutes, doors prehung in five minutes.

At the site, tilt-up partitions were set in 30 minutes, large gable ends hoisted in place by crane in four minutes, and 1.5 miles of curb and sidewalk laid by a huge special machine in one day.

Builder Andy Place of South Bend continued his demonstration of cost-saving techniques by prefabbing all parts for a 600-house project in 1964 in an on-site factory. He built wall sections, windows, components, gable ends, trusses, panel sections, and much else in the shop and moved them on low-boy trailers for fast erection in winter as well as in summer.

San Francisco builder Kenneth Hoffman was another innovative builder who put industrialized techniques to work. In 1967 he was constructing 600 homes a year on five tracts, and claimed he saved $2,000 a house by his mechanized methods. He spent $100,000 for equipment, including four-wheel drive forklifts, 24-foot reach tractors, huge dump trucks, nailing guns, impact wrenches, special drills, saws, and power equipment. He employed skillful scheduling and planning, built special racks and bins, and used packaged lumber and components. He was a good example of the power of enterprise, ingenuity, and inventiveness at work to bring down costs.

Building efficiency in the late sixties was also aided by the emergence of well-financed giants which were able to employ advanced computer technology and management techniques. One of these was the Critical Path Method, or CPM system, of job control. Some of the pioneers who used it were Charles Cheesem of St. Petersburg, Florida; Edward Bennett of Bethesda, Maryland; Richard Fox of Philadelphia; and John Minchew of Annandale, Virginia.

The Changing Prefab, Mobile, Modular, and Sectional Home Market

The biggest news in the prefab and mobile-home industries of the sixties was the emergence of the factory-built sectional house. Both prefab and mobile-home firms joined this crusade swiftly, and "Wide Load" signs were greeting highway drivers all over the country as the frighteningly large house sections were trucked to their sites.

Usually the houses were built in two or three sections which could be set easily on prepared foundations and joined together at the site. They were delivered complete with interior and exterior finish, utility connections, wiring, plumbing, carpeting, kitchen, and baths. The idea caught on rapidly, and by 1966 sales of mobile, modular, and sectional homes reached a high of 225,000 units, or about 20% of the single-family home market.

This rapid growth actually came to the housing industry's rescue by filling a horrendous gap at the low-cost end. And when floods, hurricanes, and other disasters struck, such as hurricane Camille in 1969, these miracle constructions were rushed to thousands of homeless. HUD alone supplied 5,000 units to victims in Mississippi, Louisiana, and Virginia who were in Camille's path.

The sectional-home idea was both a part and an outgrowth of what was generally called "modular construction"—a term subject to broad definition. In a wider sense, the term was applied to many types of work employing self-contained building modules. A spectacular example was Habitat '67 at the Montreal World's Fair. Here, 354 fully finished concrete cubes, or boxes, were stacked in a 13-level pyramid to produce 158 dwellings. It was the biggest attraction of the fair, and did much to focus public interest on modular building.

Another striking example of modular building was the erection of the San Antonio, Texas, Hilton Hotel in 1968, by builder Henry B. Zachry. Here the precast and prefinished concrete boxes were hoisted into place with a huge crane. Each module was fully furnished in the shop and delivered with carpeting, curtains, and pictures on the wall. Zachry completed the job in nine months and went on to use the same system in apartment and urban-renewal projects. He later manufactured and sold similar modules to Middle Eastern oil-producing countries. They were shipped by boat and delivered furnished and ready for living.

"A self-contained package of living space" was the title used to describe the modular home unveiled in spectacular fashion at the Seattle World's Fair in 1961. The completely finished and furnished units were dropped into place by crane. They were designed by architect Robert M. Englebrecht using the Panelbild system of U.S. Plywood and decorated by *American Home* magazine. The modules were flexible enough to make a variety of homes, and a typical unit was $12' \times 24' \times 9'$.

The modular-building concept was seized on by a number of home and apartment builders with varying degrees of success. The biggest splash was made in 1968 by Sterling Homes of Rochester, which for a time was the talk of the industry as well as the stock market. The compact boxes, or modules, were built in a fully automated factory—one every 45 minutes, it was claimed. They were trucked to the site and stacked with a crane to create large apartment and townhouse complexes. Technically the system appeared successful, but the firm encountered financial problems as it tried both to produce the modules and engage in developing projects in which to use them. It later went out of business amid charges of fraud and mismanagement. Its factory production methods were good, however.

The prefabricated-home manufacturing industry was able to expand its field in the late sixties by getting into the lively apartment and townhouse market. The new idea was to sell a package concept. Firms such as National, Scholz, Kingsberry, Presidential, U.S. Steel, and others offered a galaxy of special services to help builders succeed. These included feasibility studies, site evaluation, rezoning assistance, site layout, cost control, job scheduling, market-tested designs, financial aid, decorating, and marketing help.

All was not rosy in the prefab industry, however. Alside Homes of Akron built a $7 million push-button plant in 1963 to produce slick, modern, steel and glass homes. They were lovingly designed by modernists and acclaimed by architectural critics. The plan was to sell 15,000 a year. They did not sell, however. After nine months and a loss of many millions, production was stopped—they were "too modern," builders said.

One of the most interesting technical achievements of the prefab industry during the decade was the development of mechanical core units of various types. One pioneer was Albert P. Hildebrandt, president of Kingsberry Homes of Atlanta, Georgia. He built an efficient central-core unit that contained a fully equipped kitchen, two baths, and a heating/utility unit. It was designed to be trucked to a prepared site and quickly connected; the house would then be built around it. It was technically sound, but immediately encountered code and union problems. It did, however, pave the way for many later developments in mechanical and plumbing cores.

Prefab news was also made by the Air Force, which in 1965 developed a two-story relocatable house with fold-out walls. It was supposed to be compact, lightweight, and capable of being erected in 48 hours. Later the Defense Department built prototypes of a fold-out unit for military families. The walls were designed to fold from a center unit containing all utilities, kitchen, and bath. Neither were spectacularly successful.

Late in the decade the growth of large shelter conglomerates brought mergers, acquisitions, and joint ventures that blurred the lines between prefab, mobile-home, and building operations. Giant mobile-home firms bought into builder operations, and large builders bought into mobile homes. It was predicted that "total housing companies" would emerge which would produce factory-built units and develop housing projects and mobile-home parks. Some of this did take place.

A mobile-home park boom developed in 1969, partly as a result of the huge U.S. highway programs. The giant housing firms poured capital into new, better planned mobile-home parks which often had playgounds, swimming pools, and recreational areas. An estimated 100,000 such parks were developed by 1969. The housing and mobile-home industry thus made at least a token effort to meet the demand for decent housing for low-income families.

Product Upbeat

Extensive and expensive research, development, and promotion of building products continued apace during this decade. That American homes became the envy of the world for their super-equipped kitchens, elegant bathrooms, and fine heating, lighting, and air conditioning was no accident. U.S. industry worked hard, spent vast sums for research, and then perfected improved distribution and servicing systems. Since products and equipment were increasingly technical in nature, the new servicing networks manned by trained personnel were highly important, and did much to ensure satisfactory operation.

Industry leaders also did a great deal to promote the new and better products to builders and the public. One example was the "Live Better Electrically" program in which thousands of builders' model homes were awarded gold medals for meeting high standards of wiring, lighting, equipment, and kitchen planning. Millions of visitors paraded through the models, which were well publicized in trade and consumer publications.

The electrical industry also promoted underground wiring, which was aided by new cables and direct-burial trenching techniques that helped cut costs. Builders as well as buyers were happy to have their projects relieved of the maze of poles and wires that disfigured their planned communities.

Frost-free refrigerators also made strong head-way in the early sixties, as did automatic ice makers, thin-wall insulation to increase storage, separate freezer compartments, and vastly improved finishes, shelf arrangements, and interior appointments.

The gas industry, not to be outshone by electricity, also embarked on huge research and marketing programs. The rapid growth of gas pipelines increased supply and the need for new markets. Fast-moving technological change brought about cheaper, compact gas-heating units; fast, automatic gas cooking;

and more efficient water heaters and clothes dryers. To promote all of these a national model-home building and promotion program was carried on by local utilities with the cooperation of builders, product manufacturers, and trade and consumer magazines. The models were often extravagantly decorated and equipped, and included such niceties as outdoor gas lamps and gas barbecues.

The lumber and plywood industries also carried on extensive home promotions, and they had much to talk about. Grading and trademarking lumber was made mandatory by FHA in 1960, which did much to raise quality and prevent the use of substandard products. Manufactured lumber of glued and laminated pieces made its appearance. Beams, trusses, and structural members gained new capacities from laminations, connectors, glues, and adhesives.

New wood paneling of laminated layers with durable finishes appeared, as well as veneer surfaces in exotic natural woods or rough-sawed textures. Wood flooring in thin laminated sections was designed for bonding to subfloors with mastic adhesive. Plywood manufacturers researched, developed, and promoted a remarkable series of components and structural systems for homes and apartments.

Perhaps the most striking progress was made by the plastic industry which researched and developed hundreds of new products and applications. One of the most talked about houses at the 1964 New York World's Fair was the "Plastic Laminate House" built by Formica Corporation and designed by architect Emil Schmidlin of Summit, New Jersey. It dramatized the increasing uses of plastics and finishes and later was duplicated by hundreds of builders in promotional projects across the country. *Good Housekeeping* deco-

rated the models and published the plans of many of them.

Use of plastics skyrocketed. Some of the most notable uses were tubs, shower stalls, and complete one-piece bathroom units of reinforced plastic. They were colorful, easy to clean, and easy to install. Man-made marble vanities and countertops of plastics were also produced and became very popular. Plastic-coated wallboards and plastic laminates in large decorated panels were popular. Plastic waste and vent pipes made progress as well as some prefab plastic-pipe plumbing assemblies which were lightweight and easy to install. But plastic floor and wall tile, paneling, and shower-stall enclosures were the big-volume producers.

In a related field, urethane foam moved strongly into the building market. The sprayed-on foam expanded to fill space and crevices, forming a tight, rigid, weather seal. Urethane foam sheets were also widely used to insulate concrete slabs and foundation walls.

Structural panels of a variety of new types and materials were marketed by many firms. Sandwich panels had a urethane foam core with exteriors of plywood, gypsum, or aluminum. Stressed-skin plywood components were designed for use in prefab panel systems. Components such as packaged door and window units, storage walls, and trusses were marketed by large firms with a national distribution system.

A significant advance was made by heating and air-conditioning manufacturers who produced compact, efficient package units that could be slipped into place with a minimum of on-site work.

They included rooftop, attic, and closet units, and used prefab ducts and preengineered connections. The result was a reduction in air-conditioning costs as this market skyrocketed. Even the smallest homes and apartments were able to afford this popular comfort equipment.

Research by the carpet and textile industries brought another change: the use of indoor-outdoor carpets with remarkable resistance to weather or discoloration. Builders were soon putting them on terraces and patios, and in bathrooms, kitchens, and recreation rooms.

Kitchen/laundry appliance manufacturers carried on perhaps the most exhaustive technological and domestic-science research of any industry. Firms like General Motors and General Electric put all their talents—which were considerable—to work on ranges, dishwashers, refrigerators, dryers, and a host of other electrical devices. They also trained kitchen planners, home economists, and psychologists to devise the best in home appli-

ances. Some of the results were the compact, "drop-in" units that fit into standard building floor plans. They often designed the kitchen so that each piece of equipment was placed for step-saving use.

Luminous ceiling systems also contributed their glow to an increasing number of homes in the sixties. A variety of lightweight prefab systems appeared. A popular one consisted of luminous fiberglass panels suspended on an aluminum grid. It came precut and easy to install, and provided a soft fluorescent glow. Builders soon extended its use to baths, kitchens, halls, and recreation rooms.

All of these innovations did not just happen. They were the results of costly research, hard work, industry ingenuity, and skillful marketing. For that, American homeowners owe industry a vote of thanks.

How Uncle Sam Helped—Or Did He?

President Kennedy had his New Frontiers, Johnson his Great Society, and Nixon his forgotten Americans. Each pledged undying aid to low- and middle-income housing and urban renewal. But invariably the public housing/urban renewal projects became bogged down in political problems and confusion. The only real housing volume was achieved by the private sector, which produced 14 million of the 14.42 million units, or 97.5%.

In all fairness, it must be said that other national problems dwarfed housing, notably Vietnam, civil rights, and antiwar demonstrations throughout the country. Despite these, the economy was increasingly prosperous and the demand for homes great. Congress debated long and hard and succeeded in enacting

three major housing acts: the acts of 1961, 1965, and 1968. Each attempted to spur public housing and urban renewal, but ended up aiding private work through financial incentives to FHA, VA, HOLC, FNMA, and GNMA. Congress also enacted significant civil rights legislation that profoundly affected housing.

The Housing Act of 1961 was described by President Kennedy as "a giant step toward better cities and improved housing." He emphasized his campaign commitments to big-city and Negro voters and appointed Robert C. Weaver to direct the program as head of the Housing and Home Finance agency. Weaver was a cultured and highly educated black with a Harvard Ph.D., who strove hard to make the complex 1961 act work. Features of this act included:

1. A drastic cut in FHA down payments to 3% and extension of the loan period to 35 years.
2. Aid to repair and rehabilitation work, especially in run-down urban areas. Remodeling loans up to $10,000 running for 20 years at 6% interest were called for.
3. A giant $1.2-billion fund for low-cost veterans' mortgages at low interest.
4. Expanded aid to financing of condominiums, experimental housing, and housing for the elderly, and aid for farm housing.

FHA loans on condominiums were also permitted, as were aid and grants for community facilities, land acquisition, mass transit, college housing, and nursing homes. New funds for the Federal National Mortgage Association were provided, permitting it to expand its financing aids.

The act also established a controversial "below market rate" FHA insurance program for subsidized middle-income rental housing. This new Section 221-(d)3 permitted no-down payment FHA loans at $3\frac{1}{8}$% interest for 40 years.

The public housing, urban renewal, and mass-transit sections got scant attention, and Congress later cut their grants. But Section 221-(d)3, which subsidized rentals constructed by private builders, zoomed fantastically. Housing starts rose to 1.49 million in 1962 and a high of 1.64 million in 1963. Low interest rates were a major factor in this boom. At the same time, public housing dropped to 30,000 in 1962 and 32,000 in 1963 and 1964.

President Johnson set the tone of the Housing Act of 1965 when he declared that "the ul-

timate goal in our free-enterprise system must be a decent home for every American family." The act did not quite achieve this end, but it did make sweeping changes and create a bold rent-supplement plan to help the poor. Robert C. Weaver became the first black cabinet officer as the new secretary of housing and urban development.

Features of the 1965 Housing Act included:

1. No-down FHA loans up to $15,000 for veterans.
2. Sharply lower down payments for houses valued greater than $20,000.
3. FHA-insured loans for land development.
4. Larger mortgages for low-priced homes in outlying areas and near military installations.
5. Insured long-term, low-interest loans for farm homes by the Farmers' Home Administration.

President Johnson hailed the $5.3 billion Housing and Urban Development Act of 1968 as "a Magna Carta to liberate our cities," and it was called the most ambitious housing bill in the nation's history. While it did indeed aid housing, it did not make the sweeping reforms promised.

1. Section 235 provided an interest-rate subsidy for the poor that cut mortgage interest to 1%. Families earning $3,000-$7,000 could buy houses for as little as $200 down and monthly payments equal to 20% of their income. A rent-supplement plan, Section 236, also reduced rental costs for low-income families.
2. The new Government National Mortgage Association (Ginnie May) was established to guarantee securities of the

Federal National Mortgage Association (Fanny May) and other securities backed by FHA and VA loans. This paved the way for vast new sources of mortgage finance through the issuance of mortgage-backed securities.
3. FHA mortgage ceilings, as well as home improvement loan limits, were increased. FHA was also allowed to insure vacation-home mortgages.
4. Housing and Urban Development (HUD) was authorized to guarantee bonds, notes, and debentures of new-town developments up to $50 million. It was also given $1.4 billion for urban renewal and $350 million for its model-cities programs.
5. A National Housing Partnership plan was set up to encourage giant corporations to pool resources to invest in low-income housing in blighted urban areas. Edgar Kaiser of California's Kaiser Industries was appointed its first head.

During the sixties, the quality and number of housing units soared. But for the minorities, the poor, the disadvantaged, the war protestors, and many others the decade is often thought of as "the angry decade." The assassination of Martin Luther King, race riots in many cities, and violent reaction to racial discrimination had a powerful impact on builders and on housing.

In the early sixties, builders were slowly and rather painfully adjusting to the anti-bias law of 1958 and to many new state laws. Some builders resisted, acting only on the basis of court orders. But history then moved rapidly.

By 1961 the clamor against racial discrimination in housing brought the Civil Rights Act of 1961 which opened many new doors. Then in December 1961, President Kennedy issued an executive order in effect forbidding any racial bias or discrimination in FHA or VA housing. In 1963, FHA ordered an end to job bias on all its projects. In 1964 another civil rights act advanced open housing of all types. Following Martin Luther King's death on April 4, the new stringent Civil Rights Act of 1968 was passed. The bill effectively forbade discrimination in sale or rental of practically all U.S. housing.

CHAPTER FIVE

1970-1980

BIG BUSINESS AND BIG GOVERNMENT

Housing's Greatest Decade

Housing history in the seventies was sharply etched in events that reflected the tumultuous, turbulent, and sensational life of America in those years.

Home buyers and home builders were rocked by tight money, double-digit inflation, sky-high interest rates, the energy crunch, and a drastic building depression in 1973-1975 that bankrupted 1,500 building firms.

Problems and events tumbled over one another, bringing stunning changes in the affairs of builders. They were blocked and bludgeoned by new obstacles from environmental and no-growth activists, building codes, exclusionary zoning, and frenetic financial confusion, the latter caused by federal deficit financing.

Yet the years 1970-1979 were housing's greatest decade: a remarkable era when 17.8 million housing units were built—the largest number in U.S. history. Even more astonishing, the single-family home—the epitome of the American dream—became a heartening reality to millions of Americans when 12,361,000 were built—an all-time high and a surprising advance.

Housing starts topped two million units for the first time in 1971 and again in 1972, 1973, and 1978. They plunged to 1,171,000 in the "tight money" building depression of 1975, bringing despair, disaster, and bankruptcy to hundreds of builders, caused by factors beyond their control.

But home owners fared extremely well in the decade, perhaps better than any other group of Americans. The value of their homes increased faster than inflation, and the average home that sold for $25,000 in 1970 was selling for $68,000 or more in 1979.

The equity value of some 55 million single-family homes rose to $1.6 trillion. The inventory of occupied housing—single family, condominiums, co-ops, and apartments—rose to 88 million units, and citizens of the USA continued unquestionably to be better and more comfortably housed than those of any other nation in the world.

Also, millions of Americans became convinced that owning a home was the best of all investments, surpassing stocks, bonds, gold, or any other. As the decade passed, it became increasingly clear that home ownership was a prime hedge against inflation, and that property could be used and enjoyed while values rose. And as equity values increased, millions of home owners discovered they could borrow on their home's equity, or refinance to raise money to buy cars, cruises, college educations, business expansion, or a new room addition.

The soaring equity values of older homes became a powerful aid to new home buying in the seventies. Owners could easily "trade up" to better, more expensive homes by selling at the new inflationary price. The "domino effect" was neatly outlined in 1977 by Maxwell Huntoon, publisher of *House and Home* magazine: The man who bought a $100,000 house, he explained, could usually do so because he had just sold for $75,000 a house that had cost him $35,000: he had a $40,000 equity to apply. Likewise, the man who bought the $75,000 home was able to do it because he got $50,000 for the little ranch cottage he had paid $29,990 for eight years before. And so it went.

We must review the progress of housing in the seventies in the context of the harrowing but often heartening ups and downs of these ten years:

- The Vietnam war.
- The spectacle of a President conspiring to his own downfall and disgrace.
- The OPEC oil embargo—energy crunch and rampant inflation.
- Tight-money policies set forth by the Federal Reserve that often stifled building growth and development.
- A tax revolt starting in California which

spread nationwide that affected housing.
- No-growth activists who tried to stop needed building, regardless of merit.
- An increase in U.S. social and cultural values—education, art, ballet, opera, music, architecture, and creative living design.
- An enormous increase in the quality and design of American housing and the amenities of living in a good environment.
- A new maturity to building operations and firms that brought better design, planning, construction techniques, management concepts, and higher values.

We must also consider two prime factors in the change and growth of housing in the seventies. The first was a vast population movement from inner cities to suburbs, and then to outer suburbs and to close-by country and rural areas.

This movement brought industry, shopping centers, and building projects to widely dispersed rural and country areas adjacent to both towns and cities but served by an expanded highway system.

Another great population move took place: an amazing push to the so-called sun-belt areas—to the south and west. The effect on the building industry was tremendous and produced a monumental dispersal of builders and projects over wide areas.

A second and now well-known change was the striking movement of women out of the kitchen and into industry. Working women combined their income with husbands to buy more costly houses. They also became prime markets for small apartments and condominiums. Among the changes were a 50% increase in women heading households and a 100% increase in the number of unmarried couples sharing a household. The fastest growing segment of the population at the end of the decade was the 25-34 age group—a prime group of first-time home buyers.

Taken together, these changes brought new marketing targets for builders and new design concepts to serve these first-time buyers, singles, young professional couples, empty-nesters, and priced-out young families.

Of all the forces at work on housing and builders during the decade, the most powerful were the monetary and financial policies of the federal government. Dr. Arthur Burns, chairman of the Federal Reserve system for many years, was the prime villain to most building men. They saw housing starts rise or crash, time after time, as a result of the Fed's actions. Perhaps the most drastic was the tight-money building depression that brought U.S. starts tumbling from 1973's 2,058,000 level to 1,171,400 in 1975. Hundreds of building, real estate, and financial firms were forced into bankruptcy and the losses were in the multi-billions. Again the culprit was government spending funds it did not have.

Despite these problems, the industry rallied and ended the decade on a high of 2,023,000

starts in 1978 and 1,750,000 in 1979. It was a high that was, unhappily, doomed to early change. The year 1979 was a turning point of great significance, not only to housing but to the nation as a whole, and can be compared—in an economic sense—to the turning point of 1929 fifty years before.

The end of the seventies marked the end of the nation's unquestioned dominance in world affairs. The government appeared to have lost the ability to control inflation and protect the value of the dollar. It no longer controlled oil supplies and production, and its influence among foreign nations had ebbed.

Still, there was optimism that problems would be solved. Builders who had come through the seventies with flying colors were looking forward to new technologies, better design, and new approaches to financing and management, and planning for a happier environment. But then, builders are irrepressible optimists; they have to be or they could not last long in the topsy-turvy housing industry. Yet it should have been apparent that the basis for still greater crises in housing was being laid, as history so unerringly recorded later.

Demographic Changes Alter U.S. Housing and Living

A dynamic, far-reaching movement and change in U.S. population had unexpected effects on housing and life styles. Here are several of the major forces that were at work:

1. A monumental population move from urban complexes to outer suburbs and to outlying counties, small towns, and rural communities outside the metropolitan centers.

2. A major shift of home buyers to the so-called sun-belt states—especially to Arizona, California, Florida, New Mexico, Texas, and the southeastern states.

3. A sensational eruption of women from home and kitchen to office, factory, gas station, or bank.

4. A striking change in family size, formation, age, and structure—more elderly persons, buyers aged 25-34, and more small family units made up of working

women, single men, divorced parties, and single men and women living together.

The effect of these was to radically alter the market for new housing and the types and locations of structures builders were selling as the decade closed. Builders were forced to move into new areas, build smaller units—many attached, and more two-, four- and six-plex units, condominiums, and town houses. Most suprising of all was the increase in sales in mid-decade of single-family homes, fueled largely by the working wives who helped meet the monthly mortgage payments. These population changes altered the face of U.S. housing.

"Countrified cities," appeared. Although U.S. population as a whole increased only a modest 11.4% in the 1970s, the migration of people, industry, and commerce from urban areas to the countryside was immense—in fact, a major national phenomena. President Jimmy Carter highlighted the back-to-the-countryside trend in December 1979 when he enunciated a "small community and rural development" policy.

"The demographic trends of the 1950s and 1960s—the migration of people from rural areas into cities—has reversed," he said. "Since 1970 the population of the rural areas has increased 40% more than has the population of urban areas. The rural area is growing, becoming more diverse."

This unprecedented rural growth was extensively documented in a 1979 report by the Urban Land Institute (ULI) of Washington, D.C., entitled *Growth and Change in Rural America*. Glenn V. Fuguitt and Paul R. Voss, two University of Wisconsin rural sociologists prepared the basic studies, which showed that:

- For perhaps the first time in U.S. history, non-metropolitan areas were growing faster than metropolitan areas.
- The most rapid growth in the countryside was taking place in the most rural counties, i.e. those with the smallest urban centers or with none at all.
- Open country (unincorporated) communities in rural counties and townships were growing faster than small towns and cities in those counties.
- Non-metropolitan growth was a widespread phenomenon found in every U.S. census region. It was, in the words of the ULI report, "geographically pervasive," and even included the supposedly lagging Northeast.

A number of conditions came together in the 1970s to accelerate growth and change in formerly stagnant rural towns and areas.

These included the technical revolution in agriculture, freeing farm labor for other work and forcing state and local leaders to seek alternative industries; increased demand for raw materials and minerals, such as coal, produced in rural areas; federal and state government activity that channeled money, manpower, and project resources into once-isolated communities; a rapid rise in the number of people able to escape to the countryside in search of quiet, safe retirement havens and alternative life styles; the outward creep of the metropolis, which scattered low-density urbanization over ever widening circles—"urban fields," as they were called.

The ULI report also described a new form of urbanization on the U.S. scene as a result of these trends: the "countrified city"—a small town extended to the geographic scale of the county, where older rural municipalities and newer shopping centers were evolving into central business and service centers for the increasing numbers of people living along the country roads and in the mini-suburbs springing up in the countryside.

U.S. census estimates show that from 1970 to 1980, areas outside the orbit of the cities showed a net gain of three million people. The increase was stimulated by agricultural, industrial, mining, and service jobs, retirement pensions, and miles of new, easy-access highways. The growth areas became the location of thousands of new home projects and scattered lot building, and cannot be classified as rural, suburban, or urban, but a mixture of all three.

Near thousands of the nation's smaller towns and cities, U.S. industry built sophisticated plants that attracted workers from miles of surrounding rural areas—workers willing to work for lower incomes because they prefer rural and small-town living.

A fair example is Nash County, North Carolina, whose county seat is Nashville, a small but growing community. Within Nash County's 580 square miles are 120 prosperous industries, and between 5:30 a.m. and 8:00 a.m., hundreds of workers may be seen hurrying in pickup trucks, old Fords, Chevies, and some new Detroit models, heading for work. They travel along networks of good black top highways and feeder roads free of traffic jams. And they come from farm houses, rural homes, small subdivisions, trailer parks, and hundreds of country houses spread out along the rural roads.

Robert L. Bridewell, Nash County's local planning expert, reported a rash of new small-home subdivisions in 1979. Many were on land sold off by farmers. Few had water or sewer systems and most were serviced by private wells and septic tanks. Although many workers lived on farms and in rural homes, he

said, there was a strong liking for the small countryside subdivisions away from the town, and they were increasing in size and number.

This story could be repeated a thousand times about rural communities from coast to coast. It is clear that this nation-wide movement of people, industry, home projects, shopping centers, industrial parks, and educational facilities was one of the most vital changes of the decade, with major impact on the housing industry. The American public tends to think of the building industry in terms of large firms and projects in or near big cities. But a far greater volume of work nationally is carried on by tens of thousands of small building firms working in thousands of scattered locations in and around small towns and cities and in the outlying countryside.

The back-to-the-country movement of home building also contributed strongly to the high volume of single-family homes built in the seventies. Lower costs, especially land costs, contributed much. But by far the most significant factor was the basic desire of Americans for a quieter, cleaner, less hectic environment.

A few statistics from the 1980 census reinforces the view that this decade was indeed housing's greatest, with production and quality far exceeding expectations. There was a net gain of 20 million housing units, a rise of 28%, bringing the total to 88,277,000 as compared with the April 1970 total of 68,704,000. Thus the number of housing units increased at a rate more than double the population growth. And a significant decrease in the number of residents per household took place—a drop from 3.33 persons per household in 1964 to 2.75 persons in 1980. Americans, obviously, were enjoying the luxury of more living space.

Skyrocketing House Prices, Capital Gains, and Mortgage Borrowing

Of all the sensational stories of housing in the seventies, the most striking is the merry-go-round of house prices, capital gains, and mortgage borrowing practices that took place.

House values rose in astonishing fashion: they doubled between 1970 and 1977 and continued to soar into the eighties. Alan Greenspan, a nationally known economist, estimated in 1977 that the market value of the nation's entire stock of single-family, owner-occupied homes was increasing at an annual rate of $62.2 billion.

Even more striking was the impact of soaring home prices on new house sales, mortgage borrowing, and consumer spending. Home buyers found they had undreamed-of new equity values which could be used to buy a new house or car, a trip to Europe, or all three. They happily proceeded to cash in on this novel new source of wealth and consumer credit, with the result that mortgage borrowing soared astronomically.

Greenspan's studies revealed the close relationships among inflation, house prices, capital gains, mortgage borrowing, and consumer spending. He calculated that in 1977, when housing equity increased in value by $62.2 billion, new mortgages written grew at a $60.2 billion annual rate. Thus virtually the entire increase in housing value was monetized, i.e. cashed in, as mortgage debt extensions.

What this did was to pump $60.2 billion into consumers' pockets—a $60.2 billion assist to housing and the economy. It helped the U.S. climb out of the 1975 recession and spurred housing production to record levels. It also, of course, helped fuel the fires of inflation. The principle cause of inflation, however, was excessive government spending.

A vast "trade-up" movement in homes swept the country in the late seventies and was largely responsible for the sustained high level of sales. The stories of "trade-ups" are legion, in all levels of price and from coast to coast. Thousands of owners sold their houses at double or triple their original cost. They then used the proceeds to buy a bigger and better place, and often had money left over for education, travel, or a few luxuries.

The higher equities home owners found they possessed often were used to improve the old house, buy a car, or even finance a business. They could re-finance, re-negotiate, or even arrange a large second mortgage for these purposes. The new mortgage usually was at a higher rate of interest. But most home owners of the late seventies were ready to assume the cost, and they could not envision that their house's value might go down.

Contributing to the continuing housing boom in the seventies was the belief, held by millions, that a home of your own was the best possible investment and a safe hedge against inflation. Studies in 1977 indicated also that capital gains from housing were running triple the size of gains taken by private investors on the stock market. So home buyers reasoned they could live in and enjoy a home, obtain a large profit on their investment, and even borrow money for extra luxuries. Thus the "fringe benefits" of home ownership!

Financing the Housing Boom of the Seventies

The most remarkable or perhaps notable aspect of the 17.8 million starts in the seventies was that it occurred at all. And then, that which did happen was almost solely the result of private initiative and finance, not government planning or subsidy.

The obstacles to housing growth in the decade were overwhelming: political and economic chaos, war threats, the oil embargo, the energy crunch, double-digit inflation, record-high interest rates, and violent opposition to home construction projects from environmentalists, local zoning groups, and "no growth" activists who viewed any and all home building as a threat to their particular concept of life.

Overshadowing the industry at all times was what builders called "Dr. Burns' tight-money cure." This referred to the Federal Reserve's monetary policies as directed by Dr. Arthur Burns, FRB chairman from 1969 to 1978. Most housing men—and undoubtedly all of the 1,500 who went bankrupt in the 1973-1975 recession—blamed their problems on Burns' conservative tight-money policies. NAHB president George Martin protested in October, 1973: "The housing needs of our people are being sacrificed on the altars of high interest and tight money."

This was a conflict that has persisted through the years. It is true that when interest rates climb, housing usually tumbles. Certainly the 9% FHA rate, 12% prime rate, and 16% construction-loan rates of 1973-1975 brought housing starts crashing down. They dropped from a record 2.38 million in 1972 to a low 1.17 million in 1975. Hundreds of large builders and mortgage finance and investment trusts (REITs) went bankrupt or took fearful

losses in equity and stock values. The total of U.S. losses was in the billions—possibly more than those sustained in the stock market crash of 1929.

Government policies and housing laws under Presidents Nixon, Ford, and Carter also had their effect on housing. Each promised flamboyant programs to stimulate low-income housing, urban renewal, and slum clearance. And, as in the past, the public-housing portions were soon bogged down in politics and confusion. The public programs that did get under way were plagued by so many problems that few housing units were built.

It is here that we must draw some distinction between housing built by government agencies or with direct government subsidies and private housing aided indirectly by federal support to financial institutions. In the latter category, agencies such as the Federal Housing Administration, the Federal National Mortgage Association, the Government National Mortgage Association, and Federal Home Loan Mortgage Corporation all contributed mightily to the building boom of the seventies. These were essentially government-backed or insured agencies that aided the financing of private-enterprise building and stimulated the flow of mortgage funds into building. All were self supporting.

The Federal Home Loan Mortgage Corporation (called the Mortgage Corporation) was chartered by Congress in 1970 to increase the availability of residential mortgage financing, principally by developing and supporting an active secondary market in conventional residential mortgages. It buys residential mortgages from lenders and sells mortgage securities which represent undivided interests in pools of mortgages. It operates as a privately operated, government-supervised entity which showed a $25 million profit in 1978.

In 1978 the Mortgage Corporation purchased $6.5 billion of residential mortgages and sold $5.7 billion of Mortgage Participation Certificates, its principal mortgage security. It also sold $700 million of Guaranteed Mortgage Certificates. It is clear that this strong support of the secondary mortgage market helped significantly to stabilize the industry and forestall to some extent the devastating crunch of the type suffered during 1973-1974.

The huge pools of finance made available by mortgage-backed securities were an enormous aid to housing growth in the decade. Both government and privately insured institutions contributed to this growth.

Private mortgage insurance on homes zoomed upward in dazzling fashion in the last half of the decade. By 1979 it reached $85 billion and surpassed FHA—a noteworthy achievement, duly recorded by John C. Williamson of the Mortgage Insurance Companies of America, which by then had 13 agressive firms chartered.

It may be fairly stated that the private mortgage guarantee industry was inaugurated by one man—Max Karl, a Milwaukee attorney. In 1957 he founded Mortgage Guarantee Insurance Corporation (MGIC) as a way for private enterprise to step in and fill the growing needs of home buyers frustrated by the complex and lengthy process required for a government loan guarantee.

"The idea worked," says Karl, "because there was a very real hunger on the part of buyers and lenders to avoid FHA bureaucracy."

With private mortgage insurance, the top 20%-25% is guaranteed, allowing borrowers to get a home with as little as 5% down. The processing time is less, as well as are fees and other requirements.

Further developments in finance came late in the decade with the entrance of banks, savings and loans, and other financial institutions into the issuance of bonds and securities backed by residential mortgages. The Bank of America pioneered this move in 1977 with pass-through type securities backed by pooled conventional mortgages. Home Savings and Loan Association of Los Angeles also requested permission to issue mortgage backed bonds in $10,000 denominations.

Perhaps the most dazzling rise and the most disastrous fall in housing finance in the seventies were staged by those darlings of Wall Street, the Real Estate Investment Trusts.

Billions were raised by the REITs in the early decade as their stock prices soared. And billions were invested—often not too wisely—in home and apartment projects, shopping centers, and real estate development.

By 1974 double-digit inflation and high interest rates began to take their toll, and by 1975 REITs held some $3.5 billion of distressed property. Many soon took Chapter 11 bankruptcy protection. They did, however, contribute greatly to the growth of housing and in later years they revived to contribute still more to housing growth.

Another aspect of private housing finance in the era was the development of exotic mortgaging of apartments, "roll over" and "intermediate-term" loans, conversions, and syndications. New and complex financing arrangements grew up to stimulate the boom further.

Possibly the most fascinating story of this decade is the exotic growth of huge corporate ventures in housing which started in the mid-sixties, reached a dazzling peak in the mid-seventies, and suffered a disastrous decline thereafter.

The infusion of giant corporate funds into housing did much to promote growth of bigger—and sometimes better—building firms and projects. Soon there were giant shelter conglomerates covering land, building, finance, mobile homes, and much else. Wall Street loved it, and stock prices soared.

But during 1973-1975 the double-digit interest and finance costs took its toll. Many of the large corporations withdrew from building, with huge losses. Housing, REITs, and financial stocks dropped almost to zero. Losses to builders and the industry were tremendous.

It took many years to sort out the losses and the changes resulting from the REITs debacle, the giant corporate ventures, and the exotic financing methods that did not work. Yet, in the end, the nation as a whole benefited from the housing built. And the only losses were those unfortunate investors whom many said should have known better.

The Enormous Cost of the Environmentalist Movement

The dawn of a new decade of environmentalism was dramatized on April 21, 1970, by the celebration of "Earth Day." It signaled the start of a revolution in public attitudes that changed the country and the building industry to an enormous degree.

A veritable explosion of laws and regulations followed as Congress passed more than two dozen laws covering air and water pollution, toxic chemicals, strip mining, wetlands control, flood control, atomic energy control, and even noise control. A proliferation of federal, state, county, and local agencies sprang into being that soon had a finger in almost every citizen's pie—and put thousands of housing and building projects out of business.

By the end of the decade there were considerable achievements: air in cities was becoming cleaner; fish were returning to some rivers and lakes; and building developers were paying greater attention to environmental planning and the production of cleaner, quieter, more livable communities.

But the dollar cost was tremendous as land and development costs skyrocketed, and more and more builders threw in the sponge, unable to operate profitably under the maze of regulations and costly, conflicting rules. It was not until 1980 that the American public began to realize the true cost of many of the unreasonable and often capricious laws that stymied building and raised the cost of all housing.

As starts plummeted to all time lows in the early eighties, a new look was being taken to see whether the costs were indeed too high. But by then millions of builders were out of work, the economy was suffering, and Americans were finding it almost impossible to buy a new home.

The Environmental Protection Act of 1971 was the most far reaching of the federal laws affecting housing. But it was soon followed by the $25-Billion Water Pollution Control act of 1972 and the Coastal Zone Management Act, or "Wetlands" bill, which created enormous problems and delays for builders. The

Flood Disaster Act of 1973 added still further problems, controls, and delays for builders along rivers, lakes, or waterways. The confusion and delay caused by these laws and the often overzealous environmental regulators led to such builder reactions as the following:

Question: How many environmentalists does it take to change a light bulb?
Answers: Eleven. One to plug in the bulb and ten to prepare the environmental impact statement.

Bumper sticker: Have you ever met an unemployed environmentalist?

Housing was slowed and finally brought almost to a standstill in the late seventies by no-growth activists in the name of ecology and the environment. Groups such as Nader's Raiders and the Sierra Club were quick to seize on every law, rule, or regulation to bring housing growth in many areas to a halt. The resulting lawsuits and long legal delays caused hundreds of builders to give up good, well-planned projects which could have produced desperately needed housing.

The "no-growth" theme was also seized on by many towns and communities to keep out housing because they feared it would increase school costs or bring in minorities. "No-growth" proponents also took advantage of exclusionary zoning code manipulation and other devices to obstruct home building. The result: it became increasingly costly and difficult to build, and many firms stopped work.

In 1978, Ernest A. Becker, Sr., president of the National Association of Home Builders, commended the position taken by Robert Strauss on the cost of government controls and regulations:

"Recognition by the President's top inflation fighter of the enormous costs of excessive government regulations—particularly those involving environmental restrictions—is a good indication Mr. Strauss has his priorities in order," he said.

"Unnecessary government regulations are one of the main reasons housing costs have increased so much," Becker declared. He cited a Rutgers University study which concluded that regulations had forced up the price of housing by 20%. The study he referred to was conducted by the Rutgers Center for Urban Policy Research. It fixed the extra cost of a $50,000 three-bedroom home at $9,844.

"Because of the proliferation of local, state, and federal laws governing the land-development process," Becker said, "the cost of a developed lot now accounts for 25% of the sales price of a typical new home—up from 15% 20 years ago."

Becker also noted that in some fast-growing urban areas, environmental restrictions and no-growth policies had created artificial shortages of land, forcing up the price of 5,000-square-feet developed lots to as high as $40,000—including $4,000 or more for water and sewer connections.

In retrospect, it may seem a wonder that as many homes were built during the decade. One explanation may be that the full impact of no-growth opposition, environmental controls, water and sewage problems, wetlands and flood controls, zoning and building code obstructions, rent controls, tax limitation legislation, and financial legislation such as "red-lining" control did not show up until the late seventies. Then the no-growth activists had their wishes fulfilled: housing starts plummetted and housing growth stopped.

The Coastal Zone Management Act of 1972

opened a Pandora's box of complicated legislation by states and local communities. California led the way with legislation controlling building along its 1,070 miles of Pacific Ocean, and in most areas up to 1,000 yards inland. The effect on building development was catastrophic. Florida, Oregon, and Washington were also quick to adopt far-reaching laws which set up life and death powers over builders and developers. The confusion among federal, state, and local regulations enmeshed the builders in so many problems and higher costs that thousands were forced out of business.

The Flood Disaster Protection Act of 1973 was publicized as a measure to allow home owners in river-bottom areas to buy federal flood insurance. But it proved to be much more than that—in effect attempting to force 10,000 flood-prone communities along rivers, the Great Lakes, and coastlines to adopt tough new zoning ordinances and building codes. Flood-hazard maps were distributed, but the maps and the regulations were so confusing that few builders, home owners, and town officials knew what to do. As in the Wetlands laws, the effect was to strangle construction.

One of the spectacular environmental battles of the decade was over Deltona Corporation's Marco Island project near Naples, Florida. This 8,000-acre island community was started in 1964—a model of expert environmental planning of the time, and a self-contained community of 12,300 homes for about 35,000 people. Its development plans, including dredging and filling of wetlands to produce attractive homesites along canals and lakes, were approved by state and local authorities and by the U.S. Army Corps of Engineers. By 1976 the project was about half completed—a delightful tree-covered home area with golf courses, beaches, and fine community facilities.

But that year the Corps of Engineers, which had been charged by EPA with protecting wetlands, changed its position and denied Deltona permission to dredge and fill two large wetland parcels. Deltona had already sold some 3,000 lots on this land for $45 million. The land was needed not only for houses but for the churches, schools, hospital, and other structures needed for a self-sufficient small city.

The Corps' action delighted local environmentalists who claimed Marco Island was home to the bald eagle, brown pelican, and the American alligator (some of the latter were already residing comfortably in Marco's golf course water hazards).

"I am appalled," said President Frank E. Mackle, Jr., "that the carefully considered decisions of state and local officials have been overturned by the Corps' bureaucracy in Washington." A long and costly lawsuit was forecast to overturn the decision. The irony was that Deltona's dredge and fill operations were outstanding in their plan and execution, and the community was a beautiful and environmentally attractive one.

The Energy Crunch and Inflation

What some historians may call the most seismic event of the decade erupted in 1973 when a handful of oil-rich Arab nations declared an embargo, took control of about one half of the free world's oil reserves, and proceeded to effect a wholesale transfer of the world's wealth to their national treasuries.

The actions convulsed European and American markets, played havoc with the world's economy, fueled the fires of inflation everywhere, disrupted the world's balance of payments, and raised the price of gasoline in the U.S. from 38 cents a gallon to more than $1.30 by the end of the decade. Home heating costs soared, as did the cost for every other energy use. Americans learned, for the first time, that there were limits to cheap energy, and that they could not, or did not, do anything to stop the escalating cost of energy. The housing industry was one of the industries most drastically affected.

It took time for builders, developers, and the industry as a whole to react to the energy crunch. The short-term effects can be quickly pinpointed, but the confusing picture of long-term developments took years to emerge:

An immediate shift to building projects closer to jobs and urban centers took place. As driving cars became more costly, buyers tried to locate as close as possible to shopping centers, schools, and jobs.

An enormous rush to develop new or improved methods, techniques, and equipment to build energy-conserving structures started. Government programs were pushed, and NAHB and its Research Foundation built model energy-conserving homes and developed important thermoperformance guidelines. Industry manufacturers spent billions to perfect new products and equipment, including the heat pump, insulating windows, new insulating materials, solar equipment and devices, and energy-saving home equipment and appliances. Hundreds of new items of equipment and construction were rushed into production. It was perhaps one of the greatest periods of research and development in housing's history.

To say that all of this had an immediate effect on lower energy costs would be misleading. In the long run, it did. But there were many misfires; the frenetic talk about solar energy was often largely in theory only. Builders seized on solar devices and many other outright gimmicks to cash in on the energy theme to help sales. But progress eventually was made through the use of sound research and development.

A host of government actions occurred which hindered and certainly confused builders. Congress passed an Energy Conservation and Production Act in 1976 which authorized the Department of Housing and Urban Development (HUD) to develop energy-efficient guidelines for local and state building codes. The resulting local codes were often conflicting and confusing and were in conflict with state and local utility regulations on energy. Later the new Department of Energy (DOE) was given the job of developing standards and spent $20 million to do so. It was not until 1979 that DOE attempted to publish its voluminous "Building Energy Performance Standards" (BEPS) which were promptly challenged by the National Association of Home Builders and others. They were characterized as "draconian regulations that would bring the federal government into every home as never before. Their complexity and specificity go beyond the intent of the statute."

Thus we see again the confusion that often results in attempts to regulate the far-flung housing industry. For example, most rural builders are outside of code jurisdictions. Many small towns said they could not afford a building inspector to enforce the state energy code. The entire energy-enforcement program was bogged down in rules, red tape, and confusion.

Controversy over the Department of Energy's "Building Energy Performance Standards" continued for years. In 1980, DOE sent the BEPS back for revision and delayed implementation for another year. They had set "design energy budgets" for 19 different types of buildings in 78 climate zones—a confusing idea. BEPS had also established an elaborate evaluation system based on design drawings using a computer—an even more unworkable concept since few small builders had access to computers.

The most impressive gains in home energy conservation were sparked by the National Association of Home Builders and its Research Foundation. Working closely with housing industry manufacturers, and assisted by hundreds of experienced builders who were able to field test ideas, NAHB got amazing action. It built a 1200-square-foot energy-efficient demonstration house in 1977 using technology and products readily available to its thousands of members. The house was widely publicized and a checklist of energy-saving features listed. Thus the ideas, which were well researched, were quickly assimilated into small-builder practice throughout the country. Later, ten home builders across the country were selected to build "showcase energy-conserving homes" incorporating these

ideas. A checklist of energy-saving ideas was published in 1977 in connection with NAHB's energy demonstration home:

Design and Planning Features

- Compact rectangular plan minimizes heating and cooling loads.
- Unconditioned vestibule/storage room buffers end wall.
- Vestibule "air lock" entrance isolates conditioned space.
- 7'6" celing height reduces interior conditioned volume.
- Family room closes off for comfort conditioning.
- Special circulator fireplace uses outdoor air for combustion.
- South-facing windows aid heating in winter.
- Roof overhang designed to shade south-facing windows in summer.
- Deciduous trees provide summer shading at south side of house.
- North-facing windows reduced in size to 8% of floor area.

House Specifications

Foundation/Floor

- Dry basement construction with gravel and sump under slab.
- 6-mil polyethylene film under slab and behind back-filled block walls.
- Exposed walls stuccoed to seal concrete block against infiltration.
- 2" × 3", studs spaced at 24" o.c., set out from wall to accommodate insulation.
- R-19 pressure-fit insulation batts on exposed walls.
- R-11 pressure-fit insulation batts on below-grade walls.

- 2″-thick plastic foam perimeter insulation at exposed slab edges.
- 1″ glass fiber sill sealer between foundation and sill plate.
- R-19 band joist insulation.
- All utility entrances sealed with heavy caulk.

Exterior Walls

- Wall height at 7′7″ (nominal 7′6″ ceiling to reduce volume.
- 2″ × 6″ studs spaced at 24″ o.c. with single top plate.
- Bottom plate sealed to deck with construction adhesive.
- R-19 unfaced pressure-fit insulation batts in walls.
- Continuous 6-mil polyethylene vapor barrier behind drywall.
- R-5 plastic foam sheathing extends up between trusses, down over band joist.
- Plywood box-header over openings insulated as walls.
- 2-stud corner post with drywall backup clips to accommodate insulation at corner.
- No partition posts; drywall clips accommodate insulation at intersections.
- Surface-mounted electrical outlets avoid penetrating wall.

Doors/Windows

- Insulated double-glazed steel entry door has magnetic weather strip.
- Insulated, weatherstripped, inner vestibule door.
- Interior doors close off family room for comfort conditioning.
- Weatherstripped windows with double insulating glass and storm windows.
- Insulating drapes used at windows to control heat loss and gain.

Roof/Ceiling

- Trusses cantilevered over wall plate allow for insulation.
- 12″-thick R-38 pressure-fit insulation batts installed from below.
- Continuous 6-mil polyethylene vapor barrier below insulation.
- Gable-end vents give 1 square foot ventilation per 300 square feet of ceiling.
- 24″ soffit overhang provides summer shading for south-facing windows.
- Attic access door located in vestibule outside of conditioned area.
- Surface-mounted lighting fixtures avoid penetrating ceiling.

Heating/Cooling System

- Simplified duct system with low inside registers and central return.
- Special reduced-capacity heat pump with compressor installed indoors.
- Controlled bypass on inside heat-pump coil improves summer dehumidification.
- Heat-recovery device on compressor to heat domestic water with waste heat.
- Heat recirculator to discourage warm-air stratification at ceiling in family room.

Water Heating/Appliances

- Heavily insulated water heater with isolated jacket set at 120°.
- All water pipes insulated to reduce heat loss, control condensation.
- Low-water-use devices on kitchen/bathroom faucets and shower heads.
- High-efficiency refrigerator with energy-saving feature.
- Electric range with heavily insulated oven plus microwave oven.
- Energy-saving dishwasher uses less water.

- Washer uses less water, has load-size scale and selector switch.
- Bathroom vent fans exhaust through second damper in exterior wall.

Nothing caught the fancy of millions of people in the energy crusade more than solar heat—a truly ancient idea that suddenly sprang into the limelight. Socrates is said to have explained the principles of orienting buildings to the south; the Greeks did it; and builders have been doing it for years. George Fred and William Keck, architects of the Chicago World's Fair house described in the chapter on the thirties also did it: they designed and built a passive solar house in 1940. So this is not a new idea, but what a bonanza it became in the energy crunch of the seventies for magazine writers, publicists, and promoters. One observer remarked, "If publicity built houses, the country would be knee deep in solar homes."

Whatever the cause, this old-new idea sparked hundreds of exciting research projects and stimulated the building of thousands of solar homes, solar water heaters, and "passive solar" building systems. Passive solar meant modifying design and construction to make the structure receptive to the sun's heat and employ techniques to conserve energy. New definitions were needed to describe the later developments. Some of these, in addition to orienting a home for optimum solar receptivety included:

- Trombe walls—massive masonry walls on which the sun shines and which serve to hold or store that heat.
- Indoor rock beds, gravel pits, and liquid tanks (or combinations of) to provide heat-storage reservoirs.

- Greenhouse-like glazed porches or atriums to function as solar heat collectors.
- Insulating shutters and shades to minimize the heat loss through windows.
- Baffles, fencing, and earth berms to minimize the heating-loss effects of winds on the house.
- Judicious use of reflectors and shading devices to abort the sun's effects at desirable times or periods.
- Improved methods of glazing and interior daylighting.
- Natural convection or thermosiphoning of interior air.

Earth-sheltered houses became a headline-catching new trend, as did the use of mud, adobe, and massive walls of masonry—all old but now new. Underground houses were promoted and praised. TVA sponsored construction of 44 tests homes to try out passive solar designs, and three won awards from the Third Annual Passive Solar Conference of the International Solar Energy Society.

A massive federal push by the Department of Housing and Urban Development also helped put solar heat in the limelight. Some 4,000 solar homes and apartments were built with HUD grants. The government also funded 15,000 domestic solar hot-water-heater installations. It also made 162 awards in its Residential Passive Solar Design competition and demonstration which included grants of $1.4 million. Did all these efforts produce lasting results? Only time will tell.

HUD's program did get results by bringing many outstanding building leaders into solar work. An example was the Sunsation project of Perl-Mack companies of Denver, headed by President Sam Primack, a long-time innovator and leader in building research and progress. Working with a HUD grant of $9,000 each for 25 homes equipped with solar heat and hot water, Primack demonstrated public interest by selling 22 homes in one day. This and other programs helped builders test solar methods and adopt the ones most beneficial in their areas.

One of the remarkable outgrowths of the solar-home program was the burgeoning of new manufacturing firms turning out solar collectors and dozens of other solar energy products. Among home owners, a sensational interest in wood-burning stoves and fireplaces flared up. Almost overnight, long-dormant firms began turning out, once again, quaint cast-iron products. And home-owners from coast to coast began sawing up trees or anything else of wood. The increase in burning of wood and coal in fireplaces soon caused complaints from the Environmental Protection Agency that the suburban skies were about to be polluted.

In spite of the confusion and delay which was an inevitable part of such a large, complicated program involving thousands of builders and millions of home owners, many lasting benefits ultimately emerged. Houses were being better built and insulated, and they were equipped and heated with more efficient, energy-saving equipment. The development of new products and equipment was given a great push forward.

Mobies, Modulars, and Technological Progress

Advances in building technology continued during the decade on many fronts, but none startling enough to be called revolutionary. There was most certainly no dearth of exciting new ideas and concepts, but the difficulty, as always, lay in making them work under field conditions with thousands of small builders on hundreds of thousands of scattered sites.

One of the most spectacular technological projects of the decade was Operation Breakthrough in 1970—an ambitious and costly program by Housing Secretary George Romney to demonstrate the interest of the Nixon administration in lower housing costs and to promote more efficient systems and construction techniques.

This was basically an intelligently conceived attempt. From some 236 entries, 22 firms were picked to build prototype houses in 10 states on sites where 2,000 units were to be built. Local architects, builders, and site planners took part with extensive research. The units were of wood, concrete, metal, fiber and combinations thereof. There were modular, panelized, and other variations of industrialized systems.

The benefits of the program came largely from the fact that each unit or system was widely publicized and many new ideas were demonstrated. The problem was that the overall program became bogged down in confusion and delay; much of it was not completed and the end result left a bad taste and a poor image for industrialized housing. Yet who can say how many of the better concepts and methods are not today working their way into the main stream of building methods?

Perhaps the technological tone of the decade was most flamboyantly expressed in Chicago in 1971 when the first and largest Industrialized Housing Exposition in the U.S. was opened. It put under one huge roof the newest techniques in prefabrication, panelization, mobile homes, modular and sectional homes, and a wide variety of engineered building systems in steel and concrete. This was the first time the nation and its builders could see and grasp the enormous progress the industrialized housing industry had made, including the complicated equipment in field and factory that made it possible.

A striking series of research houses in 1972, 1975, 1978, and 1979 also contributed to technological progress. The 1972 house built by NAHB's Research Foundation was dedicated to Optimum Value Engineering (OVE), which literally means getting the most from the least. Its cost-cutting ideas, based on a time-study comparison with traditional methods at 1972 prices, follows:

- *Footings* 6″ × 9″ rather than 8″ × 16″. Savings: $78.60.
- *Foundation walls* 6″ instead of 8″ thick. Savings: $94.15.
- *Wood decks* at entrance (with patio doors) instead of concrete slabs. Savings: $42.41.
- *Wood girder* rather than a steel girder under the floor. Savings: $66.41.
- A *floor structure* with 2″ × 8″ continuous, spliced joists 24″ o.c. and a glue-nailed, ⅝″ single-layer plywood floor over a clear span of 13′4″. Savings: $160.74.
- *Exterior walls* with 2″ × 3″ studs spaced 24″ o.c., a 1″ × 3″ bottom plate, and a single 2″ × 3″ top plate. Also, window and door openings single framed, corner posts reduced to two members, and partition posts eliminated. Savings: $170.26.
- *Siding and sheathing* combined as a single layer of plywood. Savings: $98.93.

- *Prestained wood siding* to eliminate on-site painting. Savings: $137.95.
- *Simplified exterior trim*, including an open-soffit design and a 1″ × 6″ rake which are part of the rough-framing operation. Savings: $124.51.
- *Simplified interior trim* and smaller moldings. The rectangular section of the base trim permits simple butt joints in place of coped corners. Savings: $78.75.
- *Simplified interior framing* including drywall back-up clips to cut down on blocking and corner studs. Savings: $192.01.
- *Prefabricated DWV plumbing assembly* of PVC plastic pipe and above-floor drains for tub and toilet. Savings: $40.75.
- *Prefabricated supply plumbing* of CPVC plastic set into a prefabricated partition frame. Savings: $25.08.
- *Prefabricated wiring* including prewired service panel and wiring harness, to eliminate most drilling and field connections. Savings: $31.27.

Both the OVE house and its conventional counterpart were built in Gaithersburg, Maryland, a Washington, D.C. suburb, by David C. Smith.

Builders attending the National Association of Home Builders' Convention in Dallas in 1975 were confronted with a dazzling 3,300-square-foot contemporary ranch-style research house labeled "Discovery, 1975." Built by the Construction Research Center of The University of Texas, it was designed to save energy, resources, and maintenance costs. Among the innovations were the following:

- The first residential floor slab made of concrete reinforced with glass fibers. The CRC said this fibrous concrete performs twice as well as conventional concrete reinforced with steel, apparently eliminates shrinkage and temperature cracks, and should be cost competitive when the special alkali-resistant glass fibers are available commercially.
- Walls made of concrete block stacked without horizontal or vertical mortar joints (tripling a mason's productivity), then coated with about ⅛ inch of glass fiber-reinforced mortar. The mortar (available commercially) is said to make the concrete block wall significantly stronger than conventional walls with block set in mortar. It serves as both interior and exterior finish, and can be painted or covered with textured plaster, if desired.
- A water-repellant, free-flowing granular vermiculite, poured into cores and cavities of the masonry walls. This serves as a permanent barrier against transmission of heat and sound.
- Heating-ventilating ducts made of a flat glass-fiber sheet bonded to an aluminized fabric, then folded to form rectangular ducts. They provide an economical system completely free of noise.
- An under-foundation water system to maintain supporting soil moisture and automicaly provide water to lawns and plantings. Two parallel loops of porous pipe are made from recycled rubber tires and plastics.
- Solar bronze window glass with hermetically sealed air space between the double panes to control brightness and solar heat gain.

- A concrete-tile roof, providing long life and minimum maintenance, underlaid with a reflective coating (a waterproofing membrane with an embedded foil barrier) to reduce heating and cooling.
- Exterior doors which look like conventional wood doors, having a steel face and back—separated by wood—and a polyurethane core. This type of construction eliminates warping, bowing, and significant heat loss, and magnetic weather stripping assures no air or moisture infiltration.
- A sheathing made of extruded polystyrene foam, which is said to have superior insulation characteristics. It is used on wall and in gable areas.

A research-demonstration house featuring composite wood products and energy-saving systems greeted the Forest Products Research Society in Atlanta in 1978. Built at Marietta, Georgia, the wood-systems demonstration house was co-sponsored by the American Plywood Association and the U.S. Forest Service's Southeastern Forest Experiment Station.

Composite plywood panels, known as "comply," had wood-veneer faces and backs bonded to a solid core of reconstituted wood. Composite lumber had a similar core with several layers of veneer. Such products had the potential to use a greater percentage of the log and a wider variety of species.

The three-bedroom, single-core wood-systems demonstration house was constructed with two grades of composite plywood: ½-inch C-D exterior roof sheathing and ²³⁄₃₂-inch tongue-and-groove Sturd-I-Floor, a plywood grade specifically designed for single-layer floors. Sturd-I-Floor encompasses both composite panels and conventional plywood.

Composite lumber was furnished by the Forest Service's Southeastern Forest Experimental Station. The demonstration house was built with composite 2×8 and 2×10 floor joists spaced on 24-inch centers. Some composite 2×4s were also used for wall studs.

While the Marietta house was not the first to be built with a variety of composite wood products, it was the first to use them in conjunction with five energy-efficient or cost-effective plywood and lumber construction systems: the under-floor plenum heating/cooling system, or "Plen-Wood;" the All-Weather Wood Foundation; and Sturd-I-Wall, in this case with plywood siding over nonstructural 1-inch foamed sheathing.

The wood-systems demonstration house was built by Fred J. Estfan, Investors Services, Inc., Marietta, Georgia.

Near the end of the decade, a new breed of research homes appeared—the energy-saving systems houses. The U.S. Department of Energy (DOE) announced funding for six pre-fab panelized houses, six modular types, four mobile homes, two precut types, and one prefab log house. The houses were to test the efficiency of houses involving both passive and hybrid energy systems.

Not to be outdone by DOE, the Tennessee Valley Authority announced in December 1979 its ambitious program for 130 modular-home display models to demonstrate passive solar-heat features. Design teams were organized to include a home manufacturer, a consultant, two TVA experts, an interior decorator, and a building inspector.

Mobile- and modular-home manufacturers followed a roller-coaster course during the decade. Mobile-home sales hit a peak of 625,000 units in 1972, and ended 1979 at 270,000. Modular/sectional homes went through a severe shakeup during 1972-1973, and ended the decade at the 43,000 level.

Perhaps the outstanding development in low-cost housing was the emergence of the single, double-wide and triple-wide mobile units as permanent homes. Also the rapid move of modular/sectional manufactured homes into planned subdivisions, planned unit development projects, and condominium projects. New land-development techniques were providing ways to site both mobile and modulars in acceptable ways, and long-term financing was becoming available for such housing.

In the mid-seventies, the various interests in prefabrication and related work organized as the National Association of Home Manufacturers, with headquarters in Washington, D.C. They were active in setting new quality standards and in public relations. They adopted the term "manufactured home" to displace the somewhat tarnished prefab label. NAHM President O. Z. Oliver pointed out, in 1979, that home manufacturers market their homes through a network of small, independent, local home builders who sell and service them. He listed the three basic forms of manufactured homes:

- *The precut home:* As the name implies, all the dimensional lumber of this home is precut, assembled, and numbered in a factory for shipment as a "package" to the building site for erection. This type of home is especially popular with the "do-it-yourselfers" who are willing to perform much of the physical labor of building a home in order to reduce its total cost. In 1979 some 26,000 precut homes were shipped by this industry.

• *The panelized home:* This is the most popular and versatile form of manufactured housing. More than 314,000 panelized homes were erected by builders in communities all across the country in 1979. These homes are delivered to the building site as wall panels, 8 feet high, by whatever length is required, usually 20-30 feet. Exterior wall panels include insulated sheathing and exterior siding, with windows and doors installed in the factory. Interior panels generally consist of only the structural two-by-four lumber. Some manufacturers install interior wallboard and electrical and plumbing items in these panels, but generally these items are installed at the site by local craftsmen.

• *The modular/sectional home:* These are the most sophisticated and complete form of manufactured housing. They are nearly 95% complete before leaving the factory, and are most often shipped as two three-dimensional units which form the front and back halves of a home. At the building site they are placed on the foundation and joined at the ridge of the roof. Before leaving the factory, the interior of these homes is also completed with carpeting on the floors, paint or wall covering on the walls, and installed kitchens and baths. After the home arrives at the building site, it takes only a week to finish. More than 43,000 modular/sectional homes were produced in 1979.

Home Designs and Styles Change to Meet New Patterns of Living

The most surprising aspect of the home market of the seventies was the vigorous surge in single-family sales which took place in the last half of the decade.

Earlier, apartment building had been strong, amounting to 1,047,000 units in 1972 compared to 1,309,000 single-family units. But in 1976 the percentages changed drastically, with single-family starts rising to 1,163,000, and 374,000 for multi-family. Thereafter, single-family housing soared to 1.45 million in 1977, 1.4 million in 1978, and 1,200,000 units in 1979 out of the year's total of 1,750,000.

How shall we account for this surprising single-family home surge in the face of rising costs and high interest rates? Among the answers, consider the following:

1. Americans suddenly became more aware of the values of home ownership as a hedge against inflation, and a single-family home of their own was their favorite concept of security.

2. Buyers were able to cash in on the high equity they held in an older house and trade up to a much more exciting, livable new model.

3. Demographic movement to suburbs and outlying rural country opened new areas of land inviting to single-family home ownership and enjoyment.

4. Working wives brought in added income that made higher priced single-family homes possible.

5. Builders developed a host of new de-

signs, styles, and amenities that made single-family living more desirable.

6. Builders found new concepts for designing subdivisions to provide single-family attached units in clusters and courts with duplex and townhouse arrangements providing privacy and fine amenities.

7. To meet higher costs and energy saving requirements, many new single-family houses became smaller but more sophisticated in use of inner space. A notable advance in small-home design took place with the aid of a talented new school of architects/designers.

Architecture and design in the seventies was—as in previous decades—very much a mixed affair. There was undeniable progress in some areas due to the fact that more large project developers had the money and the will to retain top-flight architects, land planners, interior designers, and landscape architects. A description of the architectural trends in the vast and complex home-building field can be found in Robert Venturi's book *Complexity and Contradiction in Architecture,* for which he received a 1978 AIA medal. His argument, simply stated, was that human life, with all its obvious complexities and contradictions, can only flourish in a complex and contradictory environment. Thus, he concluded, complexity and contradiction are essential elements of architecture. No one has as yet made a better statement of what happened in housing design in the decade. And viewed pragmatically, there was considerable progress in housing.

The first area of progress was in the design, planning, landscaping, and building of large, environmentally planned mixed communities. These often combined single-family homes, townhouses, small apartments, duplexes or four-plexes, zero-lot line, and other concepts in communities with recreational facilities and park-like surroundings.

A second area of progress was the further development, strongly begun in the sixties, of high-density land use with skillfully designed houses on zero-lot lines, patio homes on narrow lots, planned unit development groups, clusters of townhouses, duplexes, four-plexes, and even seven-plexes. Such concepts, combined with good open-space and environmental planning produced outstanding projects.

Environmental planning became a way of life for most builders in the late seventies and they spent more money on design, planning, and landscaping than in any previous era. Many projects were built on water sites along rivers, lakes, harbors, and the oceans. Golf courses became an integral part of planning. Notable progress was made in the environmental improvement of apartment projects large and small.

A few of the outstanding projects of the decade which employed these techniques are described here:

Boca West, by Arvida Corp., is a beautiful planned unit development with townhouses, four-plexes, mid-rise and high-rise buildings, golf courses, manmade lakes, and elegant trees planted full size. There is nothing in south Florida that can touch the idyllic beauty of Boca West, and there are also adjoining office parks and industrial and commercial development.

Brookside Village at Redondo Beach, California, was built by Landmark Communities, Inc. The 385 small apartments are surrounded by landscaped areas (11.8 acres total) with artificial brooks, winding walks, and open space. Parking is located under the buildings.

Carrollwood, by Sunstate Builders in Tampa, continued its high standards of the sixties. A planned unit development with a country club and golf course, riding ring and stables, Carrollwood is ecologically elegant. The values of the houses and the worth of the community were so great that almost every other community in, around, or near this areas has the word Carrollwood in its title: Carrollwood Meadows, Carrollwood Heights, Carrollwood North, etc. Houses run the gamut from townhouses, single-family detached, and high-rises, to flats and zero-lot liners. But they were so economically sited and the land plan was so superb that Carrollwood is to this day *the* place to live in Tampa. Every kind and type of house was designed by different architects: Eugene R. Smith & Associates, Tampa; Bouterse/Borelli/Albaisa, Architects, Miami; and Rowe-Paras Associates, Architects, Tampa. This community set a new standard of land planning, design, and building for a depressed Tampa. Carrollwood literally lifted Tampa up by its bootstraps.

Castle Rock at Branford, Connecticut, was built on a 14-acre finger of land projecting into Long Island Sound. The 45 luxury condominium houses have an exceptional environmental plan that provides privacy, view, and good land use. The units include two-bedroom ranch and three-bedroom townhouses attractively clustered and lavishly landscaped. Copeland Company was the developer and builder.

Champion Forest, by the Greenwood Corporation of Houston, is a superb Texas example of luxury, excellent site planning, and a planned unit development. The houses range in price from the low $100,000s to more than $1 million. The 36-hole golf course is superb and there are 40 tennis courts, and parks, landscaped open space, and large sites for a variety of designs.

Coronado Shores is a group of striking 15-story tower condominiums on the beach at Coronado, California. They are well sited so that each apartment has a water view, with 75% of the 35-acre site for recreation, landscaping, and open space. Designed by architects Krisel, Shapiro and Association, it was built as a joint venture by Jerome Snyder and Loews Corporation.

Crow Canyon accommodates 556 townhouses and 239 zero-lot line homes on the 431-acre site near Contra Costa, California, and each and every unit opens on a golf fairway or neighborhood park. Architects Morris and Lohrbach brought new concepts of siting and design to the 1,274-2,082 square foot units priced in 1977 at $78,000 to $100,000. The builder was Broadmoor Homes.

Desert Island is a 105-acre Palm Springs luxury country club community on an island in a lake. The 388 apartments in seven-story buildings are surrounded by the golf course and lake. It was designed by Desmond Muirhead.

Eastview, by Avco Community Developers, is one of the most stunning communities of houses ever to be sold in San Diego. Eastview comprises duplex townhouses and zero-lot line houses. They are a contemporary version of angular planned houses with Tudor and Normandy design influence. The Architects were Morris & Lohrbach.

Harbor Ridge, by Irvine-Pacific, a division of the Irvine Company, is a stellar achievement in site planning and design in Newport Beach, California. The units almost doubled in value within two years. They consist of four-unit townhouses with interior galleries, dramatic staircases, vaulted ceilings, open planning, corner windows, sybaritic baths, and all of the features that have given southern California the apt sobriquet, "fountainhead of residential design." The architects were Corbin & Yamafuji.

Harbortown comprises imaginative clusters of small condominium flats and townhouses along an inlet of San Francisco Bay at San Mateo, California. Each unit has a water view, including a manmade lagoon. Design was based on an old fishing village with house exteriors in redwood, shingles, and painted clapboard. Units are from 1150-2100 square feet, priced in 1979 at $90,000 to $149,000. Excellent planning and design was done by Fischer-Friedman and Vintage Properties of San Mateo. Adjoining is Las Casitas, a community of classical four-plexes by architects Hall, Goodhue and Haisley.

Heritage Hills of Westchester is a worthy successor to Heritage Village of Southbury, Connecticut, which carried builder Henry Paparazzo's "active, adult community" concepts to a 1100-acre wooded site near Somers, New York. It has excellent environmental planning and siting of 3,000 units in rolling terrain, and good clustering of units in small garden courts. Amenities include golf courses, tennis courts, pools, club and activities buildings. Fine landscape design was done by Patricia Easterbrook Roberts.

High Hill Farm at Beckett in southern New Jersey near Philadelphia is a community of 175 detached single-family homes in zero-lot line clusters. The zero-lot line siting provides privacy while reducing land costs. The 1130-1550 square foot ranch models are grouped in 8 to 12 unit clusters separated by 45 feet of wide landscaped common areas. The developer was Glouster New Communities, Inc.

Huntington Harbour is an exotically designed and sited high-density waterside project in Southern California. The one- and two-

story townhouses are planned on a French sea village theme, with large rooms, vaulted ceilings, wet bars, master bedroom suites, and sliding glass doors leading to decks, patios, or garden areas. This was developed by Broadmoor-Grimaud, Ltd.

The Lake is located at Fullerton, California. "Waterscaping" was the key to success of this 136-acre apartment project which uses a system of pipes and pumps to circulate and aerate brooks, waterfalls, shallow lakes, and ponds that surround the buildings. Landscape architect Don Brinkerhoff created the concept and used rocks, shrubs, and wooden bridges to delight the apartment occupants.

Lake Bellevue Village has three separate 24-unit groups of three-story townhouses. It is built on a 4.62-acre site with water on three sides near Seattle. Solarium windows and sliding glass doors open the small apartments to sundecks and views. Buyers were largely well-off widows and single persons. It was designed by architect Tom Johnson and built by David McGrath.

Las Colinas, in Dallas, is one of the best planned communities in the southwest. The elegant zero-lot line homes were built by Gardinor and Williams. The design, site planning, and environmentally conceived layout are excellent. Richardson Nagy Martin of Newport Beach did the design and planning.

Lyon Farm is an old Greenwich, Connecticut, farm where single-family detached and large townhouse units are skillfully sited and clustered around open space. C.E.P. Associates were the developers and Willis Mills, Jr. the architect for the contemporary colonial project.

Madison of McLean offers luxury Colonial-style townhouses with lavishly landscaped open space and courts. Three-bedroom units have 2836 to 3215 square feet, priced in 1979 at $180,000 to $260,000. They were designed by architect Donald F. Nalley and located in McLean, Virginia. Buyers were largely "empty nesters" who moved from larger suburban homes.

McCormick Ranch, in Scottsdale, Arizona, is the outstanding planned community in the city, which is marred by too many inexpensive subdivisions. The community is developed by different builders who must heed the architectural and planning dicta laid down by the developers. There is a broad range of prices, sizes, and types of housing ranging from luxury priced townhouses to fairly low priced zero-lot line houses, flats, detached housing, and condos.

Mission Hills in Palm Springs, California, is a fine country club community with golf course, planned by Desmond Muirhead. The 680 acres have lakes, open space, 100 single-family homes, and 1,000 attached duplex townhouses with skillful siting. It was built by Max Genet, Jr.

Mission Viejo, by the Mission Viejo Co. in Mission Viejo, California, continues to become perhaps the best planned family community in the U.S. It consists of many different styles and types of houses in different village communities. There are separate communities for retirees (duplex units); detached houses on varying lot sizes for families with children; townhouses for empty nesters and professional couples, both single and married; flats; rental apartments; and, of course, the several Olympic-size swimming pools. Architects who have done work in Mission Viejo include Barry Berkus, Red Moltz, and Morris and Lohrbach.

Montbello, the "City Within a City," in Denver, Colorado, became notable as a fast growing planned community where many innovations in design, planning, and construc-

tion were carried out, not the least of which was a solar-home project of 40 houses. The Perl-Mack Companies, founded in 1952 by Jordan Perlmutter and Samuel Primack, had earlier developed the outstanding Northglen community which had received many national awards and citations, and had built large shopping centers, apartments, and commercial projects. Home costs at Montbello were kept low through new industrialized techniques including steel floor, wall, and partition components. In the late seventies Perl-Mack also developed the The Farms in Westminster, Park Village in Northglen, and Ravenshead in Westminster, as well as Regent Towers, a $15-million apartment project. The number of dwelling units produced by Perl-Mack by the end of the decade had exceeded 22,000.

Palisade's Highlands is a 1973 project that set an example for better land use, as it skillfully clustered single-family homes in groups or around culs-de-sac surrounded by open space. Good home design was by architect Barry Berkus; the builder was M. J. Brock and Sons.

Persimmon Tree offered large single-family homes (4,000 square feet) well sited on landscaped ½-acre lots near Rockville, Maryland. Carefully planned for families with children and their entertainment, there are two distinct entertainment centers—a formal adult area with sunken conversation pit, and an informal children's section in a large family room. It was designed by architects Cohen and Haft, Holz Kerxton and Associates, and built by Berger-Berman of Rockville.

The Pond, built by publicly held Writer Corp., is a planned unit development that featured cluster housing and open space and helped to set the design pace for the Denver market. Barry Berkus designed many of the units, and this California architect's influence was the beginning of a more western (vs. mid-western) influence exerted on the Denver metropolitan market. Largely as a result of his well-planned communities like the Pond, George Writer was selected Professional Builder of the Year in 1978.

Pond Place, in Avon, Connecticut, is one of the most significant single-family home projects in the East. Otto Paparazzo and FIP Corp. co-ventured to build 211 small, single-family homes on a heavily wooded, environmentally planned site in 1979. Houses designed by architect Charles Warren Callister are clustered around small courts and circles. A new sales concept allowed houses to be purchased on sites with leasehold, reducing down payment. Landscape design was by Patricia Easterbrook Roberts of Southbury, Connecticut.

Promontory Point was the most spectacular environmentally planned apartment project of the seventies. It had 30 acres on a bluff overlooking the harbor at Newport Beach, California, and was built by Irvine Co. The 520 high-rise luxury apartments are arranged in five horseshoe-shaped clusters facing the water. It offers fine site planning and landscaping with clubhouse, two pools, health club, and a private beach. The architects were Fisher, Freidman Associates.

Quail Ridge is located in Fullerton, California. Lush landscaping, exotic circular structures, 22 waterfalls, and a small rain forest made this 9.3-acre high-density apartment project an instant success. Builder John Konwiser of Newport Beach retained Donald Brinkerhoff to design the landscaping and waterscaping.

Stoney Brook by U.S. Lend Lease is an idyllic Dallas community of attached houses that simply reek of great environmental ideas. The community is overrun by rocks and rills,

and the grayish-white clapboard exteriors with a countrified air have a somewhat contemporary flair, while the interiors soar with sloping ceiling, open stairwells to basements, wide-open planning, and practical considerations like attached two-car garages. The community won a landscape planning award. The architect was Andres Aldredge, Dallas.

Sunrise Country Club and Rancho Las Palmas, in Palm Springs, by William Bone's Sunrise Corp., gave Bone the reputation of "Mr. Palm Springs Builder." Bone developed the four-plex to its highest level of luxury and architectural appointments. The units feature one-story desert living with two-car attached garages, atriums, and floor-to-ceiling glass, and sheltered by wide overhangs and a host of such comforts as breakfast nooks and sybaritic baths. Excellent site planning usually provides views of the ubiquitous golf courses that are the mark of all Bone's later communities. He also developed Deepwell Ranch, Sunrise East, and Sunrise Alejo. Another distinguishing feature of his communities is a manmade environment of lakes, and man-planted, full-sized palm trees. The original designer was Barry Berkus.

Sunset Hills comprises single-family detached houses of modest size on a site near Oceanside in San Diego County, California. These are well-sited homes from 1300 to 2400 square feet, with many amenities. They were priced at $83,000 to $110,000 in 1978. Broadmoor Homes was the builder.

Tanglewood, Wildewood Springs, and Wild Oak Bay, by Neal Communities, are undoubtedly the most ecologically elegant, environmentally sensitive communities (adjoining each other for the most part) in the Bradenton/Sarasota area of Florida. Wild Oak Bay has paired patio (duplex) housing; Tanglewood has zero-lot line houses; and Wildewood

Springs has condo flats. The Neal organization has several nurseries of its own, and an on-site nurseryman and landscape artist who adds to nature's store of flora. The architect was Richard Gillett.

Terra Granada in Walnut Creek, California, has 6,000 condominium apartments skillfully clustered in small "villages" on 1200 acres. A fine environmental plan preserves "green hills" areas, trees, and wildlife. Houses feature outdoor living, with balconies, courts, landscaped pools, club amenities, and golf course views. It was a Rossmore Leisure World project.

Tierra Antiqua Village, by Tucson developer Bruce Romano, offered 147 luxury one- and two-bedroom apartments on a well-landscaped plot of 5.25 acres. The skillful Mediterranean design and plan provided privacy even in the high-density project. Architectural Progress, Ltd. did the designing.

Treetops is located in Nanuet, New York. Builders Simon Bernstein and Martin Sherman brought San Diego architect Paul Thoryk to New York to inject California pizzazz into their large project. They responded with four-unit buildings in small clusters around open space. Wood-shingle exteriors have stained wood murals resembling old Pennsylvania hex designs.

The Villas, in Laguna Niguel, placed zero-lot line houses of Mission Moorish style on a stunning 15.75-acre site overlooking the sea. Architect Robert Jones used courtyard entries and garden walls to embrace the outdoors and angled walls, clerestory windows, skylights, and striking ceiling treatments to expand interiors. Avco Community Developers built the $133,000+ units in 1977.

Walden Woods has rustic wood townhouses clustered on a heavily wooded site at Dobbs Ferry, New York. The 116 units, priced in 1978 at $65,000 to $100,000, are surrounded by tree-covered open space, with hiking trails. The architect was Martin Ginsburg, and the builder DHI Enterprises.

Waterside has four towers rising from a platform built out over New York's East River. The $73-million project houses 1,470 families and includes a plaza, restaurant, and shopping area. One of New York's few rental projects, it took builder Richard Ravitch 12 years to fight through municipal red tape. It opened in 1973 with rentals at $720 for a three-bedroom unit.

Weatherstone in Paoli, Pennsylvania, is a 23.5-acre Main Line estate, skillfully landscaped with 115 sites for elegant Pennsylvania farmhouse townhouses arranged in small clusters around tree-lined open space. Fine traditional styling was by architect Victor Barr. The 1900-2300 square foot units are popular with wealthy retireees and empty nesters. It was developed by Environmental Shelters, Inc.

Westridge community is located in the foothills near Denver, Colorado. It was planned around an exceptional recreational center with handball and racquetball courts, exercise room, hydro-whirlpool, party room, and a deck overlooking an Olympic-size swimming pool. The club has tennis, basketball, and volleyball courts. It received awards for design and landscaping.

Willow Creek is a housing mix of single-family detached, townhouses, and apartments which works smoothly together in this planned unit development project near Denver. The single-family homes are designed to suit a broad range of family types. Houses were designed and built by the Writer Corp. of Englewood, Colorado.

Windemere, in Mount Soledad in LaJolla, by Avco Community Developers, started a southern California trend to luxury, custom-styled houses in a planned community. The combination of zero-lot line houses and townhouses was sited to take advantage of Mount Soledad's great height overlooking the Pacific. The 297 units on 140 acres were priced at $100,000+. Several other communities later emulated the kind of posh luxury and architectural pizzazz of Windemere, including the Irvine Co.'s Harbor Ridge and Avco's own Eastview. The architect for Windemere was Dale Naegle.

Woodbridge is an environmentally planned lake village on the Irvine Ranch south of Los Angeles in Orange County. It shows good blending of apartments, townhouses, single-family, and attached units in various combinations along parks and lakes. The opening section of 400 units in 1976 was so successful that a lottery had to be held to select the buyers. Initial prices were $30,000 to $100,000.

Woodbury Place, in Woodbury, Connecticut, is an exciting small condo project in a conservative Connecticut community. The 24 attached townhouses and ranch-style units are clustered on six acres with landscaped courts and open space. Patricia Easterbrook Roberts, landscape designer of Southbury, Connecticut, contributed greatly to its success. Architect Drexel Yeager, of Chesire, Connecticut, designed sharply etched, classic contemporary homes. The builder was Karl Jalbert.

Industry Progress, Direction, and Leadership

We have seen that in the decade of the seventies, housing production soared to an all-time high of 17.8 million units, single-family home building reached a record volume of 12,361,000 houses, and the quality of design, environmental planning, and amenities of living improved greatly. There were many factors at work, but one not generally credited or understood by the American public was the role of industry leadership.

The housing and home-building field of the seventies had come a long way from the totally unorganized chaos that existed in the early thirties. The World War II years, 1940-1945, forcibly brought the scattered segments of home building together, which led in 1943 to the formation of the National Association of Home Builders of the United States.

As a result of the deeds of many bold men in those years, the industry organized to produce desperately needed war and defense homes and later a better housed America. The war housing and the amazing postwar building boom that followed was made possible by a better organized industry in which the National Association of Home Builders played a major role. That role was effectively continued in many ways into the seventies.

By the end of the decade, the size and influence of NAHB had expanded astronomically. Its membership had grown to 125,000, and its leadership in research, marketing, energy conservation, finance, environmental planning, design, and construction techniques had vastly increased. At its January, 1980, Convention and Exposition there were 100 educational programs, 600 exhibits of products and services, and 70,000 building-industry people in attendance. More than 50 committees, task forces, and study groups met to work out wide-ranging industry problems such as long-range planning, energy saving, multi-family construction, land development, rent control, low-cost housing, rehabilitation, multi-family condominiums, mortgage finance, environmental affairs, labor relations, business management, government affairs, marketing, and research and technical development.

The size, complexity, and dispersion of building activity in thousands of widely separate locations have been frequently noted, and made the development of NAHB into a well-organized national power all the more remarkable. In 1974 it opened a new $8 million National Housing Center in Washington to house its far-flung activities. The five-story trapezoidal structure of glass and brick designed by architect Vincent G. Kling and Associates received rave reviews from architectural critics—itself no mean achievement for a builder's group. It provided a gross floor area of 148,310 square feet for the staff of 200, an auditorium, conference rooms, and a large library. To many, this building was the symbol of the "new professionalism" of the home-building industry.

The National Association of Home Builders, as its name implies, is composed of some 700 affiliated local and state associations. It is governed by a president, four senior officers, 15 vice presidents, and 1500-member board of directors. Since builders are notoriously individualistic, it takes a large, well-organized body such as this to get all facets of the industry represented in a democratic way. NAHB's operating budget in 1979 was in excess of $14.1 million.

The Association staff includes outstanding experts on housing legislation, zoning, codes, environmental and land planning, research, business management, marketing, and much else. It provides extensive technical data for its members, and conducts seminars and workshops in many cities. NAHB has its own research laboratory in Rockville, Maryland, and operates a wholly owned subsidiary, the NAHB Research Foundation, which does NAHB and government-sponsored research as well as projects for leading manufacturers of building materials and equipment, and for individual builders.

Through its legislative committee, legal staff, and large "grass-roots" membership, NAHB has exercised a strong national influence on housing legislation. Led by vigorous state associations in each state capital and backed by well-organized and vocal local affiliates in hundreds of towns and cities, NAHB has maintained a strong and persistent voice in both state and national legislative bodies. It has worked effectively to oppose harmful and what many considered socialistic political actions that would hinder home building. In the seventies it helped achieve a long-sought goal—a Central Mortgage Facility—and later an effective secondary mortgage market. Three new agencies contributed mightily to housing finance: the Federal National Mortgage Association, the Government National Mortgage Association, and the Federal Home Loan Mortgage Corporation.

While NAHB did much single-handedly to affect the activities, problems, and solutions of issues affecting the housing industry, it was also often joined by other strong trade associations, such as the Mortgage Banker's Association, the U.S. Savings and Loan League, the National Association of Real Estate Boards, the Urban Land Institute, the National Retail Lumber Dealers Association, and others. Together they achieved goals that advanced housing production.

The emergence of political action committees among these groups was also instrumental in making the viewpoints of the industry known.

NAHB's industry leadership record must also include its marketing and merchandising efforts, which stimulated not only sales of houses but also sales of new products, systems, and home improvements. Its grand Exposition/Convention each year became a showcase of industry progress in new products, materials, and equipment. The 1980 Exposition of some 600 products, materials, equipment, and services included a striking array of solar exhibits as well as materials and methods to produce energy-efficient homes. The impact on the energy-conservation movement in housing was considerable.

New products and equipment for home building are difficult to introduce because of the widely dispersed nature of the industry and its complex distribution system. So the annual NAHB Convention/Exposition fills a particularly important need. In addition, NAHB, its chapters, and its members stage hundreds of model-home exhibits, model-home shows, and its National Home Week and Parade of Homes programs. All add up to an effective national and local system of getting new home designs, products, and developments before the American public.

Perhaps the most outstanding achievement of the decade by NAHB was the the establishment of its Home Owners' Warranty Program—a much needed attempt to protect home buyers from building defects or defaults. The idea was forcefully presented and pushed through NAHB in 1973 by then president George C. Martin of Louisville, Kentucky. Patterned after the British program of home warranties, HOW, as it quickly became dubbed, set up a ten-year warranty-insurance plan backed up by a strong national insurance plan.

This revolutionary plan obviously filled a much needed spot in consumer affairs. In an industry as diverse as housing, many complaints were bound to surface. The HOW program did much to build confidence and perhaps forestall a possible move by government institutions into this field.

The HOW program is entirely voluntary and works through 130 local councils who register builders and screen them for technical competence, financial stability, and customer service. By decade's end there were some 800,000 homes protected by the program, and 17,000 builders enrolled.

The ten-year buyer protection program states that the builder warrants the home to be free from defects in workmanship and materials in the first year. He continues the warrant against malfunctioning of wiring, piping, ductwork, and electrical, plumbing, heating, and cooling in the second year. The builder warrants against major structural defects in the first two years, and an insurance company backs his warranty. During the third through tenth years, the insurance company directly insures the home against major structural defects.

The Home Owners' Warranty Corporation was created as a wholly owned subsidiary of NAHB with its own board of directors, officers, and a staff of insurance experts. Later it became a mutual company. It has devised unique dispute-settlement procedures which offer conciliation and arbitration as alternatives to litigation. More than 80% of cases that reach information mediation are settled at that stage. The rest go on to arbitration before the American Arbitration Association, whose decision is binding. Few cases have gone to court. Claims have been less than 1.5% of houses enrolled. By the end of the decade one in four homes being built carried the HOW coverage.

Housing Hall of Fame

Through the five decades covered by this history, a recurring theme has been that in every crisis or emergency caused by war, material shortages, depression, tight money, or confused government policies, hard-working, creative builders have emerged to keep the production of needed homes alive and growing. The housing industry is illuminated by the deeds of such men.

To honor them, a Housing Hall of Fame was established. The idea had germinated earlier in talks between Edward R. Pratt, Lewis Cenker, Mildred Druckery, George Martin and others. In 1976, Pratt presented a program, then endorsed by NAHB president John C. Hart, to the board of governors of NAHB's National Housing Center, and an impressive Housing Hall of Fame program got under way. An extensive research was carried on in which the careers of some 400 leaders in the industry were studied. Through a computerized voting procedure, 18 were nominated and later elected, and the first induction ceremonies were held in May 1977 at the National Housing Center in Washington.

Membership in the Housing Hall of Fame was granted "in recognition of those who have made significant and lasting contributions to the housing of America." At the Washington installation ceremonies, Robert Arquilla, the president of NAHB, placed a ribbon with a bronze medallion around the neck of each recipient. He declared: "It is fitting to look back, take stock, and call attention to the part our housing leaders have played. They are individuals of giant stature who have served housing and the nation well." A permanent Housing Hall of Fame memorial area was established in the National Housing Center in Washington. Here, those singled out for recognition are portrayed on engraved metal plaques

bearing bas-relief portraits. Bronze inscriptions briefly describe the highlights of their careers and their contributions to a better housed America. Following are those honored to date:

James M. Albert, Miami Beach, Florida. Albert was an untiring and dedicated worker of NAHB for more than a quarter of a century at the local, state and national level. Albert was a leader in the drive to build affordable housing in the South. In 1952, his Golf Estates subdivision pioneered the use of low-cost construction techniques and assembly-line methods to provide the opportunity of attractive, affordable housing for first-time buyers. Subsequent housing projects led the way into the Florida boom years.

George Arquilla, Sr., Chicago, Ilinois. He founded Burnside Construction Company in 1911. He guided the company through the Great Depression and two major recessions. By 1974 his company had produced more than 12,000 single-family homes and 1500 apartment units, none under any federal program. He was one of the pioneering founders of the Chicago Builders' Association and its president for two years. Arquilla was among the group of visionary builders who helped found and organize NAHB in the early 1940s.

William P. Atkinson, Midwest City, Oklahoma. A man for all seasons, Atkinson was a founder-director of the first National Center for organized builders, a nominee for Governor of Oklahoma, a university president, a newspaper publisher, and a home builder. He developed Midwest City, Oklahoma, which in 1950 won top honors from the Urban Land Institute for neighborhood development. He was president of NAHB in 1951.

Albert Balch, Seattle, Washington. Friends and home owners remember this benevolent builder and developer of residential communities in the Seattle area. His wondrous laugh and tall tales enlivened the industry. He took part in the Emergency Committee and early builder meetings that led to the founding of NAHB. Balch built 10,000 homes and developed ten of Seattle's finest communities, including Wedgewood Park. His record casts a tall shadow.

Louis R. Barba, Chatham, New Jersey. Long active in homebuilding, Barba built custom and tract housing, apartment complexes, large office buildings, and shopping centers. He served as president of the New Jersey State and Metro HBAs prior to being elected to the presidency of NAHB in 1970. He was a member of the U.S. Mission to the United Nations' Economic Commission for Europe in 1970, and a member of the FNMA Board of Directors, 1971-1973. He was appointed a member of the FNMA and GNMA and FHLB advisory boards.

Martin L. Bartling Jr., Knoxville, Tennessee. Bartling was NAHB president in 1960, and known for his creative, innovative, and imaginative approaches to lowering housing costs. He was founder/trustee of NAHB Research Institute; builder of NAHB Research Houses; pioneer electric-heat manufacturer; housing consultant and building materials executive; honorary trustee, National Council of the Housing Industry; and twice chairman, National Housing Center Council.

James Stanley Baughman, Washington, D.C. As dynamic president of the Federal National Mortgage Association until 1966, his leadership helped Fannie Mae greatly expand home financing for Americans, and set a milestone of housing progress. During his tenure, 30% of the existing United States home inventory was built. He received the President Kennedy Award for Distinguished Federal Service.

Albert Farwell Bemis, Newton, Massachusetts. Bemis was a builder, a researcher, and an innovator in housing and building systems. Bemis devoted a lifetime to the improvement of housing construction. He conceived and fathered the Cubical Modular Method of building layout and the four-inch (or ten centimeter) module, which has become the accepted standard for coordinating and standardizing the sizes of building materials and components throughout the world.

William Blackfield, San Francisco, California. He is an industry giant and the first builder recognized by the California State Legislature for adding to the state's economy by building 25,000 homes. He was the first builder to bring mass-produced housing to Hawaii, and was publicly recognized for contributions to that state's economy. As NAHB president in 1964, he launched the Registered Builders Program, the first industry effort to control quality in new home construction.

Larry Blackmon, Fort Worth, Texas. He began his career at full throttle, building almost 1,000 homes his first year in the business. He later diversified into multi-family, commercial, and industrial operations throughout Texas. Blackmon compiled a long record of high-level service and leadership in the industry. He was elected president of NAHB in 1966, and through persuasion, reason and cooperation, achieved solid results in housing legislation.

David D. Bohannon, San Mateo, California. A giant among men, he built desperately needed war and postwar homes in well-planned communities; pioneered new and faster production methods; and was a key organizer and founder of the National Association of Home Builders and its president in 1942. His work has vastly enriched the quality of American life.

Milton J. Brock, Sr., Los Angeles, California. The fine homes and communities he built in a long career are living testaments to the vision of Milton J. Brock, respected California builder whose sons have continued his traditions. He was president of NAHB in 1948, and during his term as president, National Home Week was initiated.

Alan E. Brockbank, Salt Lake City, Utah. He was a founder-director of the first National Housing Center; he helped found NAHB Research Foundation and Research Institute; and was NAHB president in 1952. His contributions to housing research have left a lasting influence. He was also a member of the Building Research Advisory Board; the National Bureau of Standards; and director, Building Research Institute; and was a credit-rating and appraisal specialist with FHA.

W. Evans Buchanan, Silver Spring, Maryland. His inspired leadership caused major advances in land use research, legislation, and efficient building techniques. As president of NAHB in 1963, he advocated a healthy housing industry through a strong NAHB. He was a builder of quality subdivisions, apartments, and townhouses, and constructed the 1962 experimental house and instituted on-site "Muddy Shoe" tours for product manufacturers and lenders.

Elmo James Burke, Jr., San Antonio, Texas. Burke is a third-generation home builder. While a lawyer by education, he is a home builder by choice. His "Sarah" project in San Antonio led a national effort toward mass production of low-income housing. An active participant in industry affairs, he was a local and state housing leader before being elected NAHB president in 1961. While NAHB legislative chairman he helped lower the FHA down payment to 3%.

Franklin L. Burns, Denver, Colorado. A builder of war and postwar homes and communities, he served on NAHB's Home Builders' Emergency Committee in 1942 to help the war-housing effort. In 1945 he pioneered 500 solar homes, and in 1946 built 1400 prefab houses for veterans. He has held many NAHB posts, including that of secretary/treasurer and tax studies chairman.

Fritz B. Burns, Los Angeles, California. His homes, apartments, and fine communities have enriched and beautified the land. He was one of the leading founders of NAHB and became its president in 1943. He built badly needed war houses quickly with new production methods, and his postwar homes set high planning and design concepts that influenced other builders and elevated public taste.

Edward R. Carr, Sr., Springfield, Virginia. Much loved builder and developer of Springfield, Virginia, and fine metropolitan Washington communities. His wit and good humor made him popular not only with the buyers of his homes but famous as toastmaster and raconteur at NAHB banquets and civic affairs. He was president of NAHB in 1947, and founder and director of the National Housing Center.

Lewis Cenker, Atlanta, Georgia. Cenker's housing career began in 1947, building single-family homes. His dual role of lawyer and builder allowed him to serve the industry through NAHB and numerous city and state planning agencies in Georgia. As president of the Georgia HBA he led a successful drive for the investment of state pension funds in housing mortgages. He was NAHB president in 1974 and housing's representative at President Ford's Economic Summit Meeting. In 1975 he served on the FNMA Board of Directors.

Lloyd E. Clarke, Des Moines, Iowa. As a builder, developer, and realtor, he has produced more than 10,000 units in quality residential communities in four states. He has also been active in commercial and industrial endeavors, and was the youngest president in NAHB's history (1968). As a member of the Home Owners' Warranty Corporation during its first three years, and chairman for two years, he helped guide its early efforts. He was also a member of the FNMA board of directors and executive committee for the first three years of its existence.

Albert M. Cole, Washington, D.C. Cole has been a United States Congressman; Administrator of the Housing and Home Finance Agency during the Eisenhower years; and private developer. As one of the most influential public figures on the housing scene, Cole championed the causes of decent housing for all Americans, for low-income and elderly families, urban renewal including revitalization and rebuilding of decaying urban areas as well as the clearing of slums and private initiative.

Miles L. Colean, Washington, D.C. Colean was an advisor to Presidents Franklin Delano Roosevelt and Dwight D. Eisenhower, a

framer of legislation creating the Federal Housing Administration, responsible for establishing national technical standards for FHA-financed homes, a highly respected housing economist and an economic historian. In his book *Renewing Our Cities* Colean coined the phrase "urban renewal." He began his long and outstanding housing career in Chicago as an architect.

Herbert S. Colton, Washington, D.C. For four decades he steered NAHB through numerous legal shoals as general counsel and advisor on legislation, labor, taxes, and law, and was legal counsel to many large home-building organizations throughout the country. As former chief counsel to Rental Housing Division of the FHA, he was responsible during World War II for adapting federal housing legislation to accelerate home production for defense activities.

Thomas P. Coogan, Miami, Florida. Coogan was a World War I flying ace, World War II developer in Arkansas, and developer of Hialeah and other residential and commercial properties in Florida. He worked diligently for the creation of a National Housing Center and the establishment of a Cabinet-level department for housing a central mortgage bank. He was NAHB president in 1950, a leader in efforts to stabilize mortgage sources, assistant secretary of defense for housing in 1951, and director, Armed Forces Housing Agency in 1961.

Frank W. Cortright, Pebble Beach, California. He was an executive, organizer, and leader dedicated to the advancement of free-enterprise building through a strong National Association. He was the first Executive Vice-President of NAHB, and served from 1942 to 1953. Working with men of vision and courage, he helped immeasurably to build the Association to its present high stature.

W. Hamilton Crawford, Baton Rouge, Louisiana. He was an outstanding leader and organizer of new community concepts, and a large-scale developer, builder, and prefab manufacturer. Involved in all aspects of the industry, Crawford built low-cost tract housing as well as custom homes. He built imaginative projects in Atlanta, Baton Rouge, New Orleans, Louisville, and Florida, and developed and built the newtown of Crofton, Maryland, a comprehensively planned community.

John M. Dickerman, Washington, D.C. Joining the fledgling NAHB as legislative director in 1947, he was elevated to chief of staff in 1952. Under his direction NAHB became one of the nation's largest and most influential trade associations with landmark legislative, educational, and research achievements. He earned national renown as one of the most astute men in housing. Retiring after 17 years, he was elected Honorary Life Director in recognition of his outstanding service to the housing industry.

Donal Dise, Chicago, Illinois. An innovator and creator of environmentally sound communities, Dise gained notable distinction as a builder on the national and international scenes. He has run the gamut from stick builder to prefabricated plant owner-operator. He has built in South America and developed a planned community on Grand Cayman Island. An NAHB Life Director, Dise has served on countless NAHB committees and has been president of the HBA of Greater Chicago.

Harry J. Durbin, Livonia, Michigan. He was dedicated to better housing for all Americans and worked diligently throughout a long career to that end. Durbin was one of the founders of NAHB and helped bring together the three groups from which it was formed. He became president in 1941. For ten years he served as active director/secretary of the Detroit Housing Commission.

Marriner Stoddard Eccles, Salt Lake City, Utah. Eccles was an FDR advisor and the framer of legislation creating the Federal Housing Administration. His concept of the long-term mortgage revolutionized home financing practices. Eccles was Federal Reserve Board chairman, 1936-1946; a member of the Board of Economic Stabilization, 1942-1946; and U.S. delegate to the Bretton Woods Conference, which created the World Bank and International Monetary Fund in 1944.

Sylvanus G. Felix, Oklahoma City, Oklahoma. A man of wide-ranging interests, Felix, an ardent friend of the housing industry, was attorney, builder, developer, and real estate investor. A charter member of NAHB and Life Director, he founded a law firm which gained national prominence for its specialization in tax and business consultation for builders and land developers. Felix was a charter member of the Central Oklahoma HBA and served as its president in 1955. He began his home building career in 1938.

David G. Fox, Dallas, Texas. Fox was one of the most successful home builders and merchandisers in the 1960s and 1970s. A trend setter in component use, production systems, and quality homes at a moderate price, he originated a host of marketing techniques and merchandising concepts. He began building in the Dallas area in 1949, and his innovative production techniques have been widely imitated.

Leonard L. Frank, Roslyn, New York. Frank began his housing career at the age of 19. His early homes were "adjudged best for families with children" by a national publication. An active, energetic member of his profession, he served the industry in many capacities at many levels. President of NAHB in 1962, he was a strong advocate of housing renewal. One of his major developments was Rockville Centre, New York, an early renewal project.

Ernest G. Fritsche, Columbus, Ohio. A builder of quality communities, he pioneered the concept of service after the sale. He is credited with being the first major home builder to provide a substantive five-year warranty on his homes. He was an early participant in the "Sweat Equity" program, a workable plan which enabled large numbers of people to become first-time home owners.

R. Buckminster Fuller, Milton, Massachusetts. World renowned for his geodesic dome design, Fuller was a leading figure for new building concepts. In 1927, he invented the Dymaxion House—a mass-producible, energy-efficient "dwelling machine" that could be delivered by air. His countless innovations in the construction field opened new ground and explored the vast potential of housing alternatives for a new age.

Edward G. Gavin, Chicago, Illinois. Gavin was an editor, and the creator of National Home Week. For three decades he spoke with a golden tongue to builders, dealers, and civic groups. His message: Build a strong industry through a strong NAHB, and create housing through unfettered private enterprise. He was an editor of *American Builder,* and received NAHB's Distinguished Service Award.

Carl Gellert, San Francisco, California. Gellert is the dean of San Francisco's home builders. Gellert built thousands of new homes in Northern California during his career. He worked diligently to forge planning and zoning policies to promote the construction of affordable houses in San Francisco throughout five decades. Gellert founded the HBA of San Francisco, and served as its president in 1948. He was a key organizer behind the creation of NAHB.

Robert P. Gerholz, Flint, Michigan. This leader and industry spokesman's espousal of private enterprise and the benefits of industry cooperation won wide hearing. He was successively president of NAHB, 1944, the National Association of Real Estate Boards and the U.S. Chamber of Commerce. His clear voice was heard throughout the land on many worthy causes.

George S. Goodyear, Charlotte, North Carolina. Goodyear was a dynamic builder of war and postwar homes in Pittsburgh, Pennsylvania, and Charlotte, North Carolina. He was NAHB president in 1957, and he pioneered low-cost ideas and systems. As president of both Pittsburgh and Charlotte HBA, he participated in the formation of the Home Builders' Association Emergency Committe and Home Builders' Institute, resulting in the founding of NAHB.

Alfred Gross, Palm Beach, Florida. His career began in the slow handicraft days of housing and encompassed years of innovations in production techniques, factory-built components, and huge projects. In four decades he and his brother George built more than 15,000 houses and 10,000 apartments. His Gross-Morton Company's 3,000-unit Glen Oaks

Village garden apartments, designed around courts, was a landmark.

Eugene A. Gulledge, Greensboro, North Carolina. Effective administrator and builder, he organized the Greensboro, North Carolina, and North Carolina State Home Builders' Association. He was active in local Mormon Church and civic affairs, was NAHB president in 1969, was appointed to the Housing Center Commission that built NAHB's present headquarters, and was the first builder to be named FHA commissioner, 1969-1973. While assistant secretary of HUD, annual housing starts exceeded 2,400,000, proving that the private sector can produce America's housing needs.

Foster Gunnison, New Albany, Indiana. Remembered as the "Father of Prefab," he experimented with numerous techniques and systems which added to the advance of prefabricated housing. His strength and determination were shown when he founded Houses, Inc., in the depths of the depression. To advance research, promote consumer acceptance, and offer low-cost quality alternatives to traditional housing, he founded the Prefab Home Institute in 1942.

Conrad "Pat" Harness, Houston, Texas. Harness began his housing career in 1946 as a real estate editor. He made the successful transition from writing about housing to making housing news as a Houston home builder. An excellent administrator, he held every elective post in the Greater Houston Builders' Association and reorganized a faltering Home Manufacturers' Association. He was a trend setter in small business parks, is an NAHB Life Director, and was Houston's 1976 "Builder of the Year."

Joseph B. Haverstick, Dayton, Ohio. His rise from carpenter, cement finisher, and self-made, small-volume builder to president of NAHB in 1956, testifies to the greatness of the U.S. private-enterprise system. He built 1,500 homes as well as motels, restaurants, and commercial buildings. He was a member of the Merger Committee that established NAHB.

Kimball Hill, Rolling Meadows, Illinois. A pioneer and activist in housing research, his name is honored for the homes and livable communities he created. His Oak Meadows and Rolling Meadows projects—more than 6,000 units—set new high standards in design and in production, using component sections built on site. He is a life Director of NAHB and is past president of Greater Chicago HBA, and has held many posts in NAHB.

Herbert C. Hoover, West Branch, Iowa. The nations' thirty-first president, Hoover worked tirelessly to impove the quantity and quality of housing in America. The principles of home ownership which he championed were promoted in his "Better Homes for America" program. His ideas for insuring mortgage funds for housing led to the creation of a federal home loan banking system. As secretary of commerce, he revolutionized the industry by standardizing sizes of brick, lumber, plumbing, and numerous other building materials.

Richard G. Hughes, Pampa, Texas. Born in a dugout in Texas, he worked 18 hours a day and fought all his life to bring better housing to low-income groups, minority groups, and all Americans. As NAHB president in 1954 he possessed a rare blend of vision and action. He advanced air-conditioning research in moderately priced housing. He is credited with awakening builders and Congress to urgent urban needs.

Ralph J. Johnson, Bethesda, Maryland. Johnson is president of NAHB's Research Foundation. His career spans four decades of housing and home-building research. He pioneered numerous building systems, methods, and techniques which resulted in homes of improved value, function and comfort; and he is responsible for ten innovative research houses. His continuing goal has been to provide better homes at lower costs and of higher quality.

Wallace E. Johnson, Memphis, Tennessee. Johnson was an activist in the formation of NAHB. Due largely to his capable, persuasive efforts in NAHB's behalf, most of the nation's housing during World War II and in subsequent years was built by the private-enterprise system. Although he found time to help build the greatest motel chain in the world as co-founder of Holiday Inns, the building industry remained his first love. He engaged actively in building single-family, rental, condominium and nursing homes, and hospitals and industrials.

Max H. Karl, Milwaukee, Wisconsin. Karl founded America's first private mortgage insurance company in 1957—an achievement without precedent in the housing industry. By protecting mortgage lenders against default, Karl's Mortgage Guaranty Insurance Corporation enabled millions of families to obtain home mortgages with small down payments. Throughout his career, Karl has been a relentless champion of affordable financing for the nations' home buyers.

George Fred Keck, Watertown, Wisconsin. The first American architect to demonstrate the potential of passive solar home energy, Keck foresaw in the 1930s the need for thermally efficient and functional modern design in housing. Keck was head of the architectural department of Moholy-Nagy's Chicago School of Design. His House of Tomorrow in 1933 and the Crystal House in 1934 were highlights of the 1933-1934 World's Fair.

James M. Lange, Deerfield, Illinois. A long-time editorial supporter of housing, he promoted vast new marketing ideas, including national product advertising. Originated and implemented numerous programs to stimulate builders' thinking, such as national competitions for low-cost housing and innovative campaigns to encourage the exchange of "know-how" among builders to reduce construction costs.

William Levitt, Long Island, New York. A housing trend setter since 1930, he created an entirely new system of home building. His first Levittown built on Long Island, to be followed by many others, was the most significant postwar housing project of the fifties. Levitt raised new standards for large-scale planned communities with innovative new production techniques which set a pattern for builders everywhere. His successful planning and construction concepts had a powerful worldwide influence.

Maxine Livingston, New York, New York. For many years as family home editor of *Parents'* magazine she prodded, cajoled, and sometimes cudgeled builders into designing and building the type of housing she felt was needed—homes for families with young and growing children. Her model-home promotions made history. Since the 1930s, she has carried on her objectives through editorial comment in respected industry publications.

Rodney Martin Lockwood, Birmingham, Michigan. Major advances in legislative, labor, tax, and financial policies of the housing industry are the results of his brilliant legal mind and leadership. He was elected president of NAHB in 1949. His World War II "Lockwood Report" did much to alleviate material shortages. He led NAHB's move to found FNMA, and later guided task forces on labor and tax policies.

Nathan Manilow, Chicago, Illinois. A national officer of NAHB in its formative years, he helped establish the first Home Builders Convention-Exposition in 1945. He was chairman of the first committee to construct a National Housing Center. He developed Forest Park in Chicago, and was one of the leading developers of high-rise complexes in Miami. For his years of dedicated service to the housing industry, Manilow was made an Honorary Life Member of the NAHB Executive Committee.

George C. Martin, Anchorage, Kentucky. Martin, designated the founder and prime mover in the creation of NAHB's Home Owner's Warranty Corporation, was elected its first chairman and Honorary Life Director. In the industry he was known as a marketing leader. His award winning, quality, low-cost homes set the trend for townhouse, cluster, and condo development in the seventies. In 1973 as NAHB president, he instituted the first Consumer Affairs Department and a special department to fight exclusionary zoning and no-growth.

William McChesney Martin, Washington, D.C. From his keen understanding of the economic needs of America following World War II, Martin galvanized the nation's banking system for the long-term capital expansion of business and industry. He served under five presidents as chairman of the Federal Reserve System, 1951-1970. During his tenure in that office, Martin's monetary policies ushered in the greatest boom in single-family home production in U.S. history.

Joseph B. Mason, Southbury, Connecticut. His distinguished career as an editor of national building publications spanned a historic 50-year period, during which he led many editorial crusades, including those for the founding of FHA and NAHB. He was awarded NAHB's "Presidential Citation" for the advancement of good housing through his perceptive writing and editorial contributions.

Norman P. Mason, Harwich, Massachusetts. Mason was FHA commissioner, 1954-1959; HHFA administrator, 1959-1961; former U.S. Chamber of Commerce director; a friend and supporter of the private-enterprise approach to solving housing problems; and an outstanding, realistic administrator and negotiator. He attracted much attention by securing a compromise that assured passage of twice-vetoed housing legislation in 1959.

Joseph E. Merrion, Chicago, Illinois. A respected builder of homes, apartments, and communities in the Chicago area, he was active in World War II housing, and in 1944, became chairman of the potent Home Builders' Emergency Committee that did much to help private builders get war houses built. A founder and organizer of NAHB, he became president in 1945.

Joseph Meyerhoff, Baltimore, Maryland. Meyerhoff was a founder and president of NAHB in 1946, and built 25,000 homes. As developer of communities and major shopping centers, the "quality-of-life" communities he created testify to his vision. He was founder-director of the first National Housing Center; was honored for his civic and philanthropic activities; and was national chairman, United Jewish Appeal, 1961-1964.

Carl T. Mitnick, Somers Point, New Jersey. His deep-felt concern for the elderly and all Americans who need good homes has been expressed in a dedicated lifetime of building, real estate development, and mortgage finance. He brought new luster to retirement-home building with his Cape May projects. President of NAHB in 1959, he supported the formation of a central mortgage bank. He served on the FHA Industry Advisory Board in 1960, and was a builder delegate to the U.S.S.R.

John McC. Mowbray, Baltimore, Maryland. Mowbray was a dedicated pioneer developer of outstanding planned communities, including Roland Park in Baltimore. An Urban Land Institute founder, he was an early proponent of sensible land development and sound environmental planning. As a member of the Home Builders' Emergency Committee, in 1941 he saw the need for a central voice to represent home builders and home buyers.

Herbert U. Nelson, Chicago, Illinois. Executive vice president of the National Association of Real Estate Boards for 12 years, Nelson's ambition was to provide all Americans with decent, affordable homes. He was an original thinker, powerful leader, gifted organizer, and an early pioneer in city planning. Playing a pivotal role in the creation of many independent building-oriented councils and institutes including NAHB and ULI, he performed a lasting service to the home builders and home buyers of America.

Jesse Clyde Nichols, Kansas City, Missouri. Nichols built and developed famous

Kansas City Country Club District and Country CLub Plaza. He built fashionable neighborhoods as well as communities for low- and moderate-income families, including Prairie Village, Kansas. A founder of Urban Land Institute and early developer of large-scale planned residential communities, his advanced concepts of siting and landscaping still inspire builders throughout the world.

George F. Nixon, Chicago, Illinois. Builder, realtor, and land developer par excellence, he was one of the small group of dedicated men who formed NAHB, and became its president in 1940. He was a founder and past president of HBA of Chicago, and a past president of the Chicago Real Estate Board. The homes and communities he built reveal his greatness.

James S. Norman, Jr., Houston Texas. Norman is a man of many professions—Houston builder, developer, engineer and attorney. The hallmark of his career was his 1975 NAHB presidency in which he led an industry-wide assault against high interest rates, tight money, and deep unemployment in the housing industry. An inveterate friend of the consumer, Norman worked diligently in the formation of NAHB Home Owners' Warranty program.

Frederick Law Olmsted, Jr., Brookline, Massachusetts. The father of the National Park Service, Olmsted was a leading U.S. landscape architect and city planner during the first half of the century. Under appointment by President Theodore Roosevelt, he restored L'Enfant's plans for the nation's capital, and later designed the Mall, the Jefferson Memorial grounds, and Rock Creek Park. His projects to enhance residential development included Roland Park, Baltimore, and Palos Verdes Estates on the California coast.

Wright Patman, Texarkana, Texas. Patman was statesman, legislative leader, and staunch advocate of programs to bring good housing to all Americans. For 50 years he was an implacable foe of high interest rates and policies that would impede building. As chairman of the House Banking Committee for many years, he left his imprint on most major housing legislation.

Andrew S. Place, South Bend, Indiana. He is an outstanding homebuilder, a creative innovator, a leader in housing research, and an Honorary Life Director of HAHB. A 24-year member and past chairman of NAHB's Research Foundation and Research Institute, his contribution to cost reduction and production techniques advanced better housing in America.

Hugh Morris Potter, Houston, Texas. A preeminent authority in the field of city planning, his River Oaks community has been hailed as "the showplace of Houston" since the early forties. As 1934 president of the National Association of Real Estate Boards, and 1943-1944 president of the Urban Land Institute, Potter made significant strides in educating builders to the importance of land, site, and open-space planning. He was a key housing adviser to Presidents Franklin Delano Roosevelt and Harry Truman, and a firm believer in the need for a strong housing industry to lead the nation's economy.

Edward W. Pratt, Troy, Michigan. An active industry leader in education and research, he has been a builder in the Detroit area since 1946. His towering influence has been felt in efforts to improve construction techniques, build better homes with more housing value at lower costs by private enterprise, and create better labor relations for the industry. He served as NAHB's national treasurer; chairman of numerous key committees; trustee and

chairman, National Housing Center Council; and director and chairman, Home Owners Warranty Corporation. For his years of dedicated service, Pratt was made an Honorary Life Member of the NAHB Executive Committee.

Perry I. Prentice, New York, New York. Prentice was editor, publisher, and crusader for housing ideals and progress, and housing consultant to the Defense Department for overseas housing. His *House and Home* round tables, symposiums, housing tours, and *Time-Life* conferences brought together for the first time builders, government officials, manufacturers, and finance leaders to work for progress and improvements in the housing industry.

James R. Price, Lafayette, Indiana. His career was part and parcel of the rise of a great industrialized housing development in the U.S. His vision, production skill, and marketing and financial acumen helped build the National Homes Corporation to the largest prefabricated home manufacturing firm in the world. In so doing, he brought better, low-cost housing to millions of Americans.

Albert M. Rains, Gadsden, Alabama. Following 20 productive years in Congress, Rep. Albert Rains, Alabama Democrat, voluntarily retired in 1965. As chairman of the Special Subcommittee on Housing, he authored and secured the passage of landmark housing legislation during his tenure. Eloquent in speech, gifted in intellect, a master of parliamentary procedure, Rep. Rains earned and deserved the title, "Mr. Housing, USA."

Nathaniel H. Rogg, Washington, D.C. Economist and lawyer, Rogg was executive vice president of NAHB for 11 years, chief economist for 12 years, and elected Honorary Life Member of the Executive Committee upon retirement. A tower of strength, he carried housing's message into the most influential sectors of the nation. Upon his NAHB retirement, Rogg continued his quest to ensure decent, affordable housing for all Americans, concentrating upon urban rehabilitation.

Robert F. Schmitt, Berea, Ohio. His housing contributions go far beyond his home community, where he provided his buyers with quality homes. A "Professional Builder of the Year," he pioneered energy-saving, cost-cutting techniques. He earned a national reputation for improved building methods, and worked for uniform, realistic building codes. He was appointed by President Ford to the board of the National Institute of Building Sciences.

Donald J. Scholz, Scottsdale, Arizona. As a builder, designer, and home manufacturer, he exerted a major influence on many sectors of the housing industry. He built more than 20,000 homes in award-winning communities from coast to coast. A trend setter in production and marketing techniques, his contributions to increased quality of manufactured homes led the prefab housing industry to new heights.

Nels G. Severin, San Diego, California. Severin was a dedicated builder of 6,000 homes, a mortgage banker, developer of fine retirement-recreational communities, and strong protagonist of a central mortgage facility to offset cyclical tight-money problems. As President of NAHB in 1958, he vigorously assisted better land use and housing research, including construction of two NAHB research houses.

Paul B. Shoemaker, Evanston, Illinois. Distinguished as one of America's creative industrialists and producer of quality products for the housing industry, he worked unceasingly to bring about better understanding and working relationships between builders, distributors, and product manufacturers. He helped advance housing research, and is an honorary Trustee of NAHB's National Council of the Housing Industry.

Earl W. Smith, El Cerrito, California. Actor, artist, designer, carpenter, son and grandson of builders, he built 25,000 homes, including the revolutionary, low-cost, "flat-top" house. His "compact house" project was an early version of the planned unit development. An innovator in housing research, he was president of NAHB in 1955. He chaired the Resolutions Committee in 1958, drafting a strong housing policy statement on the heels of the 1957 building recession.

William R. Smolkin, New Orleans, Louisiana. Unmatched in his expertise on home marketing, Bill Smolkin is widely recognized for his innovations in real estate research. He has been consulted in the planning and marketing of more than 30,000 homes in 42 states and three foreign countries. His market analyses have provided an invaluable resource to the nation's builders. He has written several books and numerous articles for NAHB in the marketing field.

John Sparkman, Huntsville, Alabama. Statesman, Senator, Congressman, candidate for Vice President, and chairman of the Joint Economic Committee, Banking Committee, Housing Sub-Committee, and Foreign Relations Committee—he has authored many major housing bills since World War II, including the G.I. Bill of Rights which raised the standard of living for millions of Americans.

Emanuel Spiegel, New Brunswick, New Jersey. One of the gentlest and brightest of men, he was a skilled lawyer, negotiator, and conciliator who achieved progress and reform through persuasion. As president of NAHB in 1953, he brought vision and depth to the concepts, purposes, and objectives of NAHB. A second-generation builder, he concentrated on producing affordable housing.

John A. Stastny, Chicago, Illinois. He was involved in construction ranging from low-cost to luxury homes, apartments, institutional, and inner-city projects; and was NAHB president in 1971. His Housing-related posts held include Presidential Commission appointee; advisory member FNMA; and six-term chairman, Federal Home Loan Bank, Chicago. Deeply committed to public service, his greatest quest was continued private opportunity of home ownership and production in the face of growing governmental encroachment.

Waverly Taylor, Washington, D.C. He was a member of the Home Builders' Emergency Committee in 1941 and a worker during the formative years of NAHB. He served as a Life Council member, a Trustee, and officer of the Urban Land Institute. As a pioneering proponent of the planned community concept, he set new high standards for design and community planning in the development of Dumbarton, Foxall Village, and other communities in the Washington area.

James W. Walter, Tampa, Florida. The Jim Walter home was an unparalleled success during the 1950s. His concept offered inexpensive housing to home buyers in the southern United States willing to use "Sweat Equity" to finish their homes. Walter parlayed a $900 investment into a multi-billion-dollar business. His corporation has since become one of the nation's largest manufacturers of building materials—giving testimony to the crucial role of the entrepreneur in the housing industry.

Stanley Waranch, Norfolk, Virginia. A dedicated and respected community and business leader and builder of single-family, apartment, and commercial properties, he was NAHB president in 1972, Virginia BA president in 1963, and the founder and first president of Tidewater HBA. He was active in the creation of HOW, served on its first board, and was elected chairman of the board, 1976. He was a member of the Atlanta FHLBB and was appointed to numerous government advisory boards including those of FNMA, FHLB, and FHLMC.

Leon N. Weiner, Wilmington, Delaware. Weiner was a strong voice for, and a builder of, housing for Americans of all income levels. The many awards accorded this 1967 NAHB president are an indication of his industry prestige. He is noted for his problem-solving approaches to suburban community development, as well as for strongly advocating the revitalization of American cities. He has effectively helped to bridge the gap between the private sector and public interest.

Perry E. Willits, Sarasota, Florida. During his outstanding career he built schools, churches, apartments, condominiums, and more than 4,000 single-family homes in all price ranges. He was a leader in promoting the use of components in home building, and was active in legislative affairs at the local, state, and national levels. As 1965 NAHB president, he forcefully advocated housing legislation. He was vitally instrumental in getting condominium legislation passed in Florida, and built many outstanding projects.

F. Vaux Wilson, Jr., Yardley, Pennsylvania. His Precision-Built system gave complete flexibility to house design due to the use of the Bemis four-inch cubical module, and proved faster than any other system because the 8 × 14 feet Homosote panels allowed the average room wall to be built in one piece. One project of 5,000 homes was built in less than five months. Other emergency housing was built in Canada, Argentina, and Mexico. His book *Tomorrow's Homes* gives the complete details.

Jesse P. Wolcott, Port Huron, Michigan. As a member of the 72nd through 84th Congress, and as chairman of the House Banking and Currency Committee during the 79th, 80th, and 83rd Congress, Rep. Wolcott proved a great friend of private enterprise—and housing in particular—drafting and guiding needed legislation through the House. In 1946 he won the distinguished congressional services award for working to remove wartime controls and to stimulate industrial production.

Frank Lloyd Wright, Phoenix, Arizona. Wright was the most influential architect of the twentieth century. During a career spanning seven decades, he designed more than 400 buildings including the Robie House, Chicago, 1909; the Guggenheim Museum, New York, 1959. His "organic" architecture stressed open, flowing space, horizontal planes, and integration of wood, stone, glass, and stucco. The Wright tradition was continued in an apprenticeship program at his desert home, Taliesin West.

Angus G. Wynne, Jr., Dallas, Texas. Wynne was one of the great, early, large-scale developers. He built and developed Wynnewood in Dallas, a premier multi-use development. He developed the Great Southwest Industrial District, adding to the economy of Dallas-Fort Worth, and planned and built the Six Flags amusement parks in Dallas, Atlanta, and St. Louis.

Herman H. York, Oyster Bay, New York. An architect with more than 750,000 homes built from his plans. For 30 years, York designs were syndicated in 300 U.S. newspapers. He designed the first subdivision split-level house built in the Northeast. York bridged the gap between homebuilders and architects with his valuable counsel to the industry. He worked actively on behalf of NAHB Research Foundation and the Research Institute, and for efficient design.

Fifty Fabulous Years: End of an Era?

The close of the decade of the seventies also marked the end of a dramatic 50-year cycle in housing—one in which America's shelter provisions advanced beyond all expectations and became the envy of the world.

But as the decade closed, there were major economic and political forces at work that appeared to foreshadow an end to what many were calling the Golden Age of Housing. The major causes were the disruptive effect of high interest rates, double-digit inflation, and fiscal policies resulting from uncontrolled government spending. The complex and vital system that provided cheap mortgage money was in great disarray.

Conditions in 1979 were a far cry from the 1930s when the Federal Housing Administration, Federal Home Loan Bank Board, the Federal Savings and Loan Insurance Corporation, and others were churned out by a government highly concerned about housing growth. During the 1940s, 1950s, and 1960s, this concern was expressed by increasingly liberal long-term mortgages at very low interest and low down payments. In the seventies such agencies as the Federal National Mortgage Association, the Government National Mortgage Association, and the Federal Home Loan Corporation greatly stimulated the flow of mortgage funds and developed active secondary markets and a system of mortgage-backed securities.

By the end of the decade, much of this favorable climate for the financing of home construction had drastically changed. Sky-high interest rates and inflation caused by federal spending and huge budget deficits brought an end to the system that fueled home ownership. Savings institutions found they could no longer operate profitably making long-term fixed-rate loans at less than they paid their depositors. Many, if not most, began losing money and cut their mortgage business. Thus ended the era of easy home finance.

Whether 1979 marked the end of the Golden Age of Housing remains to be seen. But there can be no doubt that the period 1930-1980 produced an outstanding and perhaps amazing advance in the homes and housing of the United States, unequalled in any other land. The American Dream—"to own a home of your own on your own piece of land"—was increasingly fulfilled. There were 88,277,000 occupied housing units at the end of the decade, of which 55 million were single-family homes. The single-family home—the very epitome of the American Dream—increased at the rate of a million a year in the seventies.

In 50 fabulous years of housing from 1930 to 1980, the bare-bones record of housing starts shows 57+ million. But to this may be added rehabilitated buildings, remodeling, additions, and subdividing of large houses and structures into smaller homes. There were also several million mobile homes added, which brought the census record of occupied mobile homes to four million in 1980.

A striking development near the end of these 50 years was the growth of housing rehabilitation. Hundreds of thousands of older structures were rebuilt, restored, and often expanded. The old brick row houses of Baltimore and Philadelphia are examples. But throughout the older section of many other towns and cities there was much activity—the brownstones of New York and Chicago in particular. The census reports clearly indicate a healthy condition in U.S. housing everywhere, except for a possible 5% of below-standard units in isolated sections.

After 50 years, what can be expected in housing? The problems are great, but solutions in an aggressive, inventive, unfettered private-enterprise society are not impossible.

First of all, despite the huge production of the seventies and earlier years, there was still a pressing need in 1980, for more housing. Millions of young Americans who were part of the postwar baby boom were reaching home-buying age. The need was for 21 million units in the next decade, or an average of 2.1 million a year. Need is one thing, however; fulfillment another.

There were many problems at the end of the decade, but happily, new answers were being forged. The oft repeated story of Challenge being met by new Inventiveness and Enterprise was at work. The genius of the American system in housing is that problems often represent opportunity and stimulate solutions. This is of course, as long as enterprise, ingenuity, and risk taking are encouraged, not penalized. Fortunately, the political climate in the U.S. began swinging to the right in favor of housing growth. Other problems and challenges presented themselves, solutions were emerging.

A swing in public sentiment to the right was taking place. The new conservative position favored a return to conditions that would encourage building.

A stronger attempt to control inflation and government spending was developing. Since inflation with its high interest rates had become the arch-enemy of housing, this was encouraging to business entrepreneurs.

New approaches to mortgage finance were emerging. One was the variable-rate mortgage which allows rates to fluctuate with the cost of money. Another was the shared appreciation mortgage: the lender gives up chances for higher interest rates, but in return he shares some of the profit if the house increases in value when sold. Still another plan would call for the lender to hold the monthly payments constant if the owner could not meet higher rates. The payments would accrue and be tacked on at the end of the mortgage.

The consumerism and environmentalism movements of the seventies which hindered and often stopped needed housing began to be tempered and restrained by reason. The public reaction to excessive and often harmful demands was heard in the political halls. Relaxation of many inhibiting requirements began to make it more possible for building to proceed. At the same time, the building industry moved to strengthen and improve its services. A notable example was the Home Owners' Warranty Program of the National Association of Home builders.

An amazing burst of research, development and advance in solar systems took place. Builders developed new techniques that greatly increased the energy efficiency of homes.

Builders began to face up to the fact that buyers could no longer afford everything they wanted and would have to scale down their expectations. They began to plan and produce more zero-lot line homes, townhouses, and small condominium units that used less land and cost less to own and operate. They adopted cost saving techniques, and built increasingly energy-efficient homes.

It should again be noted that housing progress is usually individualistic, unsystematic, and often accidental in its effects on people and areas. The work of builders, as we often pointed out, is carried on by small firms in thousands of isolated and separate locations and communities. But we affirm that the genius of their spirit of achievement will survive and carry the record of these last 50 years to still greater heights. Then, we can hope, the American Dream of a decent home for every American will come to fruition.

INDEX

in 40s, 31, 34, 44, 47, 49, 53
in 70s, 136, 138, 162
in 60s, 98
in 30s, 6-7, 30
"Built in America" exhibition, 58
Burchard, John E., 25, 54, 58
Burke, Elmo James, Jr., 167
Burke, Jim, 125
Burns, Arthur, 138, 142
Burns, Franklin L., 45, 48, 122, 167
Burns, Fritz B., 31, 33-34, 37, 44,
   47-48, 59, 72, 167
Butler, Nicholas Murray, 6

Cabot, Cabot & Forbes, 123
Callendar, John H., 53
Callister, Charles Warren, 110, 117,
   120, 122-123, 160
Canavaral, 101
Capehart, Homer, 68
Capital (see Equity capital)
Capital gains in 70s, 141
Carderock Springs, 121-122
Carmel Valley Manor, 122
Carpenter-Subtle Wood, 73
Carr, Edward R., Sr., 167
Carraige Hill, 122
Carrollwood, 122, 157
Castle Rock, 157
Cenker, Lewis, 165, 168
C.E.P. Associates, 158
Chamberlin House, 58
Champion Forest, 157
Champion Homes, 101
Channel Heights, 37, 57-59
Chatham Village, 18
Cheesem, Charles, 129
Chiarelli and Kirk, 53
Chicago World's Fair, 1933, 22-23
   28-29
Church, Thomas D., 16, 59
City Housing Corp., 21
City Investing, 101
Civil Works Administration, 10
Civilian Conservation Corps, 8, 10
Clark, Gilmore B., 50
Clarke, Lloyd E., 168, 105
Cluster housing, 110-112
   recreational facilities in, 112-114
Coate, Roland E., 15
Cohen and Haft, 159
Cole, Albert M., 67, 168
Colean, Miles L., 12-13, 70, 168
Collier, Barron, Jr., 105
Colomb, C. Earl, 33, 50

Colton, Herbert S., 168
Columbia (MD), 115-116, 122
Community planning in 40s, 59-60
Computers, use of, 99, 129
Concrete Frame and Glass, 73
Condominiums
   definition of, 118
   for elderly, 117-121
   in 60s, 110-112
      recreational facilities in, 112-114
Conejo Village, 110, 122
Connor, Neil, 65
Construction
   industry statistics, 3
   locations, 2
   materials
      of 60s, 124-129, 132-133
      of 30s, 27, 30
Controls, 45
Coogan, Thomas P., 50, 72, 168
Copeland Co., 157
Corbin & Yamafuji, 158
Corcoran, Tom, 12
Coronado Shores, 157
Corporations in building, 102-106
Cortese, Ross, 117, 123
Cortright, Frank W., 33, 168
Council of Housing Producers, 99, 101
   members of, 102
Country Club District, Kansas City, 20,
   50, 60
Crane, Cyrus, 33
Crash (*see* Stock market crash)
Crawford Corp., 100
Crawford, W. Hamilton, 57, 116, 122,
   169
Creedon, Frank R., 49
Crofton (MD), 116-117, 122
Crow Canyon, 157
Curved House Traps Sun, 73

Daiger, Matt, 12
Dailey, Gardener, 58
Dally, C. Fred, 57
Davison, Robert L., 27, 37
Deane, Albert, 12
Decio, Arthur, 105
Defense housing, 31, 34-44
   reduction of controls, 45
Deltona, 101
Demographic changes, 138-141
Demonstration homes, 69, 151-155
Department of Energy, 147-148, 154
Depression, 1-2, 6-8
   effect on architects, 15

Desert Island, 157
Design, importance of
   in 70s, 156
   in 60s, 109
Designers
   of the 40s, 57-59
Developers
   of the 30s, 20
DHI Enterprises, 161
Dickerman, John M., 169
Dise, Donal, 169
Dome Roof Rotating, 73
Douglas Fir Plywood Association, 57
Douglas, Lewis, 9
Dow, Alden B., 53
Dowley, Robert, 124
Druckery, Mildred, 165
Durbin, Harry J., 33-34, 169

Eames, Charles, 73
Earth-sheltered homes, 150
Eastview, 157, 162
Eccles, Marriner Stoddard, 9, 12, 169
Eckbo, Garrett, 59
Eichler Homes, 100
Eichler, Joseph, 66
Elderly, housing for, 117-121
El Dorado Hills, 116
Electricity, promotion of, 131
Emergency Banking Relief Act, 9
Emmons, Fred, 73
Energy saving techniques, 147-151
Englebrecht, Robert M., 130
Environmental planning in 40s, 59-60
Environmental Shelters, Inc., 161
Environmentalist movement, 144-146
Equity capital
   sources of, 99-108
   value in homes of 70s, 136-137, 141
Estfan, Fred J., 154
Evans, Irving, 123
Evans, Randolph W., 16-17, 57
Evolving House, The, 25-26
Exquisite Form Industries, 103

Fahey, John H., 11-12, 35
Fairway Homes, 20
Falling Waters, 58
Fannie Mae, 51, 135
Farm Credit Administration, 8, 10
Farrington, William G., 48
Federal Deposit Insurance Corp., 9
Federal Emergency Relief Act, 9
Federal Farm Mortgage Corp., 10
Federal Home Loan Bank, 5, 11-12, 29

Taliesin West, 58
TAMAP, 125-126
Tanglewood, 160
Tassone, Aurelio, 42
Taylor, Waverly, 33-34, 59, 177
Tennessee Valley Authority, 8, 10, 55, 154
Terra Granada, 161
Thiry, Paul, 70
Thomas, Grainger and Thomas, 37
Thompson, Benjamin, 75
Tierra Antiqua Village, 161
Tight money, 3
  of 70s, 138, 142
Tishman, 101
Todd & Brown Inc., 24
Tomahawk Road, 20
Townhouse construction, 110-112
  recreational facilities, 112-114
Trading up, 70, 137, 141
Treetops, 161
Trousdale, Paul, 49
Trump, Fred C., 37, 50
Tugwell, Rexford, 9
Twitchell, Ralph, 53
Twitchell and Rudolph, 72

Underwood, William, 96
Unemployment during 30s, 7
United Homes Corp., 102
U.S. Army Corps of Engineers, 44
U.S. Forest Products Laboratories, 26, 124
U.S. Homes, 101
U.S. Lend Lease, 160
U.S. monetary policy, 3
U.S. Plywood Co., 104
Urban Land Institute, 19-21, 59, 109
Urban renewal in 50s, 65-66
Urethane foam, use of, 132
Usonia Community, 58

Vacation homes, 113-114, 118
Valencia Gardens, 37-38, 58
Van der Rohe, Mies, 58, 74
Vanderlip, Frank, 22
Vanderlip Syndicate, 22
Venture capital, sources of, 99-108
Vermilya, Howard P., 58
Veterans' Administration, 5
Veterans' Emergency Housing Program, 45-46, 49
Veterans' home building, 45
Veterans' home financing, 44
Villas, The, 161
Vintage Properties, 158
Voss, Paul R., 139

Walden Woods, 161
Walker, Bruce, 72
Walker, Frank C., 9, 12
Wallace, Henry, 9
Walnut Creek, 110, 117, 120
Walter, James W., 101, 177
War housing, 31, 34-44
War Production Board, 45
Waranch, Stanley, 177
Warranty programs, 164
Washington, George, Bridge, 7
Waterside, 161
Weatherstone, 161
Weaver, Robert C., 14, 133
Webb, Del E., 53, 101, 117
Webb & Knapp, 66
Weber, Bertram, 53
Wedgewood Park, 36
Weiner, Leon N., 66, 177
Westchester, 48
Westinghouse, 104
Westridge, 161
Wild Oak Bay, 160
Wildewood Springs, 160

Will, Phillip, Jr., 72
Williams & Burroughs, 122
Williams, Cy, 49, 72
Williamsburg restoration, 23-24
Willits, Perry E., 177
Willow Creek, 161
Wills, Royal Barry, 15-16, 53, 57, 59, 73
Wilson, Charles E., 62
Wilson, F. Vaux Jr., 26, 37, 55, 178
Wilson, Morris & Crane, 51
Wilson, Talbott W., 74
Windemere, 161
Winn, Dawson, 56
Witt, William, 66
Wolcott, Jesse P., 178
Women, working, effect on housing industry, 138-141
Woodbury Place, 162
Works Progress Administration, 8, 10
Wren, Christopher, 24
Wright, Frank Lloyd, 15-16, 57-58, 73, 178
Wright, Henry, 18, 21, 108
Writer Corp., 159, 161
Writer, George, 160
Wurster, Bernardi & Evans, 122
Wurster, William Wilson, 15, 16, 38, 49, 53, 57-59, 73, 110
Wyatt, Wilson W., 45-46, 49
Wynewood, 51
Wynne, Angus G. Jr., 51, 178

Yeager, Drexel, 162
Yeon, John, 74
Yeonas, Steve, 96
York, Herman H., 57, 178
Yost, L. Morgan, 53

Zachry, Henry B., 130
Zero-lot line, 108